GNVQ Leisure and Tourism

**Gillian Dale, Rose O'Mahoney
and David Gaster**

To Fionnuala, for her patience and resourcefulness R.O'M.

PUBLISHED BY THE PRESS SYNDICATE OF THE UNIVERSITY OF CAMBRIDGE
The Pitt Building, Trumpington Street, Cambridge CB2 1RP, United Kingdom

CAMBRIDGE UNIVERSITY PRESS
The Edinburgh Building, Cambridge CB2 2RU, United Kingdom
40 West 20th Street, New York, NY 10011–4211, USA
10 Stamford Road, Oakleigh, Melbourne 3166, Australia

First published 1996

Printed in the United Kingdom by Scotprint Limited, Musselburgh, Scotland

Typeset in Swift 11/13 pt

A catalogue record for this book is available from the British Library

ISBN 0 521 49809 0 paperback

Contents

Introduction

Welcome to GNVQ leisure and tourism.

This book is your essential text and will guide you through the work you need to cover. It is also a useful resource for students on BTEC First Diploma courses and related GCSE subjects. If you are already working in the world of leisure or tourism you should find it a helpful introduction to the industry in which you have chosen to make a living.

Take a moment to look through the book and familiarise yourself with its layout.

Units Each of the course units that you need to cover for your GNVQ qualification is dealt with in a separate section. The first four units are mandatory, that is you are required to work through them as part of your course. The final four units are optional; you work through two of your own choice to complete your coursework.

The units are listed below.

Mandatory
Unit 1	Investigating the leisure and tourism industries
Unit 2	Marketing and promoting leisure and tourism products
Unit 3	Customer service in leisure and tourism
Unit 4	Contributing to the running of an event

Optional
Unit 5	The sport and fitness business
Unit 6	Researching tourist destinations
Unit 7	Operational practices in the leisure and tourism industry
Unit 8	The environmental impact of leisure and tourism in the UK

Elements and performance criteria
For the purpose of assessing your work throughout the course, each unit is broken down into 'elements' and 'performance criteria'. Each unit begins with a list of its elements and performance criteria.

Assignment activities

Finally, throughout the course you are asked to take on activities designed to extend your knowledge in preparation for the end of unit 'assignment activities'. These assignment activities provide the material by which your coursework will be assessed. You should keep all your assignment activity work in a folder, known as your 'Portfolio of Evidence'. Any work from unit activities can be kept as evidence if you wish.

When you have completed all the assignments you will have gained sufficient material in your Portfolio of Evidence for you to present it for the award of your GNVQ.

To enable you to find relevant activities quickly and easily, the following logos have been used:

 Individual activity

 Group activity

Enjoy your course!

Gillian Dale
Rose O'Mahoney
David Gaster

Acknowledgements

The authors would like to thank the following personnel for their help in the preparation of the material.

The students at Cambridge Regional College who have piloted many activities. Ian Blake, CRC Sports Centre Manager, for information and advice. Management and staff at the Cambridgeshire Moat House Hotel and Tina France for word processing.

In addition, the authors and publishers would like to acknowledge the help and support of the following organisations in the preparation and illustration of this book.

Figure 1 Social Trends 1996 Office for National Statistics. Crown Copyright 1996. Reproduced by permission of the Controller of HMSO and the Office for National Statistics

Figure 2 Jungle Jungle Indoor Adventure Land, Andover, Hants

Figure 4 English Heritage Photographic Library

Figures 5 and 11 The Rapids of Romsey (Test Valley Leisure Ltd)

Figure 7 The Gleneagles Hotel, Perthshire

Figure 8 Flagship Portsmouth Trust. A GNVQ Education Pack is available on receipt of £5 from Flagship Portsmouth, Porter's Lodge, 1/7 College Road, HM Naval Base, Portsmouth, PO1 3LJ. Tel. 01705 870999.

Figure 9 Wembley Stadium Ltd

Figures 10 and 62 *Visits to Tourist Attractions 1992* (British Tourist Authority) London W6

Figures 17, 22 and 52 Lunn Poly, Leamington Spa, Warwicks

Figure 17 Trust House Forte, London WC1

Figure 18 Cunard Crown, Southampton

Figure 19 Audit Bureau of Circulations Ltd, Berkhamsted

Figure 20 Cosmopolitan, March 1994

Figure 21 Hoar Cross Hall, nr Yoxall, Staffs

Figures 26 and 34 Airtours plc, Rossendale, Lancs

Figure 28 P&O European Ferries

Figure 30 Marks & Spencer plc, London W1

Figure 31 Cadogan Travel Ltd, Southampton

Figure 35 Eclipse Direct, Crawley, W Sussex

Figure 48 *Which?* March 1995. *Which?* is published by CA and is available only on subscription. For details please write to *Which?*, Freepost, Hertford SG14 1YB

Figure 52 *Household Survey 1993* Office for National Statistics. Crown Copyright 1996. Reproduced by permission of the Controller of HMSO and the Office for National Statistics

Figures 55 and 58 The Exercise Association of England Ltd, London EC1

Figures 56 and 57 Reebok UK, Lancaster

Figure 59 Office for National Statistics. Crown Copyright 1996. Reproduced by permission of the Controller of HMSO and the Office for National Statistics

Figure 60 *Factfile 1995*, Carel Press, Carlisle

Figure 61 The National Coaching Foundation

Figure 66 North West Tourist Board, Wigan

Figures 68 and 103 The Countryside Commission, Cheltenham, Glos

National Parks in England and Wales 1992 ISBN 086170 3472

Heritage Coasts in England and Wales 1993 ISBN 086170 3766

Areas of Outstanding Natural Beauty in England and Wales ISBN 086170 4207. All 50p where sold

Figures 70 and 78 The British National Travel Survey (British Tourist Authority)

Figure 84 Springs Hydro, Nr Ashby-de-la-Zouch, Leics

Figure 87 The Barbican Centre, London EC2

Figure 88 Henlow Grange Health Farm, Henlow, Beds

Figure 97 Office for National Statistics. Crown Copyright 1996. Reproduced by permission of the Controller of HMSO and the Office for National Statistics

Figure 100 Green Flag International Ltd, Cambridge

Figure 101 Kuoni Travel Ltd (1995 brochure), Dorking, Surrey

Figure 102 Cm 2674 : Royal Commission on Environmental Pollution Eighteenth Report, HMSO. Reproduced with the permission of the Controller of Her Majesty's Stationery Office. © Crown Copyright

Figure 104 British Trust for Conservation Volunteers Summer 1996 Natural Breaks brochure. 36 St Mary's Street, Wallingford, Oxfordshire OX10 0EU. Tel: 01491 839766

The descriptions of units, elements and performance criteria are reproduced by kind permission of the Business & Technology Education Council from *Leisure and Tourism Intermediate GNVQ, [Mandatory/Optional] Units.*

Unit ❶ Investigating the Leisure and Tourism Industries

• •

Introduction to the unit

This unit comprises the following elements required by the course and gives you practice in all the performance criteria that prove your understanding of each of these elements.

Element 1.1 Investigate the leisure and recreation industry nationally and locally

Element 1.2 Investigate the travel and tourism industry nationally and locally

Element 1.3 Prepare for employment in the leisure and tourism industries

▣ Element 1.1 Investigate the Leisure and Recreation Industry Nationally and Locally

About this element This element looks at the leisure and recreation industry nationally and locally. By the end of this element you should be able to:

1 describe the main components of the leisure and recreation industry in the UK (performance criterion 1.1.1);
2 give an example of a facility for each of the main components (performance criterion 1.1.2);
3 compare the characteristics of public, private and voluntary sectors in the leisure and recreation industry, supporting the comparison with examples (performance criterion 1.1.3);
4 give examples of leisure and recreation products and services available nationally (performance criterion 1.1.4);
5 give examples of leisure and recreation facilities of national significance (performance criterion 1.1.5);
6 describe leisure and recreation facilities, products and services in a locality.

Defining leisure

 Activities

1 In groups of four, write down your own definition of what the word 'leisure' means. Now look at each others' definitions. Are there words which occur more than once? Make of note of them. Now, as a group, agree on one acceptable definition.

How does it compare to the definition given below?

Leisure is the opportunity available to an individual after completing the immediate necessities of life, when she or he has the freedom to choose and engage in an activity which is expected to be personally satisfying.

2 Individually, write down what you consider to be the 'immediate necessities of life'. Write down some examples of activities which you consider to be 'personally satisfying'. Now compare your ideas with a partner.

3 Calculate how much leisure time you have each day over a typical week. Remember to be realistic about the time

needed to see to the immediate necessities you identified. Now calculate the average number of hours you have free time:

a per weekday
b per weekend day.

$$\frac{\text{Average time}}{\text{per weekday}} = \frac{\text{Total number of hours of leisure Mon to Fri}}{5}$$

$$\frac{\text{Average time}}{\text{per weekend day}} = \frac{\text{Total number of hours of leisure Sat + Sun}}{2}$$

How do your averages compare to the rest of your group? How can you account for the differences?
How does the time you have available for leisure compare to the rest of your family?

4 Now look at Figure 1, which illustrates the time used per week for different groups of people.

United Kingdom   Hours

Weekly hours spent on	In full-time employment		In part-time employment		Retired		All adults
	Males	Females	Males	Females	Males	Females	
Sleep	57	57	62	60	67	66	61
Free time	34	31	48	32	59	52	40
Work, study and travel	53	48	28	26	3	4	32
Housework, cooking and shopping	7	15	12	26	15	26	16
Eating, personal hygiene and caring	13	13	13	21	15	17	15
Household maintenance and pet care	4	2	6	3	9	3	4
Free time per weekday	4	4	6	4	8	7	5
Free time per weekend day	8	6	8	6	10	8	8

Sources: Social Trends 1996 ESRC Research Centre on Micro-social Change, from Omnibus Survey

FIGURE 1 Time use in a typical week: by employment status and gender 1995

Write down your answers to the questions which follow.

a Look at the figures for full-time employees. Which activities do females spend more time on than males?
b Do males or females have more free time? Why do you think this is?
c Draw a bar chart to show the differences in time use per week for males and females (in full-time employment).

d Now look at the figures for retired people. Which activities do females spend more time on than males? Who has more free time? Why do you think this is?

e Now draw a different type of graph (e.g. pie chart or line graph) to compare the use of time made by retired males and females.

Providing for leisure time

The fact that people have time that they wish to devote to leisure provides opportunities for other people to earn a living. This is the leisure industry, which has grown up over the last century to offer people an extensive range of activities designed to provide pleasure, mental and physical stimulation and challenge.

The leisure and tourism industries are closely connected as both rely on people taking time away from the business of working for a living, studying, giving childcare, shopping for essential food and clothes and maintaining the roof over their heads.

Where do people go to enjoy their leisure?

Sports and physical activities

In most towns you will find a swimming pool. There is usually a leisure centre which offers a range of indoor and outdoor team or individual sports. Some centres may include a gymnasium or health club. Other places which often run organised sports are community centres and schools during evenings and weekends.

Arts and entertainment

The provision of entertainment accounts for a significant proportion of the leisure industry. Most towns offer a cinema, some a theatre. Many will have nightclubs and discotheques. Major cities will offer concert halls, sports grounds with seating for many thousands of spectators and large cinema complexes.

Less obvious places of entertainment which nevertheless cater for leisure pursuits are libraries where exhibitions and lectures, as well as books, are provided. Church halls and community centres hold smaller concerts, lectures and exhibitions.

Accommodation

With the development of quick methods of travel at home and abroad, staying away from home in a hotel has become a popular way of spending leisure time. A hotel provides all the meals and does all the cleaning leaving the customer free to do what he or she wants.

'Self-catering' accommodation, where no meals are provided but just a place to live for a time, has become increasingly popular as an alternative to the hotel. Country cottages, flats and chalets, caravans and camping parks are all offered to people wanting a leisure base in an area away from their homes.

Catering
Eating out is a very popular leisure activity. Places which offer meals vary from fast-food outlets to expensive restaurants in which the surroundings and the quality of the service are as important a part of the experience as the food itself.

Eating is also a significant part of the enjoyment of leisure in sports and entertainment venues. Leisure centres and swimming pools offer snack bars and vending machines. Cinemas offer food to take with you into a film. Pubs are increasingly offering eating facilities, from bar snacks to quite formal restaurant facilities. Family meals out are offered by pubs. Hotels have bars and restaurants open to 'non-residents', people who are not staying in a room.

Outdoor activities
In urban areas, parks and playing fields provide opportunities for outdoor activities ranging from a family picnic to an organised game of football.

Country parks are often located near urban areas; some have been created from the sites of former quarries or even rubbish tips. They provide opportunities for people to observe wildlife, walk and cycle, as well as areas for play and picnicking. Reservoirs are also available for activities on the water such as windsurfing or water-skiing.

Natural features such as rivers, the sea, mountains, forests and lakes are well established locations for outdoor activities and often have outdoor activity centres situated nearby.

Here, facilities are provided for canoeing, sailing, windsurfing, climbing, mountain-biking and many other sports.

Investigating heritage
A great many people enjoy visiting attractions and facilities which have a historical connection. Castles, stately homes,

and monuments are typical examples of heritage attractions although industrial heritage attractions are also increasingly popular. An example is Wheal Prosper Mine in Cornwall, a former tin or coal mine developed into a heritage attraction when industry declined in the area.

Play

Learning through play is an important part of making friends for young children. They develop physical and social skills by learning to play with other children; through their make-believe games, they also develop creative abilities. Many groups and facilities exist to provide opportunities for play, such as mother and toddler groups, play groups and nurseries.

Organisations such as Tumbletots and Gymbobs offer young children special equipment to help them explore their physical capabilities. Parks with specially equipped playgrounds are provided in all towns and villages.

For older children and adults, the element of play remains in many of the leisure activities in which they participate; having fun is important. If people do not enjoy themselves and have fun in their chosen leisure activities they are less likely to continue.

There are three main types of play in which adults participate:

- games of skill, such as football and hockey;
- games of chance, such as betting, gambling;
- escapism, such as computer games or the many attractions offered by theme parks (see pages 24 and 164).

FIGURE 2 Children enjoying a 'soft play' area

Sectors in the leisure and recreation and tourism industries

Funding leisure, recreation and tourism

There are two main sources of finance for organisations providing leisure and tourism activities.

1   The public sector – where government money is provided via taxation and given as grants to support organisations providing a public service.
2   The private sector – where money is provided by private individuals who wish to run a business that earns them a living.

The public sector

The aim of the public sector is to provide a service open to everyone. This service is not normally designed to be profit-making. All types of public service facilities (for instance hospitals) are funded through central government grants and local community taxes. Your local council will decide, on behalf of the public, how the money for your area should be spent. Some councils give greater priority to leisure spending than others so that the quality of provision differs for each part of the country.

Some local leisure facilities provided by local councils are owned by the council but managed by private organisations who have a contract with the council to provide certain activities and facilities at reasonable prices. In return, they receive a management fee. These organisations employ their own staff. Their main sources of income are through entrance charges, course fees and membership fees.

The private sector

Organisations in the private sector are run by individuals or groups of people in order to make a profit whilst providing a service.

Public limited companies (plcs)

They may be large public limited companies such as Tottenham Football Club, Mecca Leisure or Wembley Arena. These organisations are funded with the money of shareholders who invest it in the hope that they will be paid dividends (a share of the profits) if the company makes money.

Partnerships

On a smaller scale, there are partnerships. Two or more people own a business with the intention of making a profit. They may have obtained a bank loan to set up in business to run a health club or open a café or restaurant.

Sole traders

Individuals, known as sole traders, are completely responsible for ensuring that the service they provide will pay its way. They need to cover their own expenses and pay themselves money to live on. If they have no customers, they will not be able to go on running their business. Freelance aerobics instructors and personal fitness trainers are examples of sole traders. They often borrow money from a bank to set up in business and interest on this loan has to be paid on top of the amount borrowed.

The voluntary sector

Largely staffed by volunteers, voluntary sector organisations are funded through grants, donations, fund-raising events and fees from customers. They can operate on a national level, such as The National Trust, on an international level, such as the Young Men's Christian Association (YMCA), or a local level, such as an amateur sports club.

Comparing public, private and voluntary sectors in the leisure industry

Figure 3 summarises the important differences in the characteristics of the sectors of the industry.

	Public	Private	Voluntary
Main aims	Provide a service	Profit-making	Bridge the gap between public and private sector Non-profit-making
Local examples	Swimming pools Leisure centres	Theme parks Health clubs, Pubs, Night clubs	Amateur football clubs
Employment	Paid employees	Paid employees	Mixture of paid employees and many volunteers
Sources of funding	Government grants, Local council taxes National Lottery	Private capital and National Lottery	Donations, fees, fund raising grants from National Lottery

FIGURE 3 Aims of the public, private and voluntary sectors of the leisure industry

National leisure and recreation: products and services

What is meant by 'products' and 'services'?

Sports equipment is a 'tangible' product – that is, you can touch it and call it yours if you pay for it. An aerobics class, however, cannot be touched or owned as an object can be. It is an 'intangible' product. Many leisure products are intangible and include 'services' to the customer. For example, a person who buys a product such as a yearly membership to a health and fitness club will expect to receive services. These could be free or reduced rate classes, access to qualified gym instructors, and refreshment and shower facilities. Additionally, a sauna or steam room could be included as well as crêche facilities and optional beauty treatments. All these services are offered as part of a product.

A person buying a product such as a weekend break will probably be offered accommodation, food and possibly recreation and entertainment.

Arts and entertainment products and services

London has traditionally been the focal point for arts venues of national significance such as the Covent Garden Opera House and the Barbican where the National Theatre is based. The Victoria and Albert Museum, the Science Museum and the National History museum attract visitors from all over the world, as do performances of plays given in the many theatres found in London's most famous area for entertainment, the West End.

These museums and theatres provide nationally important products and services to persuade you, and people from overseas, to visit them.

In recent years arts and entertainment products from other regions of the UK have grown in importance. The focus has been drawn away from London to some extent because people wanted access to music, dance and theatre in their own cities. Birmingham City Ballet is now recognised as one of the best ballet companies in the country. Manchester is the home of the Hallé orchestra and the Edinburgh Festival of fringe arts and entertainments attracts visitors from all over the world.

One provincial theatre which has a national and international reputation is the Swan in Stratford-upon-Avon, Warwickshire. The famous Elizabethan playwright, William Shakespeare, is said to have been born at Stratford and a whole Shakespeare industry has grown up around the theatre and the house said to be his birthplace. Packages typically offer accommodation with a trip to the theatre to see one of Shakespeare's plays.

Musicals from the West End, ballet and opera performances are now all staged in the provinces as well as in London by touring companies who travel from city to city.

Outdoor activities

There are many centres for outdoor activities in the UK, where expert training in a skill is offered as part of a product which includes accommodation and food. Holme Pierrepoint near Nottingham, the National Sailing Centre, Cowes on the Isle of Wight and the National Mountaineering Centre in North Wales are all funded by central government to provide such skill-training services as part of an outdoor activity product to anyone from the unfit walker to Olympic athlete.

Heritage sites

Stonehenge, a prehistoric stone circle in Wiltshire, is probably one of the UK's most famous heritage sites. It is managed by the Department of National Heritage. St Paul's Cathedral, Westminster Abbey and York Minster are examples of Christian churches of great national religious and architectural importance which are also attractions for tourists. Caernarfon Castle in Wales and Edinburgh Castle in Scotland attract national and international visitors.

Hadrian's Wall, a Roman wall built to mark the border between England and Scotland, is a heritage site which also offers the opportunity to walk long distances through beautiful countryside.

The Albert Dock in Liverpool, from which many pilgrims set out for a new life in America, now offers a museum featuring the history of these emigrants to America and an art gallery.

FIGURE 4 Stonehenge, the famous prehistoric stone circle near Salisbury in Wiltshire

Sports spectating

Some people enjoy a more passive approach to leisure and enjoy spectating rather than participating in sports. Many football clubs, for example, have spectator supporters' clubs attached to them. Horse-racing is another big spectator sport which has the added attraction of the excitement of betting on the winner.

Television now covers a wide range of sports, especially since the arrival of satellite and cable provision. As a result, sports such as darts, snooker, bowls, rugby and ice-skating are gaining increased interest nationally because people who might never have thought of going out to watch such sports have been able to do so at home.

Catering products and services

There are many catering services operating in the UK. Perhaps the best-known are 'chains' of restaurants such as McDonald's and Burger King. A chain organisation is one which operates exactly the same type of shop or restaurant with exactly the same products in towns and cities all over the country. Some even operate world-wide. Their standardised quality of food and service (fast-food) is a major attraction to their customers.

Trusthouse Forte owns the Little Chef and Happy Eater chains of roadside restaurants. Both restaurants place strong emphasis on catering for people with young families as well as business and leisure travellers.

In the UK, Indian and Chinese restaurants and take-aways have been available since the arrival in the UK of people from these countries.

Italian restaurants have also become popular: chains such as Pizza Express and Pizza Hut have a wide appeal and a reputation for fast, efficient service. They offer a product which aims for convenience with a younger, slightly more stylish image. Restaurants which attract customers by identifying themselves with a particular style and image (1950s rock and roll, 1970s grunge for example) have become increasingly popular.

For leisure centres and health clubs in-house catering is often an important part of the product on offer. Many people like to have a snack or drink after participating in a leisure activity. It is also a good opportunity to talk with others and make friends.

FIGURE 5 Enjoying a snack in the leisure centre

FIGURE 6 The changing face of the pub

Many pubs are no longer simply a bar offering adults alcoholic drinks and packets of crisps. Providing good family food has become an increasingly important part of their product. In the following activity you will investigate this.

The Changing Face of the Pub

Going to the pub remains the most popular pastime after watching TV; it seems that pubs are still the best loved places in which to pass leisure time outside the home.

However, pubs in the 1990s are being put under enormous pressure to maintain their attraction. There has been a decline in beer drinking as a result of the fall in numbers of young adults, who are typically heavier beer drinkers. The increased use of (illegal) recreational drugs by some youngsters has also hit the pub trade. Meanwhile, the trend towards a healthier lifestyle by other youngsters has taken a further toll.

Other factors which have affected pubs include the increasing popularity of imported wines and beers and increased competition from the expansion of wine bars, restaurants and fast food outlets. There is also an increasing trend for people to drink at home, rather than going out to a pub. This trend corresponds with the rise in popularity of home-based pastimes such as watching TV and hiring videos.

In its traditional form, the pub may have little future. But there is scope for new types of outlets based on the pub. Twenty five per cent of all pub takings are now spent on food, and family spending is thought to be the main growth area for expenditure on pub food.

In response to the growth in the family market, Whitbread continue to expand their Brewers Fayre chain (280 outlets in 1996). Brewers Fayre cater particularly for families by providing nappy changing facilities, children's menus, and the Charlie Chalk Fun Factories which enable children to play under supervision whilst their parents have a quiet drink.

The introduction of children's certificates has made it easier for pubs to encourage families.

Some pubs are also targeting older people, the fastest growing group in society. Early retirement and reasonable pension provision means they are increasingly likely to eat out at lunchtime. Bass has therefore created the 'Folk and Pitcher' chain to accommodate this segment.

The pub, then, has an important potential role as a form of community entertainment and activity centre. The children of today, who are introduced to the pub through Charlie Chalk Fun Factories, could be the new youth market of tomorrow. A final, encouraging side for breweries to look forward to, is the likelihood that the number of teenagers is likely to start growing again at the turn of the century.

Activity Read the article in Figure 6 'The Changing Face of the Pub' and answer the questions which follow.

1 Why do you think that going to the pub remains the 'most popular pastime after watching television?

2 The article states that pubs are having to put much more effort into maintaining their pulling power.
   a List the changing social trends which have led to a decline in the pub trade.
   b What are the other threats to the pub trade?

3 Although beer drinking is declining in pubs, more money is being spent on pub food by families. Why is this? What are pubs doing to attract the family market? What are the pros and cons of pubs increasing the numbers of family groups?

4 Why are older people also a growing market for pubs?

5 What other types of themes/pub activities do you think would be successful?

Accommodation products and services
The range of accommodation available in the UK includes:

- serviced (hotels, bed and breakfast, guesthouses)
- self-catering (holiday cottages, campsites, caravan parks and timeshare properties).

Some organisations such as youth hostels or holiday camps (e.g. Butlins, Pontins) offer guests the option of self-catering or serviced accommodation. Those who opt for self-catering packages benefit from greater flexibility (e.g. meal times) and the cheaper cost of the holiday.

Grading holiday accommodation
The English Tourist Board operates a national grading and classification scheme for different types of accommodation

Crowns   *Scale 1–6.* Guesthouses, hotels, inns, bed and breakfast, farmhouses, lodges

Keys   *Scale 1–5.* Self-catering homes (e.g. cottages, flats, bungalows, houseboats, houses and chalets)

Moons   *Scale 1–5.* Motels

Ticks   Caravan and camping parks, caravan holiday homes and chalets

The more crowns (or appropriate symbols) awarded, the greater the range of facilities and services being offered.

The **quality** of the accommodation is reflected by the grading scheme as follows.

- Approved
- Commended
- Highly commended
- Deluxe

The classification and grading of accommodation in the UK is still voluntary. In many other European countries, compulsory registration schemes are operated by the state.

Cheaper hotels providing clean, good-quality basic family accommodation have been in short supply in the UK until recently. However, the dramatic rise in car ownership has made it possible for large numbers of families to go on an independent holiday with the result that many holiday hotels and chain organisations like Forte Travelodge now offer simple affordable accommodation. This is called the 'budget' end of the market.

FIGURE 7 Gleneagles Hotel in Auchterarder, a hotel at the luxury end of the market

The very expensive hotel is said to be at the 'luxury' end of the market. The Ritz and the Savoy hotels in London offer every luxury and service that you are prepared to pay for. These hotels could, for example, expect to be awarded five crowns and a deluxe grade by the English Tourist Board.

National leisure and recreation: facilities

Natural landscape facilities for leisure are classified as 'national' if they are unique in some way. The Lake District, for example, is unique for its lakes and mountains: there is nothing quite like them elsewhere in the country.

A man-made facility of national significance is unique if it has one particular quality for which it is known – in the case of Wembley Stadium its size is unique. It is currently regarded as the UK's national football ground and can accommodate 80,000 people seated. It is therefore capable of staging entertainment events on an enormous scale.

Other unique national sports facilities which cater for more exclusive interests include the Bisham Abbey training centre for top athletes and Wimbledon tennis club, which hosts the UK's most famous international tennis tournament.

Places which are interesting to visit for their historical significance can also be called national facilities; they are numerous in the UK. Examples are the Roman Baths in Bath, the Tower of London, which dates from mediaeval times, and in Portsmouth HMS *Victory*, the ship sailed by the famous eighteenth-century naval commander Lord Nelson.

Location

The location of leisure and recreation products and facilities is vitally important to their success. As you will have noted, many of the facilities and places discussed above are of interest to both local people seeking recreation and tourists from other countries. Both the visitor from France and the family having a few hours out at their local attraction need to be able to get there with ease. This applies particularly to man-made facilities like theme parks, for instance Chessington World of Adventures in Surrey. A big park like this has to be sited away from urban areas because land is so expensive in built-up cities. In this case easy access by road is ensured by the near presence of the M25 London orbital, with many large, distinctive signs directing the motorist where to go. Easy accessibility by public transport also needs to be considered for local users.

On the other hand, the remote location of some natural facilities may be part of their attraction. The very popular ones like the Lake District, however, have become so precisely because roads and cars have made them so much easier to visit.

Case study

Flagship Portsmouth

Portsmouth, located on the South coast of the UK, used to be a thriving naval port employing thousands of dockyard workers. In 1981, as a result of government defence cuts, many dockyard jobs were lost. Instead of allowing the port to decline, it was decided to develop the redundant dockyard land as a recreation and tourist facility. It is now known as 'Flagship Portsmouth'.

It was created by setting up a series of trusts. A trust is a non-profit-making voluntary organisation qualifying for tax exemption. These trusts leased land from the Ministry of Defence. The *Victory,* Admiral Nelson's flagship, dating from 1778 had was already in residence in the port and had been a tourist attraction for some years. In 1982 she was joined by the *Mary Rose*, Henry VIII's flagship, which sank in the English channel in 1545 and was raised from the sea bed amid great publicity in 1982. Other ex-naval boats are also on display and a number of naval museums complete the facility.

Ideally located for day visitors from Hampshire, Surrey, Hertfordshire and London, it has a large, convenient car park and is within an easy distance of Portsmouth Harbour train station. Overseas visitors travelling on the European ferry links arrive in Portsmouth docks. In fact, overseas visitors now account for seven to eight per cent of the total number of people visiting the Flagship, and this percentage is rising. Signposting in different European languages enables them to find their way around the attractions more easily.

A computerised booking system in the visitors' centre means that entry to the attractions at Flagship Portsmouth is efficient, and the amount of time spent queuing has been reduced. A flexible pricing system allows people to choose individual attractions to visit and there are discounts for visits to more than one attraction (e.g. *Mary Rose* combined with the *Victory*). Family and group tickets are also offered at discounted prices.

A large privately-run restaurant with a local theme has been built in one of the renovated warehouses and even offers a mock ship play area for children.

A visitors' shop sells maritime souvenirs, which provide an important source of income for the trusts.

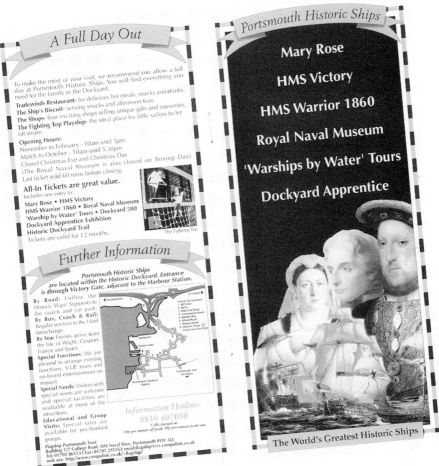

FIGURE 8 Part of a leaflet provided to visitors to Portsmouth's historic ships

---

Activity

1 What are the positive aspects of the Flagship Portsmouth's location?

2 What services are particularly important to the family market?

3 What services are particularly important to the overseas visitor market?

4 What additional source of revenue is mentioned in the case study?

5 Why do you think the attraction could have a positive economic impact on the area? (See page 25)

6 Which environmental issues need to be considered in relation to the Flagship Portsmouth attraction? (See page 26)

Case study

Wembley Park

Built in 1922 in north-west London as a showpiece for the British Empire Exhibition, the Wembley complex is made up of an enormous outdoor stadium and an indoor arena capable of staging sporting events as diverse as show-jumping and ice-skating.

It also offers a conference centre which can be hired by businesses and exhibition halls of various sizes.

The Wembley complex is a public limited company, which means that its funding comes from shareholders, people who have invested their money in the expectation that it will make them a profit. These shares pay dividends out of any profit at the end of the year, and anyone with some capital to invest can buy them.

Location
North-west London is accessible by car via the M25, which has direct links to other major motorways like the M4 to the west and the M1 to the north. There is a large car park capable of holding 7,000 cars and coaches.

It is well served by public transport, including buses and the London Underground taking people to and from central London. Rail links are provided by Wembley Central and Wembley stadium station. Wembley is also within easy travelling distance from Heathrow, Gatwick and Stansted airports.

The stadium
Although it is most commonly associated with football events, the first being the FA cup final in 1923, the stadium is also associated with a diverse programme of non-sporting events. On average, eight stadium concerts are held a year: this enables big name pop stars to perform in front of enormous audiences, which is only possible in large venues such as Wembley Stadium.

Other events held there in recent years include the Live Aid concert in 1985 and a mass celebrated by Pope John II in 1982.

In 1993 a successful ten year sponsorship deal was secured with Coca-Cola. This means that Coca-Cola provide money to help with the funding of the Stadium's upkeep in return for promotion and advertising of all kinds at events.

FIGURE 9 Wembley stadium

Wembley Arena
This facility offers a flexible programme which ranges from basketball to Disney on Ice and concerts. A Take That concert was the Arena's biggest revenue earner in 1993.

Conference centre and exhibition halls
Apart from business conferences, sporting events such as Master Snooker and the British Open Squash championships are in the centre.

Music shows and gardening fairs are examples of the types of exhibitions staged in the exhibition halls.

The Wembley Tour
A guided tour of the complex is available to anyone who is interested. It includes a mini-train ride, an opportunity to see the famous changing rooms, the royal box and a behind-the-scenes look at the media rooms. For some, the highlight of the tour is being presented with a mock FA cup after walking up the 39 steps to collect it! Desmond Lynam, a BBC sports presenter, currently acts as a guide through audio-visual screens. You can even hear cheering crowds in the stadium – on tape!

Employment
Although the 187 full-time staff are permanently employed, an extra 3,000 part-time employees may be recruited on major event days. The extra staff are employed in catering, merchandising (selling programmes and souvenirs) and stewarding.

Activity

1 What makes Wembley unique?

2 As a public limited company, what are the sources of funding available? List any other sources of revenue illustrated in the case study.

3 Consider the location of Wembley as a National Stadium. What are the advantages and disadvantages? How accessible is it? Find out how a visitor can get there from the Newcastle by coach, by train and by car. How long will the journey take? Which of these methods of transport would you prefer from the north? Why?

4 What qualities do you think the stewards need to have? Why? Prepare a list of their duties when working at a major event such as a rock concert.

5 Find out exactly what a Wembley tour guide has to do. What qualities do you think the guides conducting this two-hour tour need?

Element 1.2 Investigate the Travel and Tourism Industry Nationally and Locally

This element looks at the travel and tourism industry nationally and locally. By the end of this element you should be able to:

1 describe the main components of the UK travel and tourism industry (performance criterion 1.2.1);
2 give examples of products and services available through the travel and tourism industry nationally (performance criterion 1.2.2);
3 compare the characteristics of public, private and voluntary sectors in the travel and tourism industry, supporting the comparison with examples (performance criterion 1.2.3);
4 give examples of the positive and negative impacts in the UK of the travel and tourism industry (performance criterion 1.2.4);
5 describe the characteristics and explain the economic impact of the travel and tourism industry in a locality (performance criterion 1.2.5).

Defining travel and tourism

 Activities

1 Write down several examples of times when you considered yourself to be a tourist? Where were you? What did you do? How long were you there for?

Now compare your experience with two or three others in your group, or ask some other people you know.

Now answer the questions below.
a Did everyone consider themselves to be a tourist only when they were away from the town or area where they normally live?
b What was the shortest period of time that someone was away from home as a tourist?
c What activities were participated in as tourists?

Now write down a definition of tourism which illustrates your understanding so far.

Compare your definition with the one on the next page.

'Tourism is about the temporary short-term movement of people to destinations outside the places where they normally live and work, and about their activities during their stay at these destinations; it includes travel for all purposes as well as day visits or excursions. An essential part of tourism is the intention of the traveller to return, whether this is from a day trip, a holiday or a short business trip.'

2   In which of the examples below would a person be classified as a tourist? Why?

- Someone on a day trip to a theme park.
- Someone who moves to another part of the country to live.
- A person who travels to another town for a two day business conference.
- A person who goes to stay with friends or relatives in another town.
- Someone who visits the local museum in their home town.

Travel services

There is a range of organisations now in existence to help you to travel. Whether you want to travel 100 kilometres by car or 10,000 by aeroplane there is an organisation hoping to help smooth your way.

The main providers of travel services to tourists are as follows.

- Airlines
- Railways
- Sea transport companies (e.g. ferries)
- Road transport companies (e.g. coach companies)

These organisations are known as 'transport principals' as they provide the actual means of transport from one place to another.

There are also organisations whose purpose is to help you decide where to go. They provide information and sell products that offer travel, accommodation, food and entertainment as part of a package for your journey and stay. The two main categories of this type of organisation are as follows.

- Travel agents
- Tour operators

Travel agent
A travel agent is a shop for travel and tourism products. These shops are often part of 'chains' (e.g. Lunn Poly). They hold a

range of information on all the possibilities for travel from a simple train journey to Birmingham from Manchester through to an all-inclusive package holiday to the Caribbean. The people who work in a travel agency are in a position to give you advice on travel and holiday arrangements and also sell you products offered by tour operators whose brochures they carry. They make their money on commissions from tour operators when they sell holidays advertised in brochures. As independents, commission is also made on airline tickets, ferry tickets, coach tickets and so on. One of the biggest sources of commission is holiday insurance, often sold as a compulsory part of overseas package holidays.

Tour operator

A tour operator may specialise in hotel holidays on the Costa del Sol in Spain, another may sell self-catering villa holidays in Tuscany, Italy. Tour operators sell their products through travel agencies or direct to the public by mail, phone, or computer link. Their main method of promotion is through brochures.

The biggest tour operator in the UK is Thomsons, which owns Horizon and Sky Tours brands. They also own their own airline (Britannia) and chain of travel agencies (Lunn Poly). Portland Holidays, also owned by Thomsons, sells packages directly to the public, therefore they are a 'direct-sell' operator (see page 89).

Tours

These are organised trips, which may be UK based, or made to attractions abroad, and people on them expect to travel to different destinations or areas every day or two. Some tour operators specialise in them. Tours which consist of UK residents who go abroad by coach, car or other means of transport are known as outgoing tours. Tours which overseas visitors take through the UK are known as incoming tours; an example is a coach tour for Japanese visitors which takes in Bath, Oxford, Cambridge, York, London and Stratford-upon-Avon.

These kinds of trips are often undertaken by a party in a coach and are popular with older people who enjoy the experience of seeing as many places as possible within a short period.

Information

In the UK national tourist boards such as the English Tourist Board, the British Tourist Authority and the Scottish Tourist Board provide information, through research reports, written guides and information leaflets. Regional tourist boards offer similar services at a regional level. At a local level, tourist information centres provide information on local attractions and facilities as well as accommodation. The Association of British Travel Agents offers advice and help to travel agents and the general public who may be dissatisfied with a holiday booked through a travel agent. The addresses of all these organisations can be found in Useful Addresses on page 246 at the end of this book.

Independent transport

Increasing private car ownership has encouraged people to travel independently on holiday. Some rural areas are poorly served by buses so it is essential for visitors to have a car if they visit these areas. Motoring organisations like the AA and RAC offer rescue services to members whose cars break down. Membership fees can cover a range of benefits including rescue and repair while travelling independently abroad. Car-hire services are used particularly by incoming visitors who wish to tour independently.

Travel and tourism: visitor attractions

We have already seen on page 4 that leisure attractions and tourism attractions are often one and the same thing. If you visit a theme park such as Alton Towers in North Staffordshire you will meet people visiting from all over the UK and from abroad.

'Themed' attractions, for example Disneyland in Paris in which all the entertainments revolve around Disney characters, are increasingly popular with tourists. These rely greatly on technology and include simulated experiences such as flying in a space ship or being in a haunted house.

Zoos, rare animal parks and sealife centres are also successful tourist attractions. In the UK there is now a greater focus on animal sanctuaries and zoos devoted to breeding rare animals than earlier in the century. This is due to increased public concern for animal rights.

Industrial attractions such as Ford Motor Company in Essex and nuclear power stations such as Sellafield in Cumbria are likely to increase in popularity in the future as they help to create public interest in the industries concerned and promote a positive image for them. Tourists can now visit breweries and distilleries and factories (e.g. The Body Shop, Wedgwood pottery); a guided tour and sample wares are often on offer.

Activity   In groups of four, make a list of all the attractions listed in Figure 10 which one of the group members has visited. What sort of experience did they have? What were the enjoyable aspects of the attraction; what where the less enjoyable aspects?

Now appoint a spokesperson and share your conclusions with the other groups.

Look at the recent trends for each attraction (the pattern of visitor numbers for the past years).

List the attractions which have:

a shown an increase in numbers in recent years;

FIGURE 10 Attendances at the most popular tourist attractions in 1995

b shown a decrease;

c remained fairly steady.

What conclusions can you draw from these findings?

United Kingdom   Millions

	1981	1991	1993		1981	1991	1993
Museums and galleries				**Historic houses and monuments**			
British Museum	2.6	5.1	5.8	Tower of London	2.1	1.9	2.3
National Gallery	2.7	4.3	3.9	Edinburgh Castle	0.8	1.0	1.0
Tate Gallery	0.9	1.8	1.8	Roman Baths, Bath	0.6	0.8	0.9
Natural History Museum	3.7	1.6	1.7	Warwick Castle	0.4	0.7	0.8
Science Museum	3.8	1.3	1.3	Windsor Castle,			
				State Apartments	0.7	0.6	0.8
Theme parks				**Wildlife parks and zoos**			
Blackpool Leisure Beach	7.5	6.5	6.8	London Zoo	1.1	1.1	0.9
Alton Towers	1.6	2.0	2.6	Chester Zoo	–	0.9	0.8
Pleasure Beach,				Sea Life Centre,			
Great Yarmouth	–	2.5	2.4	Blackpool	–	0.7	0.6
Pleasureland, Southport	–	1.8	2.0	Edinburgh Zoo	–	0.5	0.5
Chessington World of				Whipsnade Wild			
Adventures	0.5	1.4	1.5	Animal Park	–	0.6	0.4

Source: Social Trends 1995, Visits to Tourist Attractions 1992, British Tourist Authority

The economic impact of tourism   When an area develops as a tourist destination it is often good for the local economy. New jobs are created and, with the increase in visitors to the area, more money is spent in shops and restaurants: generally this benefits local trade.

On the other hand, areas which develop a tourist trade as a result of the decline in a traditional industry such as mining find themselves dependent on an industry which in the UK is often seasonal. This means that many jobs are available only in the summer (or winter in skiing areas); such jobs are often low paid.

When an economy is in recession the tourist industry suffers more than many as people have less money to spend on luxuries and holidays are not seen as a priority.

Environmental impact

Increased numbers of visitors to an area may be good for the economy, but there can be damage to the environment. Increased traffic volume and traffic congestion result in more pollution and increased noise levels. There is often a litter problem. Erosion of natural landscapes by numerous visitors walking on the same paths is a big problem in areas such as the Peak District and The Lake District.

In some countries, visitors pay a tourist tax when they stay overnight in an area in order to help pay for the upkeep of local facilities and attractions, natural and man-made. This may happen in the UK in the future; currently visitors are charged to visit Stonehenge, but are restricted as to where they can walk in order to minimise the effects of soil erosion. Some visitors were also found to be trying to remove chunks of the Stonehenge rocks to take home as souvenirs!

Social impact

A sudden influx of tourists into their area in the summer months may not be welcomed by all the permanent residents, who can feel resentful of the extra traffic congestion, noise and litter which is created.

Locals may feel that visitors are 'taking over' and swamping local community life. This has become a problem in some areas such as Wales where people have bought second homes as weekend or summer retreats. The demand for these second homes in certain favoured areas has forced house prices up and locals can resent this.

For more information on the environmental impacts of tourism, you should refer to Unit 8 on pages 219–39.

Element 1.3 Prepare for Employment in the Leisure and Tourism Industries

About this element This element looks at employment in the leisure and tourism industries. By the end of this element you should be able to:

1 identify, using main sources of information, jobs within the leisure and tourism industries which are likely to suit you and explain why (performance criterion 1.3.1);
2 identify and describe the qualifications, skills and experience required for these jobs (performance criterion 1.3.2);
3 describe how to acquire qualifications, skills and experience required for these jobs (performance criterion 1.3.3);
4 describe different ways of presenting personal information to prospective employers (performance criterion 1.3.4);
5 produce a curriculum vitae suitable for submission to prospective employers (performance criterion 1.3.5).

As the scope of the leisure and tourism industry is very broad, so, too, is the range of jobs which come under the leisure and tourism umbrella. Some of these jobs and careers are listed below.

Leisure
- Sports coaching
- Recreation assistant
- Life-guard
- Personal fitness trainer
- Professional athlete
- Hotel manager
- Venue manager
- Outdoor pursuits instructor
- Chef

Tourism
- Travel agent
- Tour operator's reservations assistant
- Tourist information assistant

- Air steward
- Tour guide
- Overseas resort representative
- Children's representative
- Cruise ship entertainment organiser

FIGURE 11 A leisure centre assistant oversees the use of a pool complex

Where do I start?

If you are still undecided as to which field of leisure and tourism you wish to go into, you can have a careers advice interview, free of charge. This is usually available at your school or college, but you can also arrange an interview through your local careers advice centre. Their address is available in the telephone book or through your local library.

If you would like to work in the area where you live, you need to gain a realistic idea of what the local job opportunities are for leisure and tourism. Perhaps you could talk to local employees, such as an assistant in the sports centre or someone who works in the local travel agency. Most areas have a leisure services and tourism department which you can contact for advice. Try the telephone book or your local library for the address. Many areas also produce tourism and leisure plans which are available from these departments. These will give you some idea about the future of tourism and leisure in your locality.

You should visit local job centres and employment agencies. You can look at the jobs on offer and talk to one of the assistants who will ask you to fill in a form so that you can be contacted if anything suitable arises.

The 'classified' advertisements section of the local paper is another useful source of information on available jobs; you should look through it regularly.

Professional organisations in leisure and tourism also offer advice and information on training in the industry. Refer to the Useful Addresses list on page 246.

Further sources of information

If you are prepared to move away from home to work in another part of the country, or even to go abroad, you need to look at a wider range of information sources.

National papers which carry recruitment advertising on certain days each week are *The Guardian, The Times, The Daily Telegraph* and *The Independent.*

Both the leisure and tourism industries also have trade journals where specialist jobs are advertised. These are available in your area's main reference library. They include the following publications.

- *Hotel and Caterer*
- *Leisure Manager*
- *Leisure Opportunities*
- *Sports and Leisure*
- *Handbook of Tourism and Leisure*
- *Travel Trade Gazette*

How do I gain skills, qualifications and experience?

GNVQs and NVQs

An advanced GNVQ in leisure and tourism is likely to be available at your local college on a full or part-time basis. If you gain sufficient units on an advanced GNVQ, you will be eligible to apply for higher education at a university leading, for example, to a degree or HND (Higher National Diploma) in leisure studies or tourism.

NVQs (National Vocational Qualifications) are closely related to the world of work and to particular jobs. They are based on national standards set by lead bodies, representing employers. In the leisure and tourism industries, lead bodies include ABTA (The Association of British Travel Agents), Sport and Recreation, The Hotel and Catering Training Company and The Museums Training Institute.

NVQs assess a person's competence to perform a range of tasks in the workplace. They are available at a variety of levels, from 1–5, where 1 is foundation and 5 is post-graduate level. In a travel agency for example, you might be expected to gain an NVQ in Travel Services. In a leisure centre the relevant NVQs you could work towards include 'Coaching Adults' and 'Coaching Children'.

Open learning

Courses run on an open-learning basis are increasingly being offered by employers as part of continuing education. They are particularly convenient for people working in the leisure and tourism industries because the amount of shift work and anti-social hours often makes it hard for them to attend conventional courses. Open learning gives people a chance to study at their own pace in their own time; the fees and books are often paid for by employers.

'I want to work in a travel agency.'

Some agencies employ young people as youth trainees. You will then receive a mixture of on-the-job training in addition to working towards an NVQ in travel services. The British Airways NVQ in air ticketing is another qualification you may be expected to achieve.

'I want to work in a tourist information centre.'

Working for a tourist information centre requires good customer-care skills and a thorough general knowledge of the facilities, products and services available locally.

'I want to work for a tour operator.'

Tour operators employ either office workers dealing with administration, such as telephone reservations staff, or people who work abroad in the tourist destination, for instance overseas representatives. If you wish to work as an overseas representative you will need to have a working knowledge of a major European language. Many tour operators recruit 'reps' to work just for a summer, or winter, and put them on an in-house training course prior to starting. This will include selling and customer-care skills, plus the company's administration procedures. Some tour operators also employ children's representatives to run activity schemes in family resorts. This job has the advantage of a lower starting age, that is 18 instead of 21, which is the minimum age for many representative jobs.

'I want to be a recreation assistant.'

Leisure centres often give on-the-job training, such as awards for competent sports coaching or an exercise to music teacher's certificate. Obviously, it would be helpful if you could gain some relevant preliminary sporting awards before applying to a leisure centre. The Community Sports Leaders Award, for instance, is a basic introduction to sports coaching and is run at various centres around the country. Most sports lead bodies have their own coaching qualifications, which start off at a leaders level and progress to senior coach level.

'I want to work in outdoor pursuits.'

If you are interested in outdoor recreation, there are relevant coaching awards in individual sports such as windsurfing, sailing, canoeing, and mountaineering. The Central Council for Physical Recreation (see page 246) also offers leaders awards in outdoor activities, which provide a basic introduction to the outdoor environment. An NVQ in outdoor education is also available.

Work experience

Many vocational courses have work experience built in to the programme: this is a good way of trying out a job to see if it really suits you. If it is not possible to gain work experience in this way, you could try work shadowing for a day. This would involve you contacting a suitable employer and asking if you could accompany an employee for a day to give you an idea of what their job involves.

Applying for a job

Once you have found a job to apply for you need to be confident that you can produce a good letter of application. Some employers will send an application form, or they will ask for a curriculum vitae (c.v.).

How do I write a curriculum vitae?

A c.v. is a summary of your qualifications and achievements to date. It also gives an employer some indication of what you are like as a person (see Figure 12).

Presenting a c.v.

1   A c.v. should always be typed or should fit on one side of one A4 piece of paper only.
2   Never send out a c.v. containing any mistakes or corrections.
3   After you have written your c.v. get a friend to read it through and make sure it is clear.

Look at the sample c.v. given in Figure 12 below.

CURRICULUM VITAE

Name: Susan Catherine White

Address: 26 Thelby Road, Anytown, Northamptonshire NH2 YW2

Tel: 01690 999999

Education and Qualifications
Anytown Secondary School 1990–1995
Examinations gained: GCSE Maths Grade E
                        GCSE English Grade C
                        GCSE Geography Grade D
                        GCSE French Grade D
                        GCSE Social Studies Grade E

Currently studying at: Anytown College 1996 GNVQ Intermediate Leisure and Tourism

Work Experience
Anytown Jeans and Jumpers   Summer 1995
High Street, Anytown   Sales assistant (part-time)

Personal Interests
Skiing: I have an older married brother who works in France as a skiing representative. He is married to a French woman and my family visit him every winter to ski.
Camping: I helped to organise the forthcoming college camping holiday to Austria.

Other Information
I have shadowed a sales consultant at ABC Travel for one day in April 1996, and feel that I would be suited to the job. I can speak French to conversational standard as a result of my family's frequent winter skiing holidays in France.

Referees
Mrs J Brown, Manager
ABC Travel
2 The High Street
Anytown, Northants NH3 8VW
Tel 01690 888000

FIGURE 12 A sample curriculum vitae

Presenting a letter

1   A letter may be handwritten or typed. If you write it, make sure that your writing is neat and legible.

2   Use good quality white or blue writing paper and write in black or blue ink only. Do not write letters on lined paper, or in red ink or pencil.

FIGURE 13 A sample letter of application

Now look at the sample letter of application written by Susan White.

Mrs J Brown
Manager
XYZ Travel
3 Main Street
Somerton
Nr Anytown
Northamptonshire
NT1 AK4

Susan White
26 Thelby Road
Anytown
Northamptonshire
NH2 YW2

Tel 01690 999999

10 June 1996

Dear Mrs Brown

Trainee Sales Consultant

I would like to apply for the job of Trainee Sales Consultant as advertised in the Journal of 8 June 1996.

I am seventeen years old and at the moment I am completing a GNVQ Intermediate course in Leisure and Tourism at Anytown College. My grades to date have been good passes and I expect to complete the course successfully at the end of June.

I have long been interested in making a career in the travel agency business and have tried to find out as much as possible about the work of a travel consultant. I feel that I would really enjoy dealing with the public, advising them on their travel and holiday requirements and contributing towards the success of a travel agency business.

I have already had some experience of working in a clothes shop during the evenings and weekends where I was a sales assistant. This involved dealing with the public both in person and by telephone.

I enjoy skiing and camping and have been on several holidays of this nature to France, Austria and Spain.

I enclose my c.v. which gives you more details about myself. If you feel I would be suitable for this position I would be very pleased to attend an interview.

Yours sincerely

Susan White

Susan White   Enclosed: c.v.

The interview   If your application is successful and you are invited for an interview, you need to bear in mind the following points in order to make the best impression.

1   Prepare for the interview by finding out about the organisation beforehand. They may ask you questions about its work and if you are knowledgeable you will demonstrate real interest. Prepare answers for obvious questions which are likely to arise, such as:

- 'Why have you applied for his job?'
- 'What relevant experience have you got?'
- 'What relevant skills have you got?'

2   Have some questions prepared which you can ask at the end of the interview. You could enquire about training and prospects for promotion.

3   Dress appropriately. A cared-for appearance is very important in the leisure and tourism industry as it helps to convey your health and vitality, sociability and efficiency.

4   Make sure that you arrive in good time. If you are late, it will create a bad first impression.

5   It is normal to be nervous, but try to think about your body language during the interview. Do not slouch in the chair and look down. Keep good eye contact with the interviewer as this will help you to be confident. Shake hands firmly.

6   Answer questions truthfully but as positively as you can. Try not to give one word answers, but expand on your answers where you can and make them interesting.

Assignment activity Unit 1   You should keep all your assignment activity work, clearly labelled, in your Portfolio of Evidence. This work provides evidence of coverage of all the elements and performance criteria covered in Unit 1.

1   Choose a week in which you are able to investigate all the sources of information listed on page 29. Choose a number of jobs which you think might suit you and at the end of the week carry out the following pieces of written work.

   a   Make a list of all the jobs which have interested you. Include their advertisements if appropriate.
   b   Write a brief summary of why you think each job you have chosen would suit you.
   c   List the qualifications, skills and experience required for each job you have chosen. You will need to read the advertisements, where given, quite closely. If you need

additional information you can contact the employer for a job description.

Having carried out your job search, you may feel that you need to gain extra qualifications, skills or experience in order to be eligible to apply for the career of your choice. Make a note of this if necessary.

2 Look at the jobs advertised in Figure 14 and select one which interests you. Alternatively, you may use one of the job advertisements that interested you in assignment activity number 1 above.
   a Prepare your curriculum vitae.
   b Prepare a letter of application for your chosen job.

3 With a partner, take it in turns to interview each other for the jobs you have applied for.

   To prepare this, exchange letters and c.v.s and make a list of questions you will ask as interviewer and interviewee.

   Make notes during each interview and give feedback on each others' performance using the guidelines given.

4 This part of the assignment requires group co-operation to mount an exhibition. Here is the brief.

   A group of leisure and tourism students from another European country will shortly be visiting your organisation as part of an exchange programme. They are eager to find out as much as they can about the UK leisure and tourism industry.

   In groups of three or four you are to build up a portfolio of material to create an exhibition which will be on display in your library. The aim is to give a general overview of national leisure and tourism industries and to focus in detail on a locality.

   Each group of three or four will be allocated a display board and table for the presentation of material. Remember that the information must look attractive and make people want to visit your stand. You should try to produce your text on a wordprocessor.

   a Describe the components of the leisure industry given below and give one example of a facility from each component.

      • Arts and entertainment
      • Sports and physical activities
      • Outdoor activities

Waves Leisure Pool
RIPPLES HEALTH AND FITNESS
Are you looking for a career in Leisure?

We need two new members of staff to join our team responsible for the safe operation of this very busy complex. Situated on the banks of the River Thames, the centre comprises of a leisure pool with waves and giant waterslides, river run and many other water features. The centre has a substantial health and fitness facility including gym, activity studio and health suite, as well as a catering and bar operation.

Recreation Assistant
£9,000 p.a.
+ profit share scheme
If you feel you can meet the challenge of delivering the highest standards of service we provide to all our customers and have a current life saving qualification, you could be part of a team responsible for the safe operation of the pool. This could be your first step towards a career in leisure.

Fitness Instructor
£9,500 p.a.
+ profit share scheme
We are seeking a highly motivated individual with the ability to deliver a service that exceeds our customers' expectations. You will need a YMCA or RSA fitness qualification or equivalent and ideally experience in exercise prescription.

Contact Jo Black for an informal chat or application details at Waves Leisure Pool on 01758 99999.
Closing date 10th June 1996. Interviews – week commencing 24th June 1996.

Airline Cabin Crew

required by Major International Airline

Ideally you will be aged 21–30 years, a minimum height of 5'3" (with weight in proportion) with a good basic education, excellent health and good eyesight. Fluency in English is essential and an additional language would be an advantage.

We invite applicants both with and without previous experience.

To arrange agency interview phone   Crew

Trainee Sales Consultants – Travel
Wimbledon
Full and part time

Our Sales Consultants work hard at helping people enjoy their holidays. So our Travel Shops have a lively atmosphere which is enjoyed not just by our customers but also by our staff.

As part of our effective, efficient team you'll use your friendly outgoing personality to make customers feel welcome, build a rapport and achieve sales. Ideally, you'll be CRS/SABRE trained, although this is not essential as full training will be given.

We offer excellent training, a negotiable starting salary, profit share and excellent discounts on holidays.

If you would like to be part of a forward looking company, please phone 0181 010 987 6 for an application form between 8.30 am and 5.30 pm Monday to Friday.

Closing date for completed applications: Friday 21st June

FIGURE 14 A selection of job advertisements

- Heritage
- Play
- Catering and accommodation

b Give examples of at least one leisure product or service from each component which is available nationally

c Select four examples of leisure and recreation facilities which are of national significance. Each of the facilities chosen should be unique for one of the following reasons. Your answers should be summarised in a table similar to the table below.

Unique qualities	National example	Explanation
• Unique in natural landscape features	Lake District	Only mountainous area in UK with large area of lakes
• Unique physical size or in numbers of people attending		
• Unique in historical significance		
• Unique in cultural significance		
• Whether the location relates to natural or historical features (e.g. sailing club near a lake)		

d Choose an example of a leisure or recreation facility and a travel and tourism facility from each of the public, private and voluntary sectors. Compare the three facilities in terms of:

- national or local operation;
- aims (e.g. profit making);
- types of staff employed (numbers of paid or volunteer staff).

List the methods of funding for each facility.
Devise a table to summarise your findings.

e Describe the components of the tourism industry and give examples of products and services from each.

- Travel services
- Tour operators
- Transport
- Visitor attractions
- Information and services
- Accommodation and catering

f Give six examples of the positive and negative impacts which the travel and tourism industry has in the UK. Your answer should include economic, environmental and social impacts. Set your answers out as in the example on the next page.

		1	2	3	4	5	6
Economic	Negative Positive						

		1	2	3	4	5	6
Social	Negative Positive						

		1	2	3	4	5	6
Environmental	Negative Positive						

g Produce a local guide which identifies and describes the leisure and recreation industry in a locality.

- Describe the main facilities products and services available.
- Locate them on a map with a colour coding.
- Explain the reasons for the location of the facilities, products or services.

You should consider the following points:
- how easily customers can reach the facilities;
- the numbers of people who can reach them;
- whether they meet the needs of the local community.

h Prepare a presentation on the travel and tourism industry in the locality. You should:

- describe the facilities, products and services available;
- locate them on a map;
- identify which sector they belong to.

Draw up a table as in the example below.

	Private	Public	Voluntary
Name Facilities Location			

- explain the positive and negative economic impact of the Travel and Tourism Industry on your chosen locality. Use statistical evidence (e.g. numbers employed) to support your answers.

Unit ② Marketing and Promoting Leisure and Tourism Products

This unit comprises the following elements required by the course and gives you practice in all the performance criteria that prove your understanding of each of these elements.

Element 2.1   Investigate marketing and promotion in leisure and recreation, travel and tourism organisations

Element 2.2   Plan a leisure and recreation or travel and tourism promotional campaign

Element 2.3   Run and evaluate a leisure or tourism promotional campaign

▚ Element 2.1 Investigate Marketing and Promotion in Leisure and Recreation, Travel and Tourism Organisations

About this element   This element looks at marketing and promotion in the leisure and tourism industry. By the end of this element you should be able to:

1 explain how marketing applies to leisure and recreation and travel and tourism organisations (performance criterion 2.1.1);
2 describe the marketing mix and explain how promotional activities fit into it (performance criterion 2.1.2);
3 describe the main types of information gathered by market research (performance criterion 2.1.3);
4 describe how the leisure and tourism target markets are divided into market segments (performance criterion 2.1.4);
5 explain how the marketing mix relates to target markets for products and services in selected leisure and recreation and travel and tourism organisations (performance criterion 2.1.5).

What is marketing?

No organisation will survive for long unless it uses effective marketing. This means that all company policies are based on meeting customer needs, on creating satisfied customers who will return again and again to the organisation. Large leisure and tourism organisations have marketing departments with their own personnel who oversee the marketing operations of the whole company. Examples include large tour operators such as Airtours, transport companies like P&O European Ferries and large hotel groups. It is not essential to have a marketing department to practise the philosophy. An independent leisure centre can achieve success by looking after customers in every aspect of its business. The basic function of marketing is to ensure that the right product or service is delivered to the right people at the right time in the right place. Achieving these 'rights' should lead to a healthy and profitable organisation.

The example in Figure 15 shows the organisational structure for a regional venue. You can see that marketing staff are integral to the organisation although there is not a marketing department.

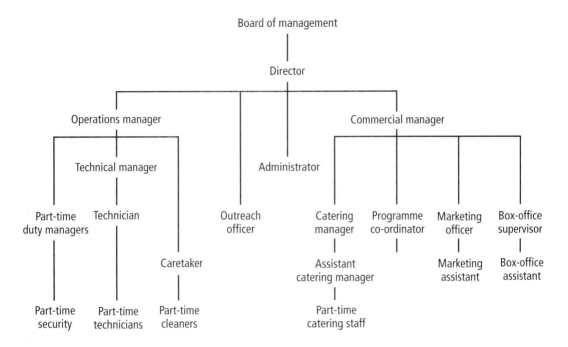

FIGURE 15 A typical staff organisation structure

Public bodies also take marketing very seriously. The British Tourist Authority (BTA) has the vital task of marketing the UK overseas as a tourist destination. To achieve this, they have offices all over the world.

The marketing mix

This term is used to cover all the activities undertaken to practise marketing. All marketing concentrates on four main areas, known as the 'Four Ps'. The Four Ps may vary in relative importance according to the particular objectives of a marketing campaign.

The Four Ps
- Price
- Product
- Place
- Promotion

Let us look at some examples of the work that goes on to serve the Four Ps. This work will include:

- market research;
- product development;
- pricing;
- advertising;
- distribution ;
- selling;
- aftersales service.

The Four Ps: Price If you wish to travel by train, for example, you will find yourself presented with a variety of fares for your journey. The most expensive will be an ordinary return. By travelling 'off peak' (that is in quieter times of the day outside business travelling hours) you will get a saver fare or a cheap day return. If you are a student you can buy a rail card entitling you to a reduction on fares. If you are a family, you can buy a family rail card offering similar reductions. This choice of fares is called a 'pricing structure'. Some leisure and tourism services have developed quite complicated pricing structures in their attempts to attract a wide range of customers.

Tour operators price their holidays according to season. The most expensive holidays always coincide with school holidays when demand is highest. This expensive period of the holiday year is known as the high season and usually coincides with Easter, school summer holidays and Christmas.

Look at Figure 16. It shows an extract from tour operator's brochure advertising hotel holidays in California. Note the difference of £200 in price between winter and summer season for the same holiday.

SUNSAND – CONTINENTAL BREAKFAST INCLUDED

NO. OF NIGHTS	01 JAN – 05 APR	06 APR – 13 APR	14 APR – 30 APR	01 MAY – 17 MAY	18 MAY – 30 JUN	01 JUL – 07 JUL	08 JUL – 31 AUG	01 SEP – 30 SEP	01 OCT – 24 OCT	25 OCT – 15 DEC	16 DEC – 24 DEC	25 DEC – 31 DEC	01 JAN – 27 MAR	CHILD DISC
7	479	599	479	539	579	639	679	579	529	499	669	499	479	35%
14	579	699	579	639	679	729	779	669	629	599	779	559	579	40%
EX NGT	14	14	14	14	14	14	14	14	14	14	14	14	14	75%
SG SUPP	14	14	14	14	14	14	14	14	14	14	14	14	14	N/A

EXTRA NIGHT PRICES ARE PER PERSON AND DO NOT INCLUDE CAR HIRE. SATURDAY FLIGHT SUPPLEMENTS £12 EACH WAY

Hotel Features

- Private facilities
- Safes
- Gift shop
- Private beach
- Air conditioning
- Free covered parking
- Rooftop swimming pool
- Colour TV with pay movie channel
- Recently refurbished rooms
- Rooms have fridge, microwave & tea/coffee server
- Discount coupons for nearby restaurants
- Continental breakfast included

FIGURE 16 The differences in price for a hotel in California – winter and summer seasons

Prices may vary according to the needs and purchasing power of different customers. A leisure centre, particularly a public facility, will have a scale of charges to cater for the unemployed, those who are retired and sometimes local residents.

Private organisations also offer discounts from time to time. This may be because they wish to increase sales or to respond to competitors who are making similar offers. The advertisements in Figure 17 show special offers being made.

FIGURE 17 Advertisements run by Lunn Poly and Forte Leisure Breaks offering discounts

The Four Ps: Product

The range of products and services offered by leisure and tourism organisations is diverse, ranging from package holidays, sports activities and travel to tickets for rock concerts. Products have to be developed to suit customer needs and fashion. As customers' tastes change, so must the products.

Theme parks, for instance, have to introduce new and exciting rides to ensure that their customers return again and again. In 1994 Alton Towers built a new ride called Nemesis and publicised it heavily to attract and regenerate custom.

Tour operators have to cater for changes in fashion in holiday destinations, even trying to lead the way in 'discovering' new areas. At the beginning of the 1980s Turkey was almost unknown as a tourist destination. Today, Turkey's coastline and major towns are a generally available as a holiday to anyone in the UK who feels inclined to go.

Companies selling products that offer to take care of every aspect of their customer's holiday need to provide more and different luxuries to be sure of offering customers something new and attractive. Look at Figure 18, advertising a Cunard cruise holiday. Notice they way in which emphasis is placed on the service and convenience you can expect.

FIGURE 18 Cunard's advertisement for a carefree Caribbean holiday

---

Activity Look again at the hotel features shown in Figure 16.

a Make a list of all the elements which make up the product.

b Can you think of anything which might be added to improve it?

c Imagine you are putting together a package holiday to your home town for tourists from California.
Design one page of a brochure to attract them to the town. Try to cost the holiday as well. Remember to show different charges for different seasons.

The Four Ps: Place

The word 'place' in the Four Ps refers to the place where a product or service is actually delivered to customers.

You can be sold a product:

- on the high street;
- in your home;
- at a specialist venue.

Where are tourism products sold?

Tour operators usually sell their holidays through travel agencies located on a busy street in the town or city. Travel agencies need a good shop site, so that they can hope to attract a wide range of shoppers. The high street site is such a good selling place that some tour operators have set up their own travel agency chains. Lunn Poly is owned by Thomson Holidays and Going Places by Airtours.

Some organisations prefer to distribute their product by direct selling. This means that advertising and encouragement to buy is addressed directly to the customer through newspaper, poster and television advertising. Portland Holidays (also part of the Thomson Group) do this. You can sit at home and watch a television advertisement, then ring and ask for details without going through a travel agency. Other holiday companies will send you advertising through the post if you have been identified as the type of customer likely to be interested in their products.

Some holiday products are deliberately distributed through very few outlets to keep the price high. These products are often associated with an 'exclusive' image which the organisation wishes to maintain.

Where are leisure and recreation products sold?

Public sports centres are usually centrally located so that they are easily accessible to a wide range of customers. Privately run ones may not be so centrally located but will certainly provide lots of car parking and special members facilities.

Some sports equipment manufacturers use the specialist venue selling technique to keep up the exclusivity image. An example is the L A Lights trainer shoe which is distributed through just a very few sports shops.

Some attractions are often unable to control their place – The National Trust has no choice over their position – but are able to advertise to the public through the post, through leaflets designed to be picked up and taken home from tourist information centres and through distinctive roadside signposting.

The Four Ps: Promotion

Promotion is the term given to all the activities which are used to bring an organisation's products and services before the general public. Advertising in the media is only one part of promotion.

Promotional activities are a very important part of the marketing mix. Promotion usually lets customers know what to expect of an organisation and its products by way of price, product and place. The examples of advertising we saw in Figure 17 are part of a promotional campaign informing the customer about prices.

Advertising in the media

You will have noticed all kinds of advertisements for leisure and tourism organisations appearing on media ranging from posters on billboards to national television. Organisations, and their advertising agencies, think very carefully about which media to use. They need to know the answers to the following questions.

- Who is the target audience (potential customers)?
- Will the media chosen reach them?
- What will the advertisement cost?
- Does this cost justify the expected return?

The following terms will help you to understand the language of advertising in the media.

Reach – the number of people an advertisement reaches in total.

Spot – the timing of a single appearance of a television commercial, for instance, before the main evening news or late at night.

Column centimetres – the width (column) and depth (centimetres) of the space booked for an advertisement in a newspaper or magazine.

Circulation – the total number of one particular newspaper or magazine distributed (that is sold or given away free) locally or nationally.

Readership – the number of people who actually read the publication (more than one person may read a single copy). This is usually calculated as three times circulation.

Ratecard – sets out the costs of insertions by sizes and positions of advertisements in newspapers and magazines or spots by time length and time of day on television.

Television

Tourist organisations are more likely than leisure organisations to use television advertising, known as a television commercial. This is because they are often large organisations who need to attract customers from all over the UK.

Some organisations use local television networks to place advertisements for tourist services in a specific region.

Why do tourist organisations like tour operators use television to advertise?

1   In any one week 91 per cent of adults in the UK watch commercial television. Did you know that *Coronation Street* attracts audiences of more than 20 million viewers?
2   Television shows moving, colour pictures and is therefore an ideal medium through which to sell the idea of an attractive, glamorous holiday.

Target audience

The audience for television varies according to the time of day and programming schedules. Adults with the ability to pay for a holiday, the tourist organisation's target audience, are likely to be watching in the evening after work. This time is also peak time: 6.30 p.m. to 10.30 p.m.

Organisations considering television advertising need to think about the increasing use of video recorders. If you record a popular programme and watch it later you may well fast forward through those expensive commercials.

Price

The high cost of television advertising means that only very large organisations are able to afford national television commercials. The cost of making the commercial itself is often very high.

National newspapers

A person in the UK is more likely to buy a daily newspaper regularly than a person from anywhere else in Europe.

According to the National Readership Survey 1995 over 60 per cent of adults in the UK buy a daily newspaper. Advertisers therefore have a wide choice of target audiences and circulations. Look at the table giving national newspaper circulation rates in Figure 19. Although newspapers are struggling to maintain circulation levels, often by discounting their prices, they still represent an attractive proposition to advertisers.

Newspaper title	Average net circulation Oct. '95–Mar. '96	October 1995	November 1995	December 1995	January 1996	February 1996	March 1996
National morning popular							
Daily Mirror	**2,499,360**	2,522,501	2,492,285	2,451,433	2,560,052	2,514,427	2,480,231
Daily Record	**740,994**	741,632	754,432	738,913	737,915	734,508	738,432
Daily Star	**667,207**	660,760	666,894	664,850	688,585	671,250	659,826
The Star – Eire	**87,502**	87,606	87,141	87,344	84,632	88,635	88,947
Sun	**4,072,971**	4,055,746	4,075,902	4,007,580	4,128,485	4,073,601	4,101,117
Total of average daily net sale	**8,068,034**	8,068,245	8,076,654	7,950,120	8,199,669	8,082,421	8,068,553
National morning mid market							
Daily Express	**1,262,920**	1,251,432	1,252,811	1,288,051	1,265,967	1,265,016	1,255,293
Daily Mail	**1,981,707**	1,853,236	1,894,242	1,987,349	2,065,985	2,039,713	2,055,775
Total of average daily net sale	**3,244,627**	3,104,668	3,147,053	3,275,400	3,331,951	3,304,729	3,311,068
National morning quality							
Daily Telegraph	**1,044,281**	1,052,592	1,052,340	1,036,906	1,053,146	1,027,882	1,042,647
Financial Times	**304,854**	297,382	305,918	310,200	295,112	308,556	308,914
Guardian	**401,988**	405,716	404,450	393,325	408,186	402,214	400,245
Independent	**288,364**	296,689	293,777	282,965	292,049	285,809	280,396
Times	**672,292**	675,032	672,521	645,303	687,992	688,205	669,366
Total of average daily net sale	**2,711,779**	2,727,591	2,729,006	2,668,699	2,736,485	2,712,666	2,701,568
Overall total of average daily net sale	**14,024,440**	13,900,504	13,952,713	13,894,219	14,268,106	14,099,816	14,081,189
National morning sporting							
Racing Post	**47,518**	45,450	44,004	41,777	46,997	56,059	54,596
Sporting Life	**68,207**	67,039	65,604	62,252	63,724	76,746	74,895
London Evening							
Evening Standard	**463,146**	468,931	460,686	432,954	479,127	463,299	473,739
National morning group							
Daily Mirror/Daily Record	**3,240,354**	3,264,133	3,246,717	3,190,346	3,297,967	3,248,935	3,218,663
Daily Star/The Star – Eire	**754,709**	748,366	754,035	752,194	773,217	759,885	748,773

FIGURE 19 National newspaper circulation rates 1993–94

Target audience

A newspaper's target audience is often described as its 'reader profile'. *The Daily Telegraph* is said to have an establishment, conservative, literary reader profile; *The Sun* is said to have a gossipy, interested in scandal among the rich and famous, reader profile.

Advertisers are able to study the reader profiles of newspapers and decide which offers the best target audience for their products. However, a company is unlikely to restrict its campaign to one newspaper only.

It is often effective to run an advertisement with a relevant feature; for instance an article about Thai culture might be accompanied by a tour operator's offers of package holidays to Thailand. Advertisements like this are often accompanied by reply coupons; the reader is asked to fill in their name and address, cut it out and post it off as a request for further information. This is called 'direct response' advertising, and provides the organisation with the actual names and addresses of the target audience.

One disadvantage of advertising in national daily newspapers is that once read they are thrown away and the advertisement will not be noticed by the target audience more than once.

Price

The cost of advertising in a newspaper is determined by its circulation. *The Sun*, for instance, as you can see from Figure 19, is able to command very high fees. Prices also vary according to where in the newspaper the advertisement is placed.

Local newspapers

For leisure centres and venues which wish to attract custom primarily from their local area local newspaper advertising is very useful. Some areas have a daily evening paper (London has the *Evening Standard*), many have a weekly paper (Salisbury has the *Salisbury Journal*) and some areas have weekly free newspapers which exist on the revenue from the advertising carried.

Weekly papers in particular are useful for advertising leisure facilities and programmes of events as people keep them for reference throughout the week. This means that there are many opportunities for an advertisement to be noticed.

Magazines

The advantage of advertising in a magazine is that the finished product is much superior to that in a newspaper. Full colour, full page, glossy advertisements can be aimed precisely at a target audience. Look at Figure 20 for an example of an advertisement targeted at women who would like to achieve a healthy, fit attractive body without strenuous exercise routines. A more discreet advertisement which is also accurately targeted in shown in Figure 21. Who do you think would be interested in this health resort?

Magazines can be categorised into two main types:

- trade magazines;
- consumer magazines.

Rating ★★★★
Health and Fitness Magazine

"It is a good, fun, safe, and effective exercise programme. I enjoyed it." – **The Sports Council.**

Plus a £50 off voucher for a luxurious weekend break at an exclusive health farm (see pack for details). **Only £10.99.**

FIGURE 20 An advertisement promising a quick way to achieve a fit, healthy and attractive body

Trade magazines

These magazines talk about issues important to a particular industry. The advertise products and services of interest to those working within that industry. The leisure and tourism industry titles include *Leisure Management* and *Travel Trade Gazette*. These are important sources of information about new initiatives in leisure and travel organisations and also carry advertisements for jobs within the trade.

Consumer magazines

These magazines are aimed at the general public who want information about hobbies, lifestyles, fashion and food. They are particularly good value for advertisers as they are often kept and re-read for at least a week after purchase. Most such magazines are read by more than one person as they are often passed on to friends and relatives before being thrown away. They even get as far as your doctor's or dentist's waiting room where you read magazines you would not normally buy!

TV Times and *Radio Times* are important consumer advertising magazines as they are so widely bought and kept specifically for information.

FIGURE 21 An advertisement for health in a stately home

Commercial radio

There are many local radio stations in both town and country areas. In addition, the 1990s brought in the era of network commercial radio with stations such as Virgin broadcasting throughout the UK.

As with television advertising, the number of listeners and the audience profile changes throughout the day and leisure and tourism organisations need to consider when their potential customers will be listening. Many local radio stations have a regular 'what's on' feature.

Posters

There are two types of poster advertising:

- roadside
- transport

Roadside posters (billboards)

These are usually used for 'reminder' campaigns, that is they are linked to a current television advertisement. They have to put across a very simple message or image because people are only going to see them briefly as they are walking or driving past.

Transport posters

Transport posters can be used to give more detail, particularly in the London Underground where the passenger has nothing to look at outside. A captive, sitting audience waiting for, or travelling on, a train or bus has nothing to do but read advertisements.

Sites for both types of poster can be booked individually or in a package. London Transport Advertising handles London buses and tube trains, but there are specialist companies which arrange poster advertising for clients.

Cinemas

The main age range of cinema goers is between 16 and 25 and much of cinema film advertising is aimed at this younger target audience. However, there is now a concerted effort by film makers to win back the family audience, age range between 25 and 45. Cinema audiences are growing and in future this target audience will make cinema advertising more interesting to organisations like tour operators.

Activity   Find a local weekly newspaper from your area and turn to the section with the 'what's on' advertisements.

Now imagine your family is host to a family of visiting Americans for a week. You have been given the task of organising their entertainment.

The family consists of the father in his 40s, a son of 18 and a daughter of 8 years old. They don't all have to do the same thing together.

Make a one -week diary starting on the Sunday and finishing on the Saturday. Fill in the activities planned for each day, using information from the newspaper advertisements only.

Other promotional activities
Exhibitions

The purpose of an exhibition is to display a wide range of goods and products to the general public, or to a specific trade, or both. The London Boat Show is a popular example of a leisure exhibition held annually at Earls Court, West London. Another famous leisure exhibition is the Ideal Home Exhibition, also held at Earls Court. Both these exhibitions allow the public to see the full range of new products on offer and be tempted into buying on the spot. Trade visitors are able to assess the products on offer from competitors.

Exhibitions such as the Caravan Show at London's Olympia are open to trade only for the first days of the exhibition and then opened to the public. This allows sales people to deal with business from trade customers before turning their attention to attracting the general public's interest.

Competitions

Competitions are usually organised to encourage people to buy a product or at least take a second look at it. The reader is often expected to read the text of an advertisement in order to be able to answer the questions, with the result that she or he takes in the information being promoted.

Discounts and money-off schemes

These schemes are very popular with travel agents. Such offers are usually made for limited periods so that people will be tempted to book holidays as soon as they notice them. Theatres sometimes offer early booking discounts for the same reason.

There may be conditions attached to discount offers particularly in the travel industry; a child must share the hotel room of two adults to qualify for a free holiday or travel insurance must be purchased to secure a discount. The important text in Figure 22 is the small print!

Incentives

These are schemes designed to encourage a customer to be loyal to one organisation's products. Hotel chains offer points to business people every time they choose to stay in one of their hotels. When sufficient points have been collected a free night's accommodation can be claimed.

Within the travel business itself sales people may be offered free trips or holidays in return for achieving their sales target.

FIGURE 22 The importance of the small print

Special events
Special events are designed to attract new customers or attract attention to a new venture opening up. A new restaurant may have a Valentine's Day candlelit dinner for two offer with a free red rose or chocolates. If the customers who come are happy with their meal they will spread the word.

When a sports or leisure centre opens it is common practice to offer a free introductory visit to try out the facilities so that the customer can be encouraged to join.

Direct mail
Organisations use their list of potential and existing customers to send out information directly to people's private addresses. Mailing lists can be built up from the customer base or bought from a mailing list agent.

Courting publicity
Publicity is gained when something happens that people want to know about and talk about. This quality is known as 'newsworthiness' and it is difficult to control. In 1992 the Hoover company promised people free flights in return for buying their vacuum cleaners and they received a great deal of favourable publicity. There was even more publicity, however, when Hoover were unable to keep their promises and it was not the sort they wanted.

Read the two items in Figure 23 opposite. The restaurant review of eating in one town is good publicity for the organisations concerned; the letters are not.

Companies and organisations often employ public relations agents (PR agents) to obtain good publicity for them. These agents are used to dealing with the media but they do not restrict themselves to buying advertising space. They 'court publicity'.

The PR agent, for instance, can arrange a celebrity actor to open a new leisure complex so that newspapers and possibly even television will take an interest. A tour operator specialising in the Bahamas will sponsor a fashion shoot of beach wear in the resort so that the resulting glossy photos of attractively clothed people are associated with a mention of the operator's business address and telephone number.

PR agents often use the press release to help get publicity for their clients. The press release is a document sent out to newspapers and magazines to let them know of a new service

Letters . . . .

I am writing to express my agreement with Mr Smithson's comments on The Someborough Hotel. The Someborough attempts to exude an atmosphere of old-time opulence, which its kitchen fails to support. My recent meal was tepid, the vegetables over-cooked and the general appearance of the plate served was most unappetising.

They should really do better.
SM, Kent

IN THE LIGHT of Mr Smithson's recent article about the Someborough Hotel, I thought I would write and tell your readers about my experience there in January of last year.

I organised a breakfast for a group of friends, a few days before my wedding, and was told by the banqueting department that I should devise a menu beforehand, in order to save time.

Forty-five minutes after my guests has arrived our breakfast was yet to appear on our table. There seemed to be an abundant shortage of kippers, but perhaps this was just the time of year!

I also let it be known that one of my guests would be in a wheelchair and that our table should be situated with easy access. When I arrived I found that we had been placed up on a platform which meant that my guest had to be carried to the table.

Like Mr Smithson, I too was offered a free meal, but I am yet to take it up.
MA, London W3

RECENTLY I had the misfortune of choosing the ABC Brasserie in the West End for a working lunch.

Our order could not have been simpler. The service could

not have been slower or less helpful. We arrived at 1 pm and ordered soup and salad. The soup came fairly quickly. Two of our main-course salads then took 45 minutes to arrive, and that was only after many enquiries to the staff who offered no explanation, except repeatedly telling us that they were 'on the way'. The third salad – a green salad – turned up so much later that I told the waitress not to bother and to bring the bill instead. By then it was 2.15 pm. Not only was this a disgrace, it was embarrassing. What should have been a pleasant working lunch turned into a shambles.

It surprised me that no effort was made either to apologise, or to make up for our poor experience. To add insult to injury, our waitress then said she did not blame us for omitting to add service to our bill.
BZ, Essex

Review · · · · · · · ·

Eating in Tourtown: to eat in style, go to the Grand Hotel. Three-course set lunch for £24. For bistro food and a bistro atmosphere (plus a collection of risqué French seaside postcards) try Chardonnay at 3 Church Row, off Queen Square. A salade landaise, bavarois de foie de volaille with roasted peppers, white and dark chocolate terrine, plus a kir, a third of a bottle of house white and a pot of coffee came to £19.60. Or you can have a plat du jour and a glass of wine for £5.80. Roses at 10 New Buildings, George Street offers set lunches from £12.95 to £14.95, and the Roses Cafe Bar at the same address is more informal and cheaper. Hills, 9–13 King Street, opposite the museum, has a set lunch at £10. You can also eat in the Vaults beneath the attractive Theatre Gallery building at Bridgworth, or in the Tap Room where a brunch costs £6.75.

SG

FIGURE 23 The power of publicity

or an event taking place. Figure 24 gives an example. Magazines find these releases quite useful to fill space and give news to their readers.

FIGURE 24 An example of a press launch

> Press Release
> **GRAND OPENING**
>
> *Cinderella's Night Club*
>
> Mill Road, Berkley
>
> *8 pm, Friday 18th November 1996*
>
> All press are invited to opening night cocktails as this
> beautiful nightclub reopens its doors to the public of
> Berkley every night of the week.
> Telephone Sarah Munt for further information
> on 01345 225167

Activity

Study the cutting in Figure 25 on the next page very carefully. This item appeared in a trade magazine, presented as a news item for readers. The information given was received in a press release.

Think about how the press release would have been laid out and try to write it as the magazine would have received it including all details as in our example.

Market research

In order to fulfil customer needs, leisure and tourism organisations must know who the customers are and what products and services they want.

They must also keep in touch with competitors' activities. To do all of this a company will undertake market research.

Market research may be:

- primary research or;
- secondary research.

Secondary research is also knows as 'desk research'. This involves looking at information which has been collected in previous research or at statistics and sales information which is already available. Primary, or field research, is that which is being done for the first time – the researcher has to start from scratch.

Discovery Zones for Kids in the UK

The giant American entertainment company Blockbuster is to develop a series of children's play centres across the UK this year. The first is due to be launched at the Merry Hill Shopping Centre in Dudley this Easter, the joint project of Blockbuster's UK arm, Blockbuster UK, and American Discovery Zone Inc. The facilities at the play centres are designed to promote physical co-ordination, develop upper body strength and balance in children under 12. Parents and guardians are actively encouraged to join in and play with the children.

Staffed by fully trained supervisors the centres are particularly safety conscious, including checking that children are always accompanied by an adult and leave with that same adult.

These Discovery Zone play centres cost around £750,000 each to build and require about 50 full and part-time staff to run them. Their turnover is expected to be in the region of £1 million a year. It is planned to have a Zone in all the major UK population centres, covering about 20,000sq ft.

Blockbuster owns approximately 20 per cent of Discovery Zone's outstanding stock and will have an option in June to increase this to 50.1 per cent. For details ring 01213 345678.

FIGURE 25 A report of Discovery Zones

For example, a sports centre may want to know what customers think of their facilities and design a questionnaire to collect this information. This is primary research.

Figure 26 shows an example of a questionnaire given out by Airtours.

Types of information
Quantitative research
One important source of research data is the sales data that has been collected by the organisation; sales data, which tells us how many people and what sort of people buy particular products, is described as 'quantitative research'. Information on competitors and their products is also included in this category of research.

Qualitative research
Qualitative research is used to find out why people buy or like particular products, what they like or dislike about them and what would need to be improved or changed to increase the product's attractiveness. This type of research is often conducted by asking potential customers to complete a written survey or attend a meeting when they will be asked

FIGURE 26 Part of a questionnaire used by Airtours to gather information about their customers

for their opinion. You can see this kind of survey being undertaken in shopping centres and high streets.

Market research forms an increasingly important part of any marketing and promotional planning. Work in this area on behalf of large organisations is now continuously carried out.

SECTION 9 **YOUR HOLIDAY AND DUTY FREE PURCHASES**

Q1 If you consume tobacco products, what do you smoke most often?

You	Cigarettes ☐	Low Tar ☐	Cigars ☐	Handroll ☐	Pipe ☐	
Your partner	Cigarettes ☐	Low Tar ☐	Cigars ☐	Handroll ☐	Pipe ☐	

How much do you both smoke (cigarettes or cigars per day OR grams of tobacco per day)?

You	5 or less ☐	6-10 ☐	11-15 ☐	16-20 ☐	21-25 ☐	26-30 ☐	30+ ☐
Your partner	5 or less ☐	6-10 ☐	11-15 ☐	16-20 ☐	21-25 ☐	26-30 ☐	30+ ☐

Q2 **Which brand do you smoke most often? IMPORTANT – Please sign that you are a smoker aged 18 or over. Each person MUST sign so that they can receive special tobacco offers.**

For office use

Your main brand_____

Your partner's main brand_____

Your signature_____

Your partner's signature_____

Q3 If you purchase suntan lotions, which brands were they?

Ambre Solaire ☐	Boots Soltan ☐	Delial ☐	Piz Buin ☐
Avon ☐	Clarins ☐	Hawaiian Tropic ☐	Uvistat ☐
Bergasol ☐	Coppertone ☐	Nivea ☐	Other ☐

Q4 **Which duty free drinks did you purchase?**

Beer ☐	Gin ☐	White Rum ☐	Cognac ☐
Lager ☐	Vodka ☐	Dark Rum ☐	Wine ☐
Whisky ☐	Liqueurs ☐	Brandy ☐	Other spirits ☐

Q5 What is your favourite brand of drink?

For office use

Your favourite brand_____

Your partner's_____

Q6 If you purchase perfume, please state the brand?

_____

Q7 Did you pay for your holiday purchases by?

Travellers cheque ☐   Cash ☐   Credit card ☐

Q8 How long before your holiday did you book?

Up to 1 month ☐	1 to 2 months ☐	3 to 4 months ☐
5 to 6 months ☐	7 to 8 months ☐	9+ months ☐

SECTION 10 **YOU AND YOUR FAMILY**

Q1 Were you or any member of your family ill at any time during your holiday?

Yes ☐   No ☐   *If yes, please specify symptons/illness*

_____

Q2 What is your month of birth? Your month ___/19___ Your partner's month ___/19___

Q3 Are you: Single ☐   Married ☐   Divorced ☐   Widowed ☐

Q4 Please indicate the age groups of your children living at home?

Boys	0-2 years ☐	3-4 years ☐	5-9 years ☐	10-14 years ☐	15-17 years ☐
Girls	0-2 years ☐	3-4 years ☐	5-9 years ☐	10-14 years ☐	15-17 years ☐

Q5 How many cars are there in your household? None ☐ 1 ☐ 2 ☐ 3+ ☐

Q6 Please answer the following questions about the MAIN car in your household?

For office use

The make (e.g. Vauxhall) _____

The model (e.g. Astra) _____

Registration letter ___ Year brought 19___ The car's annual mileage _____ ,000 miles
Was it bought new? Yes ☐ No ☐ Who owns the car? You ☐ Company ☐
Does it use? Diesel ☐ 4 star ☐ Unleaded ☐
Do you take the car abroad? Yes ☐ No ☐
In how many months will you change your car? 0-3 ☐ 4-6 ☐ 6+ ☐ Don't know ☐

Q7 In which month do you renew your car insurance? Month _____ Don't know ☐

Q8 Do you take more than one holiday per year? Yes ☐ No ☐

Q9 Which group best describes your COMBINED annual household income?

Up to £9,999 ☐	£15,000-£19,999 ☐	£25,000-£29,999 ☐	£35,000-£39,999 ☐
£10,000-£14,999 ☐	£20,000-£24,999 ☐	£30,000-£34,999 ☐	£40,000 plus ☐

Q5 Please mark all the newspapers that are REGULARLY read in your household?

Daily Express ☐	Guardian ☐	People ☐	(Scottish) Sunday Mail ☐
Daily Mail ☐	Daily Telegraph ☐	Sunday Express ☐	Sunday Mirror ☐
Independent ☐	Financial Times ☐	Mail on Sunday ☐	Independent on Sunday ☐
Mirror/Record ☐	Daily Star ☐	News of the World ☐	Regional Daily ☐
Sun ☐	The Times ☐	Sunday Telgraph ☐	Sunday Post ☐
Today ☐	Observer ☐	Sunday Times ☐	

Q11 Do you buy mail order? Cosmetics ☐ Beauty products ☐ Books ☐ Wines ☐

Q12 To which type of charity do you donate?

Children ☐	Pet welfare ☐	Overseas aid ☐	Health Research ☐
Wildlife ☐	Blind ☐	Deaf ☐	Environment ☐

Q13 What interests and hobbies do you pursue on holiday or at home?

Reading ☐	Gardening ☐	Photography ☐	Theatre/Arts ☐
Bingo ☐	Records/Tapes/CD's ☐	Cooking ☐	D-I-Y ☐
Go to pubs ☐	Keep fit classes ☐	Plates/Figurines ☐	Golf ☐

Q14 Do you have: Dogs ☐ Cats ☐

If yes, Do you put them in Kennels/Cattery whilst on holiday Yes ☐ No ☐

Independent market research organisations compile omnibus surveys which can be purchased by organisations or advertising agencies when they are planning a campaign. Omnibus surveys bring some of the benefits of market research to organisations that might not be able to fund their own.

Market segmentation

This term refers to the categorising of both existing and potential customers of leisure or tourism organisations according to common characteristics. Having defined a market segment organisations develop products and services designed to appeal to the people in it.

Demographic segmentation

Customers are categorised demographically according to their age, sex, income and socio-economic grouping. It is easy to see how various activities appeal to different age groups; we have 'Tumble Tots' gymnastics for toddlers, sports teams for different age groups rising to holidays for elderly adults under the 'Saga' brand or Thomsons 'Young at Heart'. Most sports have separate men's and women's teams.

Socio-economic grouping is a commonly used and commonly quoted form of classification and is based on the definition of social grades provided by the National Readership Survey. This survey is a form of continuous market research collecting information from a sample cross-section of the population. Socio-economic groupings are based on occupation. Figure 27 gives the NRS grades.

ADULT POPULATION BY SOCIAL GRADE & SEX – GB

Social	Total		Male		Female	
Grade	'000	%	'000	%	'000	%
A	1,400	3.1	732	1.6	669	1.5
B	8,363	18.4	4,322	9.5	4,042	8.9
C1	12,377	27.2	5,714	12.6	6,663	14.6
C2	10,441	22.9	5,548	12.2	4,893	10.8
D	7,375	16.2	3,156	7.7	3,859	8.5
E	5,543	12.2	2,158	4.7	3,385	7.4
Total	**45,500**	**100.00**	**21,990**	**48.3**	**23,510**	**51.7**

Note: Figures may not add up due to rounding.
Source: NRS Jan–Dec 1994

NRS SOCIAL GRADE DEFINITIONS

Social Grade	Social Status	Occupation
A	Upper middle class	Higher managerial, administrative or professional
B	Middle class	Intermediate managerial, administrative or professional
C1	Lower middle class	Supervisory or clerical, and junior managerial, administrative or professional
C2	Skilled working class	Skilled manual workers
D	Working class	Semi or unskilled manual workers
E	Those at lowest levels of subsistence	State pensioners or widows (no other earner), casual or lowest grade workers

FIGURE 27 The National Readership Survey social grades

Note: The social grade of an individual is normally based on the occupation of the Chief Income Earner of his or her household.
Source: NRS

These categories, and the percentage of population in each, will obviously change over time but a lot of information has been collected which provides the campaign planner with a useful insight into the buying habits and attitudes of the members of each category.

Lifestyle segmentation

Whereas demographic segmentation is based on facts and figures, lifestyle segmentation attempts to categorise customers according to their tastes and behaviour. This is a more sophisticated and more difficult method of segmenting as it is difficult to categorise people's lifestyles.

Activity   Collect copies of all the brochures from one tour operator, e.g. all Thomson's brochures or all First Choice brochures.

Make up a chart showing how the target market differs for each brochure. Use the one below to guide you.

Target market comparison

(Example)

Brochures used: Club 18–30

Target market:
Age   18–30
Sex   both

Socio-economic grouping   C1,C2

Income   low to middle

Lifestyle   likes to have fun with sports
enjoys nightlife
wants sun and company

Marital status   single

Your comments

Element 2.2 Plan a Leisure and Recreation or Travel and Tourism Promotional Campaign

This element looks at how to plan a promotional campaign. By the end of this element you should be able to:

1 describe the stages of a leisure and recreation or travel and tourism promotional campaign (performance criterion 2.2.1);
2 describe, with examples, the objectives of a leisure and recreation or travel and tourism promotional campaign (performance criterion 2.2.2);
3 explain the factors which could affect the success of a campaign (performance criterion 2.2.3);
4 prepare a detailed plan for a promotional campaign for a selected leisure and recreation or travel and tourism product (performance criterion 2.2.4).

Most large organisations who wish to launch a campaign to promote a new or existing product or service will appoint an agency to assist them. If the agency is new to the work of the organisation they usually start with research to gain an understanding of their client and its products. Once appointed, it is normal for an agency to work with the same client over a number of years.

The stages of a promotional campaign

1 Product and market research
2 Setting campaign objectives
3 Defining the target market
4 Devising a campaign strategy
5 Setting a budget
6 Creating and producing advertisements
7 Planning and buying media coverage
8 Measurement of the results

1 Product and market research
The purpose of the research, which may involve both client and agency, is to understand fully the customers the client wants to either retain or attract to its product.

2 Setting campaign objectives

The objectives for a campaign could be stated as the obvious 'increase sales', but normally the objectives will include other goals, for instance increasing market share compared with identified competitors or changing the opinion of customers about the quality of the product. The success of the campaign will be judged by the extent to which the campaign objectives are met. Post-campaign research is sometimes undertaken to evaluate the extent to which the objectives are met although of course the improvement in product sales represent the most attractive measurement of success for the organisation concerned.

3 Defining the target market

The target market is the people an organisation and its agency hope to attract to buy and use its product. Defining the target market assists the people who create the campaign to decide what form their message about the product should take. It also helps them decide where they should advertise to reach the customer they want. The size of the target market will depend a great deal on the nature of the product, for example in tourism the appeal of a holiday in Spain would be wider than an overland trip to China. An effective promotional campaign for the trip to China would have to be much more precisely targeted to reach the small audience interested.

4 Devising a campaign strategy

A campaign strategy is the development of an approach which will best present the product to the market.

The objectives might be:

- to highlight one aspect of the product which is considered to have the most appeal to the target market;
- to highlight one aspect of the product which differentiates it from competing products.

In marketing language this is the USP or Unique Selling Proposition. The advertising agency will provide a 'creative brief' suggesting directions in which the campaign could be developed; it includes all information gathered from stages 1 to 4 above.

5 Setting a budget

The budget set can be based on an 'advertising/sales ratio' which means that the amount spent on advertising is worked out as a percentage of the sales estimated or achieved.

Alternatively the level of expenditure might be set depending on the level of advertising of competitors. An obvious limit to expenditure is the overall financial position of the organisation.

The setting of a budget is very important as it will greatly influence the strength of the campaign and the media which can be used. The promotional budget is part of the marketing budget of most organisations. The relative importance it places on its various marketing activities will dictate the limit on expenditure for promotional campaigns.

6 Creating and producing advertisements

The sixth stage of the design of a promotional campaign is the creation and production of an advertisement. For many people this is the most exciting area of marketing in which to work but the pressure on those involved to create new and exciting ideas is considerable. The complexity of the advertisement required will be determined by the nature of the campaign and the choice of media to support it. Television advertising, which now features so prominently in the lives of most of us, is the most complex and expansive but also the most high-profile and effective. For many, the television advertisements we see are as significant as the programmes in terms of entertainment value. As a result, humour in all advertising in the UK has grown in significance. Many campaigns will employ a number of different forms of advertising with the emphasis being determined by the size of the budget and the nature of the product. Not every product lends itself to television advertising even if the money is available to support it.

At this creation and production stage a lot of thought will be given to the emotions the advertisement sets out to stimulate. In addition to humour, campaigns sometimes set out to shock, appeal to sentiment, demonstrate the benefits, draw comparisons or possibly increase the appeal by using well-known personalities: sports trainers advertisements often use sports celebrities to say how good the product is.

Once the advertisements have been created and the ideas agreed, the agency may undertake a pre-testing stage. A group of people from the target media will be shown 'roughs' or 'scamps' illustrating the theme and storyline of the proposed advertisement and asked for their response. This pre-testing enables the organisation and its agency to move forward to the expensive production stage with more confidence. This testing is only normally applied to large scale campaigns involving television or film but it can prove very useful in helping the agency to refine its proposed approach.

The agency will normally put together a 'creative team' to work on this part of the campaign's development. The team is responsible for creating the ideas for advertisements and organising their actual production. The production process involves an art director in addition to copywriters, illustrators, photographers, camera men and film crews, researchers and administrative staff. Agencies will often employ freelance experts as members of their team to ensure they have the best possible skills available to them.

7 Planning and buying media coverage

Planning which media outlets to use for the advertising and buying the space or spots is a job that goes hand in hand with the creation and production of the advertisements. It is this part of the campaign in which most money is spent and therefore it is very important to employ someone experienced in getting the best coverage for the least money. The person responsible in an agency is known as a media planner.

The media planner is expected to secure the most efficient combination of media for the campaign. This is known as the 'media mix'. The media mix chosen has to reach the target market decided upon and so the media planner is provided with all the information gained from work on stages 1 to 6 above.

The assessment of the media plan is based on three key factors:

- **coverage** – the percentage of the target market that will see the campaign advertisements at least once;
- **frequency** – the number of times each person will have the 'opportunity to see' (OTS) or the 'opportunity to hear' (OTH) the campaign;
- **cost per thousand** – CPT is the cost of reaching 1,000 people in the target audience.

For television based campaigns there is another form of evaluation – the 'television ratings' points (TVRs). These ratings are determined by audience research. A rating point is defined as the percentage of the target audience viewing a particular spot.

8 Measurement of the results

Measuring the results of a campaign is a very important task, although it takes place when all the excitement of planning and launching is over. If a campaign is not as successful as was hoped, the reasons can be investigated and taken into consideration in future campaigns.

Sometimes products are launched before they are fully prepared or tested or understood. Sometimes an organisation may create a demand for the advertised product which it is unable to meet. You or someone you know may have had some experience of this – perhaps being disappointed with a holiday which sold out within hours of being advertised leaving you dissatisfied with the operator concerned. Organisations try to learn from such mistakes.

Element 2.3   Run and Evaluate a Promotional Campaign

This element looks at how to run and evaluate a promotional campaign. By the end of this element you should be able to:

1 prepare appropriate promotional materials for use during the campaign (performance criterion 2.3.1);
2 participate effectively in the running of the campaign (performance criterion 2.3.2);
3 evaluate the effectiveness of the campaign and summarise the findings (performance criterion 2.3.3);
4 make and present recommendations for improving similar future campaigns (performance criterion 2.3.4).

You will now evaluate the steps taken in the preparation and delivery of a promotional campaign designed for a specific company. The company selected is P & O European Ferries and the campaign selected is one run for the period January to August 1994

Case Study

P & O European Ferries

The period of the campaign took into consideration the original planned launch of the Channel Tunnel and was put together by the marketing department of P & O European Ferries and their appointed advertising agency BSB Dorland.

Objective
The objective for the campaign was to establish P & O European Ferries as the company of first choice for crossing the English Channel and North Sea.

Strategy
The company's research had identified its position as the leading UK ferry company and therefore its declared strategy for the campaign was

'To consolidate P & O European Ferries position as Britain's No. 1 Ferry Company'

The illustrations used in the media campaign show clearly the repetition of the reference to 'Britain's No. 1 Ferry Company' as its unique selling proposition (USP). A line repeated in a campaign in this manner is sometimes referred to as the 'strap line'. Whatever eye-catching messages are used on the posters and ads the 'strap line' is always included. You can see this in Figure 28.

The objective in this campaign was to highlight the functional benefits of the service, that is more ships, more routes, greater capacity, more professional, better quality. P & O and its advertising agency felt that stressing these facts about their services established the company as the 'No. 1 Ferry Company'.

The overall message of the proposed advertising was that P & O European Ferries have the capacity to satisfy your every need when you want to cross the channel. This was the 'campaign strategy'.

FIGURE 28 Samples of advertising used in P&O's promotional campaign

Having determined the campaign strategy the next stage in the design of the campaign was the choice of media. P & O decided to utilise most elements of the media mix at some point during the eight months of the campaign. The media selected included:

- television;
- outdoor – that is poster sites;
- national press – both colour and monochrome;
- trade press.

The high costs associated with media advertising meant that the media planners were required to give careful thought to the way money was spent over the long, eight-month campaign period. They decided on the following timetable.

1 Television: March to June
The following television stations were selected.

- London
- Meridian
- HTV
- Channel 4
- Central
- Anglia
- Granada

The advertisements featured were a mixture of the 50 seconds full commercial with a series of two 20 second shortened versions.

The series of commercials were featured in two 'bursts':

- the first burst – March to April;
- the second burst – May to June.

2 Posters: January to April, June to August
The poster campaign was outdoor and based on two sizes of poster; a combination of full and half-size billboard posters. The areas selected for the poster sites were as follows.

- London
- Yorkshire
- Southern and Eastern England
- Midlands
- Wales and the West

The poster campaign was designed to run from January to August with May excluded; remember that May was the planned month for the launch of the Channel Tunnel.

3 National Press: April to May
The campaign was based on colour and monochrome (black and white) advertisements in the weekend newspapers and review sections.

The schedule for quality newspaper advertising used the following publications.

- *The Times*
- *The Sunday Times*
- *The Daily Telegraph*
- *The Sunday Telegraph*
- *Daily Express*
- *Sunday Express*
- *The Guardian*
- *The Observer*
- *Daily Mail*
- *The Mail on Sunday*
- *The Independent*
- *The Independent On Sunday*
- *Evening Standard*

The campaign was planned to run during April and May and in addition the plan provided for a permanent weekly presence throughout the year in the *London Evening Standard.*

4 Trade Press: throughout the year
The *Travel Trade Gazette* (TTG) and *Travel Weekly* were used throughout the year, creating a regular 'presence'.

Assignment activity Unit 2

You should keep all your assignment activity work, clearly labelled, in your Portfolio of Evidence. This work provides evidence of coverage of all the elements and performance criteria covered in Unit 2.

1 Consider all elements of the P & O promotional campaign very carefully. Then answer the following questions.
   a Describe the target market in detail. Use Unit 2 in general and the information on P & O's selection of media to help you.
   b Examine the examples of the poster and newspaper advertisements and list the product promises that are made.
   c What is the company logo? Why is the logo important?
   d What information is missing from the case study of the P & O campaign? How would this be useful if you were asked to evaluate its success?

2 Plan an advertising campaign for a service which you might be able to offer, for instance, babysitting, shopping for neighbours, car cleaning.

Carry out the following tasks.

a Describe your target market.

b Produce at least a brochure and a poster advertising your service. You may produce a handout, an audio or video tape if you wish.

c Choose at least five customers or potential customers and ask them their views on your campaign. Prepare some questions to find out whether your campaign:

- gives the necessary information;
- gives a good company image;
- attracts customers;
- makes them buy the service.

Write up all your findings and say how you would change your campaign in the light of your customers opinions.

Assignment   Comparing advertising campaigns

You are a marketing assistant at the Makepiece agency. Your line manager has requested a report from you evaluating two of the company's current campaigns.

The campaigns are as follows.

a Thomsons holiday advertising and promotion.

b A smaller local leisure or tourism organisation.

For (a) collect examples of Thomsons' advertising and promotion. Sources include newspapers, magazines, television and travel agencies.

For (b) choose a local leisure or tourist organisation. Collect examples of your local organisation's advertising and promotion. Sources include local newspapers and radio, leaflets from shops and libraries or from the company itself if it is a public place.

Compare the two campaigns in terms of:

- media used;
- target audience;
- overall objective of the campaign;
- purpose of individual advertisements;
- types of promotion;
- effectiveness of the campaign in your opinion.

Submit your findings in a report to the marketing manager. Refer to your collected examples by numbering them and putting them at the back of your report as an appendix.

Unit 3 Customer Service in Leisure and Tourism

•••

Introduction to the unit This unit comprises the following elements required by the course and gives you practice in all the performance criteria that prove your understanding of each of these elements.

Element 3.1   Explain the principles of customer service in leisure and tourism

Element 3.2   Investigate the provision of information as part of customer service

Element 3.3   Investigate and demonstrate sales techniques as part of customer service

Element 3.4   Provide and evaluate customer service in leisure and tourism

Element 3.1 Explain the principles of customer service in leisure and tourism

This element looks at customer service in leisure and tourism. By the end of this element you should be able to:

1 explain what customer service is (performance criterion 3.1.1);
2 explain what is achieved through effective customer service (performance criterion 3.1.2);
3 explain the importance of customer service (performance criterion 3.1.3);
4 describe, and give examples of, types of communications used in customer service (performance criterion 3.1.4);
5 give examples of customer service in selected leisure and tourism organisations (performance criterion 3.1.5).

What is customer service?

Providing customer service means looking after the customers' needs whenever they come into contact with the organisation. All successful organisations in leisure and tourism recognise the importance of customer care and are proud to advertise the emphasis they place on good service. Figure 29 shows a typical announcement.

> # CITY SPORTS CENTRE
> **Our staff will be:**
> ✓ trained and appropriately qualified
> ✓ easily identifiable by wearing their uniforms at all times
> ✓ helpful, experienced and informative to ensure that your visit is safe and enjoyable
>
> **In general we will:**
> ✓ listen and be responsive to comments, complaints and suggestions
> ✓ maintain a balanced programme of activities
> ✓ notify to our customers any forseen change by the display of an appropriate notice
> ✓ keep ancillary areas including changing rooms, showers and toilets clean, hygienic and in good working order

FIGURE 29 A typical statement of customer care

The government has helped to promote customer service in all industries by emphasising customer charters. If you belong to a college, you will have been given a copy of the student charter. This document outlines all the services the college promises to offer you.

Charters and mission statements

Government departments such as the Inland Revenue publish their charters so that the general public – for example the tax payer – can see what services the department is expected to provide.

In some organisations there may be a strategy of customer service without a formal written policy. This strategy may be summed up in a single clear objective, for instance:

The objective of this sports centre is to provide better customer service than any other sports centre.

Such an objective is known as a **mission statement**. The mission statement publicises the organisation's main aim or aims to both public and staff. The staff, at whatever level, are then aware that they are working towards that aim.

Activity   Find out what the mission statement is for your college or organisation. Write it down.

In a group, discuss whether it is what you expected and whether you feel it should be different in any way.

Remember that the aims of an organisation may constitute a series of statements. These will then form the basis of the **customer care plan**.

Activity   Study the company principles from Marks & Spencer carefully (Figure 30). Marks & Spencer is renowned world-wide for its excellent customer service.

Using their principles as a base, write a set of company principles for a UK tour operator.

Providing for customers' needs

In order to provide customer service, the organisation must recognise the needs of its customers. The specific needs of leisure and tourism customers cover many areas, including the following.

MARKS & SPENCER
COMPANY INFORMATION

COMPANY PRINCIPLES

◆ TO SELL MERCHANDISE OF THE HIGHEST QUALITY AND
   OUTSTANDING VALUE.

◆ TO OFFER THE HIGHEST STANDARD OF CUSTOMER CARE IN
   AN ATTRACTIVE SHOPPING ENVIRONMENT.

◆ TO IMPROVE QUALITY STANDARDS CONTINUALLY
   THROUGHOUT OUR OPERATIONS BY INVESTMENT IN
   MODERN TECHNOLOGY.

◆ TO SUPPORT BRITISH INDUSTRY.

◆ TO PURSUE MUTUALLY REWARDING LONG-TERM
   PARTNERSHIPS WITH SUPPLIERS.

◆ TO ENSURE STAFF AND SHAREHOLDERS SHARE IN OUR
   SUCCESS.

◆ TO NURTURE GOOD HUMAN RELATIONS WITH STAFF,
   CUSTOMERS AND THE COMMUNITY.

◆ TO MINIMISE THE ENVIRONMENTAL IMPACT OF OUR
   OPERATIONS AND MERCHANDISE.

St Michael
MARKS & SPENCER • COMPANY INFORMATION • COMPANY PRINCIPLES • PAGE 1   A/C3003/03

FIGURE 30 Marks & Spencer's company principles

Information needs
Examples are:

- opening times of a facility;
- products on offer;
- how equipment works;
- what childcare facilities are available;
- what holidays are available;
- how to get to a location.

Help and advice needs
Examples are:

- making a choice of holiday;
- how to start an exercise program;
- what the rules of a game are.

Safety and security needs
Examples are:

- to know that all safety measures are taken in a gym;
- that staff are trained in first aid;
- that holiday programmes meet with applicable legislation;
- that premises are clean and hygienic.

Look at Figure 31. This is an example of how Cadogan Holidays has provided services to meet the needs of different categories of customers.

Cadogan Holidays fo

HONEYMOONS

We pride ourselves on offering the very best resorts and accommodation in each of our destinations, which is why Cadogan is the perfect choice for honeymooners. Many of the hotels we feature provide you with extra niceties such as a free room upgrade or champagne on arrival. Look out for the Honeymoon symbol at selected hotels.

INFORMATION PACK AND DISCOUNT CARD

With Cadogan you receive more than just your tickets before you leave home. With your final invoice will be a comprehensive information pack containing a useful travel guide and a Cadogan Privilege Card that entitles you to discounts and offers at many restaurants, shops, nightspots and attractions.

EXTRA VALUE

Throughout this brochure we feature a wide range of special offers. These have been negotiated to offer you exceptional value for money and include simple niceties such as a complimentary bottle of wine or a basket of fruit on arrival.

CHILDRENS PRICES

 Cadogan offer excellent price reductions for children, see the child prices listed for each hotel. In addition, where you see the 'family value' symbol we offer particularly good value for families at that hotel.

GOLF

 Many of the resorts we feature have excellent facilities for golfers. We have indicated throughout this brochure hotels that are particularly well suited. Some hotels are actually situated on a golf course, whilst others offer free transportation to and from the clubs and/or reduced green fees. Please check the "Extra Value' section of each hotel for details.

EXTRA NIGHTS FREE

 We have negotiated with hoteliers many superb extra value offers that enable you to stay additional nights free at selected hotels. Extend your holiday at no extra cost during certain periods. Look out for the 'Free Nights' symbol for hotels where offers are available.

SINGLE SAVERS

 People travelling alone, or friends wishing to occupy separate rooms are often faced with having to pay hefty supplements. At many hotels you will find that we have been able to waive these additional costs on selected dates. These hotels are high lighted with the 'Single Saver' symbol.

EARLY BOOKING BONUS

 At selected hotels we offer reduced rates when we receive an early booking. Check the 'Extra Value' sections for details.

CADOGAN HOLIDAYS

FIGURE 31 A holiday company advertises that it provides for the needs of a wide range of customers

Activity   Joan Harris is a young mother with three children aged from six months to five years. She has joined her local sports centre as an off-peak member so that she can go every day to exercise and meet people. She is interested in using the gym equipment but has never used it before. She is a competent swimmer and would like to use the pool. She would also like to play squash but as she is new to the area, she has no partner. She has played squash before to quite a high standard, but hasn't had time since having the children. Joan knows that there are aerobics and step classes at the centre and might be interested in them.

1   Assess Joan and the children's needs using the headings given on page 75 to help you and write them down.

2   Decide what services you as her fitness trainer would recommend to her at the sports centre.

3   Compare your findings with the rest of the group.

Why is customer service so important?

Customer service is like politeness in general; it is important because people feel valued, respected and confident where service principles are observed. Satisfied customers will tell others that they are and this kind of 'word of mouth promotion' leads to increased business for the organisation concerned. In the case of privately-run organisations more business means increased sales and thus increased profits.

The image and reputation of all kinds of organisations will benefit if their commitment to customer service is made clear.

In both the public and the private sectors of the leisure and tourism industry good customer service means that:

1   the organisation's understanding of customers will increase and thus the right kinds of products and services will be offered to meet customers needs

2   the physical environment in the facility will be safe and secure contributing to the well being of staff and customers

3   staff will have increased job satisfaction and improved motivation.

The provision of customer service

Face to face contact

First impressions are very important and staff who are to come into contact with their organisation's customers must be particularly aware of this. In hotels and leisure centres particularly, a uniform may be worn to help the customer recognise who is a staff member. A uniform also helps to promote a smart corporate image for the organisation.

In a hotel

The first point of contact may be the commissionaire at the entrance or the people at the reception desk. Politeness and smartness is part of the good first impression.

The customer will also meet:

- the porter who takes the bags to the rooms;
- the staff who serve drinks at the bar;
- the housekeeping staff.

FIGURE 32 A uniformed receptionist

In a travel agency

People entering a travel agency need to be made to feel welcomed but, unlike a hotel, they may not know exactly what service they require. They need to be made to feel confident by:

- the counter staff dealing with the enquiry;
- specialist staff dealing with the supply of foreign currency or travellers cheques.

While travelling

Someone who is travelling is often quite vulnerable. They are in a strange place trying to use unfamiliar timetables or even an unfamiliar language. They need the help and professionalism of:

- bus drivers;
- ticket sales personnel;
- air crew;
- airport staff.

All these people should be trained in providing customer services. This means that they need to develop the following qualities.

Listening skills

Listening skills sound obvious but are often difficult in practice! They involve:

- concentrating on what the customer is saying;
- not interrupting;
- being objective and open minded.

Personal presentation

The dress of a staff member, perhaps uniform, should be appropriate to the job they are doing and consistent with the image of the organisation, that is smart suit for a hotel manager or neat, clean tracksuit for a fitness trainer.

Facial expression

A smile is very important as it shows that your attention has been fully focused on the customer, if only for the moment of greeting.

Eye contact

This is an important way of acknowledging someone's presence, establishing a rapport, and making them feel wanted and welcome.

Voice

The tone of voice should be warm, sincere and interested. Even if you do not always feel these emotions, it is surprising how putting them into your voice will help you to do so!

Body language

It is not what you say, it's the way that you say it! Try greeting someone while writing in a book or just looking down. The warmth will not be there.

Be careful with your posture (is it bored?) or gestures (are you scratching the back of your head as you speak?).

Written communication

The impression given by letters and invoices can be improved by using an organisation's logo on all correspondence. The principle of trying to see the customer's point of view and adopting a friendly tone apply equally strongly to written communications.

Many organisations have a policy of replying to a letter with in a given period, perhaps five days. If a query is going to take longer an acknowledgement should be sent to the customer. Remember how you felt the last time you wrote a letter that was ignored for weeks?

If you are dealing with correspondence you must possess a good standard of English and know how to write a business letter. Unit 4, pages 116–17, gives you practice in this skill.

Telephone communication

A customer's first point of contact with an organisation is often the telephone. If the telephone is answered, after many rings, with a curt 'hello' a poor impression is given: uncertainty and annoyance on the part of the person calling is often the result.

If your job is to answer the telephone you should try to do so within five rings. Organisations sometimes ask staff to use a set greeting – for example, 'good morning, Regina Hotel, Simon speaking. How may I help you?' In this way you can be sure that customers are greeted by a friendly voice, they know that they have reached the right number and they know who they are speaking to for future reference.

Surprisingly, body language is also important when you are on the telephone. Sit up straight, do not be distracted by others, and smile. The smile goes 'down' the telephone quite clearly.

If you cannot deal with the caller's needs immediately, always take details and the person's phone number and call back within the time that you say you will.

Activity   Working in pairs, you are going to do some role play. One person is a customer and the other a staff member.

The member of staff must deal with the following situations in which the customer is on the phone.

1   You work in a hotel reception. The telephone rings. Answer it correctly. Mr Brown, a guest, is requested by the caller. Mr Brown is in the bar.

2   You work in a travel agency. A customer rings, asking for information about Tunisia. She wants to know the currency and exchange rate. You do not have this information to hand. Answer the telephone correctly and deal with the enquiry.

3   A customer telephones the leisure centre when you are on reception. He wants to speak to his sister who is playing squash. He needs to rearrange a lift. You know that you should only fetch his sister if the call is urgent. Answer the telephone correctly and deal with the customer.

⬛ Element 3.2   Investigate the Provision of Information as Part of Customer Service

About this element   This element looks at how information is provided to customers. By the end of this element you should be able to:

1 explain the value to the customer of leisure and tourism employees having a broad range of knowledge (performance criterion 3.2.1);
2 explain what organisational knowledge leisure and tourism employees should have (performance criterion 3.2.1);
3 describe sources of information which are used as part of customer service (performance criterion 3.2.3);
4 explain how to give clear information to customers (performance criterion 3.2.4);
5 investigate specific information needs of different customers in selected leisure and tourism organisations and present the findings (performance criterion 3.2.5).

Providing customers with information

You cannot provide good customer service without possessing a good knowledge of your company, your industry and the products on offer. Customers will ask you for information and they will only be satisfied if accurate information is given quickly.

What do you need to know?
Obviously, the knowledge you need will vary depending on which sector of the leisure and tourism industry you work in. We will now look at some examples.

Travel agency
In order to satisfy your customer's needs you must know all about the products you sell. This means being familiar with the tour operator, their holidays and prices in all the brochures on offer. You must also know about all the other services an agency arranges: car hire, insurance and travel services or rail tickets for example. Customers will ask you questions about resorts, currencies and exchange rates. You will need to know what vaccinations are required for

particular resorts and whether passports and visas are needed. You must also know your own company's organisation and procedures inside out.

You will not be expected to display all this knowledge immediately! The important thing is to know where to get information or whom to ask, rather than give inaccurate information to a customer. By asking and reading constantly you will gain all the information you need.

Where does this information come from?
Tour operators' brochures give a lot of detail about holiday destinations. Timetables and information guides on travel are issued by ferry and air companies. Tour operators offer trips at reduced prices for 'educational' visits to resorts by people working for travel agencies. You are then able to pass on first-hand knowledge of destinations and means of travel to the client.

Helpful publications include trade magazines like *Travel Trade Gazette* or the *World Travel Guide* which gives independent resort information. *Health Advice for Travellers* is a leaflet published by the Department of Health. The Tourist Boards of countries offer a lot of promotional material and helpful data is usually on offer.

Training within the agency is often given to help ensure staff product knowledge and knowledge of procedures. This training will probably include access to computer systems which hold databases with customer details and bookings and allow direct links with operators to give you information on holiday availability.

Associations such as **ABTA (Association of British Travel Agents)** and **AITO (Association of Independent Tour Operators)** also offer trade information and updates on legislation to their members. A thorough knowledge of legislation relevant to the tourism industry is important so that you avoid misleading customers verbally or in writing.

Sports centre
The knowledge required if you work in a sports centre is of a different nature, but just as necessary to the customer.

The information you are asked for may include:

* sports venues, times, prices;
* gym equipment, use and prices;
* membership, availability and prices;

- what safety regulations you have;
- where the first aid kit is;
- sports equipment for sale;
- other facilities on offer, for instance, crèche and cafe.

You also need to know about the organisation: whom to ask if you have a problem or a complaint, what the procedures are for booking and payment. You should know about other sports centres in your area, both public and private, and what they offer.

Where does this information come from?

Training will be given to the staff of the centre you work for so knowledge about the organisation and its procedures is easily gained.

You should go to other centres and see how they are organised and presented. Scanning local newspapers will give information about the activities of centres in competition with your own.

Fixtures and events lists are produced both for information to staff who are not directly involved in their planning and for customers, detailing the sports and facilities available and when.

Manufacturers offer written guidelines and instructions for gym and sports equipment to ensure it is safely used. You should read all such material. Manufacturers' service representatives will visit the centre and you should take the opportunity to sort out any queries you may have.

Specific areas of knowledge may need special certified training, for instance first aid or coaching awards. Your sports centre will give you details of these.

Tourist information office

As the main role of anyone working in a tourist information office is that of 'knowledge giver', a wide range of knowledge is especially important. Consider the information needs a customer may have.

- What's on in this town?
- Where can I stay?
- How can I get there?
- How can I hire a car or bike?
- What attractions are there to see?
- What can my children do?
- How do I use the local bus or telephone?

You will also need to know how the tourist office fits into the overall structure of UK tourist boards both regional and national.

Where does this information come from?
The English Tourist Board in London distributes a lot of information to offices in the different regions. You should read it all.

Local attractions will provide the nearest tourist office with leaflets to give out to visitors and you should read all these. Maps and guides published by the local authority in order to attract tourists are good sources of local information. Events listings will be issued by sports and concert venues, cinemas and theatres. A list of accommodation should be compiled by the tourist office. You should, in short, have carefully read everything with which the office is provided.

Up-to-date, accurate and comprehensive information, including advice on health and safety, is essential if a tourist office is to gain the confidence of its users.

Activity

You and four friends plan to visit a theme park. You want to travel there by rail and stay overnight as you have heard that it is possible to buy a ticket and receive free entry for the next day. You will not be taking food and drink with you, so you will need to buy provisions there.

Decide what information you need. Whom will you telephone or visit to obtain it, and where do you have go to for tickets?

Make a chart following the one given below and complete it with all your information.

Information needed	From whom?	From where?
Example: rail time and places	BR station	published timetable

Giving information clearly

Your customers may not always be English speaking or easily able to understand detailed information.

The leisure and tourism employee must ensure that all information is clearly given. This is easy if the following steps are taken.

1   Use simple language and terms – the customer will probably not be familiar with airport code names or industry jargon. They will not know local landmarks.

2 Speak clearly.

3 Write down any addresses or telephone numbers, so that the customer has a record of them.

4 Use diagrams or maps where appropriate and mark maps to show exactly where the attraction or hotel asked for is located.

5 When you have given the information, check that the customer has understood it. Many do not wish to appear rude by insisting!

6 Ask if the customer wants any other information.

Activity Mr Apuzzo is an Italian tourist visiting one of England's historic cities with his family. He speaks excellent English with an Italian accent.

He is at the tourist office. He wishes to find a hotel in the city and he also wants to find the famous antique market. He meets Sharon, who is a trainee at the tourist office, momentarily unsupervised. The following conversation takes place.

'Good morning. How can I help you?' asks Sharon.

Mr Apuzzo explains that he is foreign.

'From Italy.'

'Italy! I see, well I will explain everything very clearly', says Sharon, excruciatingly slowly and loudly.

She shows Mr Apuzzo a brochure on a local bed and breakfast and says it is popular with families.

'I thought there was a Holiday Inn here', says Mr Apuzzo.

'There is,' replies Sharon, 'but it is very expensive.'

'All the same, please book me a room there', insists the Italian.

This Sharon now does and then proceeds to explain how to get to the antique market.

'Go to the Rose Column, follow the road straight ahead to Penham Place and you'll see the market', again all very slowly. 'Have a good day. Goodbye.'

As you will have noticed Sharon made a series of errors. State what they were, and then say exactly how you would have attended to Mr Apuzzo's information needs.

Element 3.3   Investigate and Demonstrate Sales Techniques as Part of Customer Service

About this element

This element looks at sales techniques in leisure and tourism. By the end of this element you should be able to:

1 explain the importance of selling as part of customer service (performance criterion 3.3.1);
2 describe, and give examples of, sales situations in leisure and tourism organisations (performance criterion 3.3.2);
3 describe sales techniques required of employees in the leisure and tourism industry (performance criterion 3.3.3);
4 demonstrate effective sales techniques, selling selected leisure and tourism products and services (performance criterion 3.3.4).

Selling

Most leisure and tourism organisations are in the private sector, commercial operations which aim to make a profit by selling a product or service. Without sales they will not make a profit and cease to trade so it is important that selling is carried out professionally. Staff are therefore often trained in sales techniques as part of customer service.

Where goods and services are sold properly customers will be satisfied. A proper sale is one in which the sales person has matched the right product or service to the needs of the person buying it.

It is a fact that satisfied customers come back, creating repeat business. They also tell their friends about the good service they have received and the friends, in turn, create new business for the organisation.

Sales situations

There are many opportunities for selling within leisure and tourism industries. We will look at several examples. In general the techniques for selling follow the same procedure, with variations according to the particular situation.

Retail outlets – shops

When we think about selling, this is the situation we first consider. Selling in a shop has the advantage of being straightforward. The customer often knows their requirements and has come prepared to make the purchase there and then. The assistant can give advice and guidance and then complete the transaction.

Travel agencies

As we have seen, travel agents are intermediaries, that is they are selling holidays on behalf of a tour operator. The agent is paid commission on each sale. In a shop, the stock is bought outright, and then resold. The travel agent is selling other organisation's products which are often very similar. The agent has to employ considerable selling skills, therefore, to help the client determine which one best meets their requirements. To do this a great deal of product knowledge is needed as we noted earlier in this unit.

Since the agent also has to compete with other travel agencies a good sales person, prepared to spend time with the customers, will give the competitive edge. The holiday brochures provided by the tour operators are important sales tools for the agent. They give both information on and, importantly, pictures of resorts and accommodation.

Remember that a travel agent does not only sell holidays; during the sales process the sales person must consider the possibility of selling their other products, such as insurance. The time taken to sell a holiday for instance, may be considerable: it is an emotional, as well as an expensive, purchase.

Bars and restaurants

As in a shop, the sales process is straightforward and quickly completed. The customer orders, from an already prepared menu, food which is eaten and paid for.

The sales person, normally either the waiter or manager, should be prepared to cater for special needs, perhaps unusual dietary requirements or cocktails not normally served.

The sales person also has the opportunity to suggest extra dishes or special wines, to ensure that the table is the one the customer wants, that it is well laid, that flowers or candles are placed upon it and that used dishes are cleared quickly. All this helps increase customer satisfaction and bring them back with friends for another meal.

Accommodation

Reservations staff in hotels and lodges do not only take bookings; they are trained to sell. Figure 33 shows the procedure one hotel follows to increase room sales. You will note how customers are asked to take alternative accommodation, or nights, when their first choice is not available.

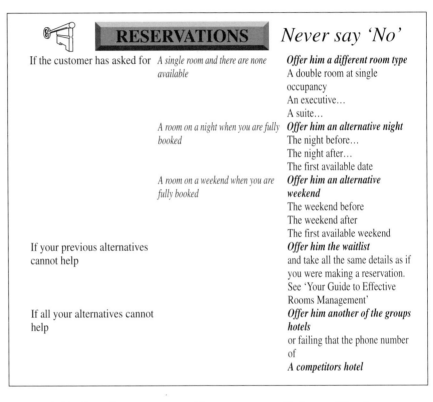

RESERVATIONS		*Never say 'No'*
If the customer has asked for	*A single room and there are none available*	**Offer him a different room type** A double room at single occupancy An executive… A suite…
	A room on a night when you are fully booked	**Offer him an alternative night** The night before… The night after… The first available date
	A room on a weekend when you are fully booked	**Offer him an alternative weekend** The weekend before The weekend after The first available weekend
If your previous alternatives cannot help		**Offer him the waitlist** and take all the same details as if you were making a reservation. See 'Your Guide to Effective Rooms Management'
If all your alternatives cannot help		**Offer him another of the groups hotels** or failing that the phone number of **A competitors hotel**

FIGURE 33 How reservations staff are trained to sell accommodation

If this hotel cannot provide a room at all they offer the telephone number of another hotel. The relieved customer (who has not had to put down the telephone feeling helpless) will remember the excellence of the service and probably come to the first hotel again.

Memberships

Private health clubs and sports centres rely heavily on membership fees for their income. Selling the membership is therefore an important part of bringing in sales.

Leaflets will be printed extolling the facilities on offer, and the benefits of membership, but the experienced sales person will not rely on leaflets alone. Membership of a club is an expensive, important purchase, not one which is bought on impulse. The sales person must be prepared to spend time showing off the facilities, perhaps on more than one occasion, and ascertaining which type of membership is really most suitable for the client; full, off-peak or corporate for example.

Trips and excursions

You may be surprised to learn that tour operators make more profit out of the 'added extras', such as insurance and trips and excursions, than they do out of the holidays themselves. It is no surprise, then, that a lot of effort is invested in persuading customers to go on excursions whilst on holiday. Excursions may be mentioned briefly in the holiday brochure to whet your appetite (Figure 34 gives an example) but the main sales pitch takes place in the resort. This type of selling is described later in this unit, on page 94.

FIGURE 34 Excursions advertised in a brochure

> ## EXCURSIONS
>
> **JAMAICA EXCURSIONS**
> Jamaica really is an island which is well worth exploring. That is why we have put together a great selection of excursions for you to choose from. Here are just a few highlights . . .
>
> **AIRTOURS BEACH PARTY**
> (Approximately £41 per person)
> (from Montego Bay)
> This is one of our most popular excursions, and it is no wonder why. Begin the evening with a sunset sail by catamaran across Montego Bay to a secluded private beach. Once here take your pick from the mouth-watering Jamaican buffet and enjoy the evening's entertainment programme as you sip from the free bar. There is modern and cultural dancing, and a great night to be had by all!
>
> **ISLAND PICNIC**
> (Approximately £25 per person)
> (from Negril)
> Travel by catamaran from the fashionable west coast resort of Negril to Booby Cay, your idyllic sunshine hideaway for the day. Here do as much or as little as Snorkel over the colourful reef

Direct selling

Direct selling in the world of tourism refers to holidays sold directly to customers rather than through travel agencies.

There are several operators who use direct sell. You have probably heard of Portland Holidays and Eclipse. As they do not use agents, they rely heavily on newspaper advertising to attract customers using direct response; a coupon to return or telephone numbers to ring. Once a customer has requested a brochure their address is on the organisation's mailing list and they will be sent another automatically every season.

A *warm welcome from*
ECLIPSE DIRECT

When you plan your well earned break you can be sure that Eclipse Direct has exactly the holiday for you, and at a surprisingly low price. Selling our own holidays keeps costs down and the savings are passed on to you. This also means that you deal directly with the experts. A call to our Holiday Helpline can answer your questions on any of the resorts we feature.

Booking your holiday yourself from the convenience of your own home is the simplest way to book. No more struggling through the High Street with dozens of heavyweight brochures and no more queuing for ages as you wait to be served. Your tickets are delivered to your door, so no trouble parking as you pop into town to pick them up. You can even arrange your foreign currency and airport car parking through us on the telephone.

What could be better – low prices, wide choice, convenience and you talk to the experts. Your holiday could not start off in a better way.

The Brighter way to book

Choose from our wide range of destinations and holidays. Booking is as simple as picking up the telephone. Call any of the numbers shown, tell us the holiday you want and we can confirm it for you there and then.

Book today to get your top value holiday from Eclipse Direct, the UK's most experienced direct sell holiday company.

SCOTLAND
041 248 4776
NORTH
061 742 2222
MIDLANDS
021 200 2920
SOUTH
0293 554 444

Triple price promise

LOWEST PRICES GUARANTEE
If you find the same adult holiday at a lower brochure price within one month of booking from this brochure, we will refund the difference.
YOU'RE REFUNDED IF WE DISCOUNT
In the unlikely event we reduce the price of your specified holiday after you have booked it from this brochure, we will refund the difference. So why wait?
NO SURCHARGES GUARANTEED
The cost of any holiday booked from this brochure is guaranteed. There will be no surcharges on the cost of your holiday.
See page 168 for full details

FIGURE 35 An example of direct selling advertising

The benefits of buying a holiday by direct sell are clearly outlined in Figure 35, an extract from Eclipse's brochure. You can study the brochure at home and pick up the telephone to arrange all the details. Notice that Eclipse also make sure that you feel you are being asked a fair price for the holiday.

Activity

Study Figure 35 again. Now write a similar piece for inclusion in a travel agent's promotional leaflet. You are competing against direct-sell organisations: stress the benefits of booking a holiday through the travel agent instead.

With other products, direct selling refers to any situation where there is direct contact, that is a face to face conversation with the customer. This can be confusing; as we have seen with direct-sell holidays there is no face to face contact with the customer!

Sales techniques

A popular theory used to describe the sales process is that of **AIDA**. AIDA stands for the four words below.

- Attention
- Interest
- Desire
- Action

Attention

The customer's attention is attracted by a colourful or surprising window display, a brochure full of photographs or an exciting newspaper advertisement. The customer's attention will be intensified if they are already considering buying that product. For example, a customer who has just booked a holiday to the sun is likely to notice a display of swimwear and beach towels. Once Christmas is over, the UK public turns its attention to summer holidays. The travel industry homes in on this with a mass of television and newspaper advertisements.

Having obtained the customer's attention you, as the person selling a product, must then take them through the further stages of interest and desire.

Interest

Interest is achieved by finding out what the customer's particular needs are and matching the need to the product. Is a value-for-money price on a squash racquet going to interest them or should the emphasis be placed on quality? The sales person must find this out through careful questioning.

Desire

The next stage, desire, is best achieved through demonstration. This is easily done with sports equipment. In the case of holiday sales the sales person can call on their own or a colleague's experiences of a resort. In an hotel you can show off the room. Timeshare sellers give a tour, or offer pictures, of a show apartment to create desire.

Action

If the sales person successfully gets this far, they must then lead the customer to action by closing the sale and completing the transaction.

We will look at these stages in more detail.

Stages of a sale

First impression

As the sales person, your body language and general presentation are very important. You may be wearing a uniform or a badge to identify you or you may be in casual sports gear if you work in a leisure centre, but you should look smart, enthusiastic and fit!

You only get one chance to make a first impression.

Greeting the customer

You can tell through experience when it is the best time to approach a customer. Allowing them to browse through the products for sale for a while first gives them a chance to relax and collect their thoughts.

However, there is no reason why every customer should not be greeted, as soon as they appear, with a smile and a cheery 'Good Morning' or 'Good Afternoon.'

The approach

Sometimes customers approach you for help with questions at the ready, but in a shop or travel agency it is often up to you to make the approach. Beware of being too pushy; you can easily frighten off a potential sale. Ask open questions rather than closed.

A **closed question** allows the customer to reply only with Yes or No. 'Can I help you?'

'No.'

What can you say next? Nothing at all!

Open questions ask for information and are difficult to answer with Yes or No.

'Which countries are you interested in for a holiday?'
'What type of holiday are you looking for?'

Assessing the customer's needs

Once you have made contact with someone you need to ask them questions in order to find out about their needs. In a travel agency the sales person will take notes as there will be quite a lot of detail, for instance dates, price range, number of people. In a shop it is not usually necessary to make notes in order to identify the right product. You should know your stock and be able to make suggestions.

Demonstrating the product

You should only show the customer the products or services which meet their needs. It is up to you to show how they meet their needs. For example, the travel agent may show a customer an apartment rather than an hotel as the apartment offers cheaper, more convenient accommodation for a family of six with small children. The waiter in a restaurant will not show a grill menu to a vegetarian, but will suggest and describe an alternative meal.

Overcoming objections

In order to achieve a sale you will often have to overcome the customer's objections to price, brand or other factor.

This is quite difficult to do effectively, but an experienced sales person will anticipate objections, that is they will have asked a lot of questions and considered the problems which might impede the sale and deal with them before they arise.

Consider the following situation. Mrs Perkins has chosen an exercise bike which is very good quality but more expensive than the price she at first said she wanted to pay. The experienced sales person anticipates that she will hesitate to buy because of the price although it is obvious she wants the bike. Even before she voices her objection the sales person is telling her about the interest free credit scheme.

Closing the sale

There are several ways to close a sale.

1	Firm close	the sales person assumes the sale and asks 'will you be paying by cash or cheque?' and completes the transaction.
2	Concessionary close	the sales person closes by offering a discount or emphasising a special offer which finishes that same day. This is a technique employed by travel agents when they have periods of discounting on holidays.
3	Limited edition close	this can be used when there are only a few seats left on a flight, or only a few items left in stock. The customer realises they may miss the purchase altogether.
4	Expert's close	this appeals to the 'snob' in many people. The indecisive customer in a restaurant can be persuaded to order if the waiter suggests the chef has recommended a dish. In a shop, the sales person may suggest that not many players have the skill to use this particular tennis racquet. The customer is sure to buy!

Other sales techniques
Add-on selling

Have you ever been in a shoe shop where they *don't* try to sell you shoe protector, or rainguard, a similar product? No, of course not!

This sales technique is used in leisure and tourism as well.

In restaurants you are asked if you want an apéritif, garlic bread, coffee, dessert – all at a small extra cost.

A travel agent will try to sell insurance and car hire as well as your holiday. They may ask if you require travellers cheques. All these services bring the agent extra revenue.

Trading up

The sales person who tries to sell a more expensive product than the customer is prepared for is trying to trade up. It doesn't always work!

Welcome meetings

This sales technique is a very important sales tool used by tour operators to sell excursions, which cost extra, to people who are already on a holiday.

If you have ever had a package holiday you will have been to a welcome meeting. It takes place the day after you arrive so that you are in a good humour and refreshed after your journey.

All new arrivals are invited, enticed by a free drink and promises of information about the resort. Once this basic information has been given the tour representative or courier gets down to the real business of selling excursions. These are described in details with photographs or slides and clients are encouraged to book there and then. Sales are good because of the warm atmosphere (free drink!) and holiday mood.

 Activity Choose a travel agency or shop. Your objective is to observe a member of staff making a sale to a customer. Do this as discreetly as you can!

There is no need to ask questions, simply watch and listen carefully. Then leave the shop or agency and, as soon as you can, make detailed notes on what you observed.

- Try to distinguish the different stages of the sale.
- Comment on them, for instance was questioning carried out? Were needs assessed? What kind of close was there?

Prepare your findings for an oral presentation to your group.

Telephone selling

Telephone selling is difficult as there is no face to face contact with your customer. A positive, enthusiastic attitude must be conveyed by your tone of voice. Telephone sales personnel usually have a script to follow. Think of the double-glazing people who call you at home. They are following a script. Most leisure industry telephone sales situations involve selling extras: the customer has made the initial phone call with enquiries about a specific product she or he wishes to buy. In this situation, a script is often helpful to allow the sales person to check that they have covered all the 'extras' on offer.

Activity

1   Draw up a script for a receptionist in a hotel who is taking a booking for accommodation.

You must cover the following information and sell as many hotel services as you can at the same time.

- Name, dates and arrival time.
- Number of rooms, types of board, special needs.
- You need confirmation in writing or a credit card payment.

You could start with the following greeting.

'Good morning, Jensens Hotel, Karen speaking. How may I help you?'

2   Practise your script with a colleague. Does it work? If not, adjust it and try again.

Element 3.4 Provide and Evaluate Customer Service in Leisure and Tourism

About this element

This element consists of activities concerned with providing and evaluating customer service. By the end of this element you should be able to:

1 identify customer needs for selected situations (performance criterion 3.4.1);
2 identify the types of information required by customers in selected situations (performance criterion 3.4.2);
3 demonstrate effective customer service in selected situations (performance criterion 3.4.3);
4 maintain accurate records for selected situations (performance criterion 3.4.4);
5 evaluate your own performance in the provision of customer service in selected situations (performance criterion 3.4.5);
6 summarise your own evaluation findings (performance criterion 3.4.6).

Assignment activity Unit 3

You should keep all your assignment activity work, clearly labelled, in your Portfolio of Evidence. This work provides evidence of coverage of all the elements and performance criteria covered in Unit 3.

Below are three situations requiring customer service.

For each situation you must:

a participate in a role play;
b complete any necessary documentation;
c make notes on the situation;
d evaluate your own performance.

1 The birthday party

Surfeet Ali is planning her 21st birthday party. She has come to you to enquire about your Passenger Cruise Service which runs using a pleasure boat on the river, catering specifically for parties.

You must find out about Surfeet's needs, and provide her with the information and service appropriate.

Role play: information for Surfeet
Your birthday is on 23rd July. You would like to invite 60 guests. You want a jazz band and a finger buffet. You would like a bar to be provided. Guests will pay for their own drinks, except for the champagne for a toast. You don't mind what time the party is as long as it is in the evening. Your budget for the party is £1,000. You are concerned about how your wheelchair-bound sister will get aboard.

Role play: information for sales person
The date Surfeet wants is available. You can provide a jazz band or disco for £120 each. Basic hire price for the boat is £400 for four hours. Maximum number of guests is 85. You have various menus available.

- Canapé menu: (e.g. cheese tartlets, rolls, choux pastry): £7 per person.
- Fork buffet: (e.g. curried chicken, stuffed eggs, salads): £10 per person.
- Hot fork buffet: (e.g. pork, chicken or ham, potatoes, profiteroles): £20 per person.
- Champagne prices:
    Lanson Black Label £25.00

    Moet et Chandon   £32.50

    Cava Extra Brut   £12.00
    (Sparkling wine)

The sales person must now fill in a copy of Figure 36, the booking sheet, and a copy of Figure 37, the evaluation form. Surfeet Ali should add comments using the evaluation form.

2 The faulty squash racquet

Jonathan Sims is an ambitious and successful squash player. He had a big league match on Friday evening and bought an expensive new racquet for the occasion. During the match a string broke. It is Saturday morning. He is furious and he is in the shop with the racquet, complaining loudly. Deal with him.

Role play: information for Jonathan
You bought the racquet last Saturday. You chose it as it is a well-known brand and has an excellent reputation for quality. It cost £159. You practised with the racquet once. Your match on Friday was your chance to become league champion. You were so upset when the racquet broke that your concentration was shattered and you lost. You are looking for someone to vent your anger on.

Jilly
Passenger Cruise Services
~~~~~~~~~~~~~~~~~~~~~~
Booking Sheet

Name of contact _____

Name of client _____

Address of client _____

_____

_____

_____

Contact Telephone No _____ Contact Fax No _____

Date of Booking _____

Time of Departure _____ Time of Return _____

Point of Departure _____ Point of Return _____

Number of Passengers _____

Menus _____ Number of Vegetarians _____

Welcome Drinks _____

_____

_____

Bar _____

_____

_____

Wine _____

_____

_____

Entertainment _____

_____

_____

Decorations _____

_____

_____

</div>

FIGURE 36 The booking sheet

Role play: information for sales person

You are renowned for your ability to deal with angry customers. You will be able to calm Jonathan. You have had three of these racquets brought in with the same problem, and intend to return them all to the manufacturers.

The sales person must now fill in a copy of the returns form, Figure 38 and the evaluation form, Figure 37. Jonathan should add comments using the evaluation form.

Evaluation: How Did I Do?

How were the customer's needs met?

Was the customer satisfied? How do I know?

What would I do differently next time?

Customer comments

FIGURE 37 The evaluation form

Racquet Sports

Returns Form

Item: _____

Product code: _____

Price: _____

Reason for return: _____
_____

Action taken: _____
_____

Customer's name and address: _____
_____
_____

Customer signature:

FIGURE 38 The returns form

3 Basketball

Mr Alan Price telephones you at the Leisure Services Department. He is looking for a basketball course for his ten year old son in the summer holidays. Deal with him on the telephone.

Information for Mr Price

You hold a 'Leisurecard B' as you are a city resident. You wish to pay by credit card over the telephone. You will need to know where and when the sessions are and how to get there.

Role play: information for sales person

Look at Figure 39 for your course information.

COURSE ONE		
	Open to	Children aged 8-14 years
	Duration	4 sessions
	Day	Tuesday to Friday
	Dates	28, 29, 30, 31 May
	Time	10 am to 12 noon
	Venue	Hazelmere School Sports Hall, Streatham Avenue
	No. places	30
	Course ref	BASK-1
	Cost full	£8.00
	Lcard B	£6.00
	Lcard A	£4.00

FIGURE 39 Basketball course information

At the end of the telephone conversation the sales person must fill in the booking form, Figure 40. It is to be sent to Mr Price to sign. The sales person should also complete the evaluation form. Mr Price should add his comments.

ENTRY FORM

NAME	Address & Post Code	Contact Phone Number	Age if under 16	Course Ref No.	Fee Paid
1					
2					
3					
4					

Total amount enclosed with this form £ [ ]

TYPE A/B

Leisurecard enclosed with form (please tick)   Yes ☐ No ☐   ☐
Leisurecard Application & documents enclosed with form Yes ☐ No ☐   ☐

Read carefully before signing

I understand that the City Council or the organisation providing facilities, their Agents, Servants and Employees accept no responsibility for loss, damage or injury caused by or during attendance on any City Council organised activity except where such loss, damage or injury can be shown to result directly from the negligence of the said Council, Agents, Servants or Employees.

Signed_____ (Parent or Guardian if under 16)
For the persons named above

You will be sent a letter of confirmation once you have been accepted onto the course.
This form can only be returned (by hand or post) to: LEISURE SERVICES

Tick here ☐ if you do not wish us to store your details on our database to receive future sports information.

FIGURE 40 The entry form

Unit ④ Contributing to the Running of an Event

· ·

Introduction to the unit

This unit comprises the following elements required by the course and gives you practice in all the performance criteria that prove your understanding of each of these elements.

Element 4.1   Plan an event with others

Element 4.2   Undertake a role in a team event

Element 4.3   Evaluate the team event

Element 4.1 Plan an Event with Others

This element looks at planning events. By the end of this element you should be able to:

1 describe the planning process for an event (performance criterion 4.1.1);
2 explain possible objectives of the planned event (performance criterion 4.1.2);
3 select, with the team, an event from a range of options which will meet the agreed objectives (performance criterion 4.1.3);
4 calculate, with the team, what resources will be needed for the event (performance criterion 4.1.4);
5 identify, with the team, constraints likely to affect the event (performance criterion 4.1.5);
6 agree, with the team, contingency actions in case of emergencies and anticipated disruptions (performance criterion 4.1.6);
7 agree and allocate roles for each team member (performance criterion 4.1.7);
8 contribute to producing a realistic team plan for the event (performance criterion 4.1.8).

World events

When Ireland's football team reached the semi-final of the World Cup in 1994 the streets were deserted as everyone watched the game on television – the pride and thrill in their team felt by all the spectators brought everyday life to a halt.

Imagine how much more of a thrill you would feel if you had helped to organise the event yourself – well, many people do just that. Obviously, an event like the World Cup is not organised by an individual; it relies for its success upon a whole team of people working together.

Major events are always the result of a team effort. You will have heard of the 'Live Aid' concert held at Wembley in 1985. For the first time many famous bands and singers got together and gave their services for free. The organisation involved was awesome: simultaneously, a similar concert was staged in Philadelphia. Phil Collins managed to appear at both concerts by jetting between the two.

These concerts succeeded in raising millions for starving Ethiopians yet they started life as a simple idea from two musicians, Bob Geldof and Midge Ure. They had seen news reports of the starving people and were moved, particularly by the plight of the children. They used all the people they knew in the music business to help plan the event and then performed in it as well, singing their 'hit' song 'Feed the World' whose sales revenue also went to feed the Africans.

Domestic events

Smaller events are often organised by one person: think about parties you have been to. They are quite complex in that there are lots of things to consider; guest list, invitations, food, drinks, where to have it, cleaning up afterwards. Again, the organiser will feel a great sense of achievement when all goes well.

You too can help organise events and in this unit we aim to show you how to do so in a professional manner. You may do so well that one day you get a job as an events organiser.

Planning an event

You may be planning an event as part of your college course, or because you wish to arrange a special celebration. If the event is part of your course, consider why you are being asked to do it.

The answer is, that you are likely to develop many organisational skills during the planning process. You will find that you have to communicate well, often in ways that you are not used to, for example via business letters or in meetings.

Defining the objectives

One of the first things you must do is determine the objectives for your event.

It is important to do this before you decide on the type of event as you have to ensure the event you decide to hold is the right way to achieve your objectives. For example, a sports centre may decide that they need an event to increase membership. Thus a sponsored swim for existing members would not be suitable as it would not achieve this objective.

Case study

A student event – Part 1

A group of leisure students at a London college has decided to produce an event as the climax of their year's course. Their tutor, Jocelyn, is pleased at their enthusiasm and ambition but is also concerned that the event be professionally organised. Jocelyn decides that the project should go ahead but that every activity and decision will be formally recorded at full meetings.

The group consists of 15 students. They know each other very well at this stage of their course and are aware of each others' strengths and weaknesses.

Jocelyn calls the first meeting in April. She explains that she will chair this meeting but expects the role to pass to a member of the group in due course. As she expects, the students have already had heated discussions about what the event should be. Jocelyn insists that the group draw up a list of objectives for the event before considering what it should be.

These are the objectives they came up with.

- To gain experience of planning and promoting a leisure event.
- To practise business skills, for instance writing memos, letters, dealing with people out of college.
- To develop organisational skills.
- To develop team skills.
- To publicise the college and their course.
- To make a profit which could be used for an educational trip.

Jocelyn is quite impressed with this list but suspects that three of the students have done most of the work. She isn't concerned by this, as she knows that the students will be tested to their limits in the course of project.

Having come up with their objectives the students are ready to hold their brainstorming session. They are not shy and soon have a list of ideas. Jocelyn likes the idea of a college sports day, but the students think this too predictable for leisure students. Instead they plump for the fashion show idea suggested by Vera. The next step is to check back to their list of objectives to make sure this event will fulfil them. They find it serves the objectives clearly and are delighted at their decision. They haven't yet considered the scale of the project ahead.

Activity   Imagine you are organising a surprise 21st party for a friend. What are your objectives? Draw up a list – obviously your objectives will differ from those of an educational project. Check your list with a member of your group to see if you agree with each other. Discuss your results and amend them if you think fit.

Brainstorming

Among any group of people there will be several ideas for the best way of achieving the event's objectives. One way of putting forward these ideas is to hold a brainstorming session.

All the ideas are put forward to the chairperson and recorded. No criticism of ideas is allowed. You need quantity of ideas rather than quality at this stage. Since no criticism is allowed, outlandish ideas may be put forward and built upon. As a result, more timid group members may not be so afraid to put forward their ideas. Once a long list of ideas is established they can be reviewed and screened according to their practicability and ability to satisfy the event's objectives.

Finding the financial resources

Once you have decided on your event you have to consider what resources will be needed. Unless you are very fortunate indeed the greatest problem you will have is raising money. Colleges cannot afford to give their hard-won budget to students for events and it is unlikely that you have any spare cash!

If you are working in a business you may find that money is already allocated in the budget for marketing and promotion and some of this can be used for special events. Otherwise you need to consider how you can raise funds for your event. There are various possibilities.

Sponsorship

Many companies have funds allocated for community projects, particularly banks. Write to a number of organisations explaining what you want to do and telling them how much money you need. Ask for slightly more than you need in the expectation they will reduce the figure. You will have to explain exactly what the money is for and give an indication of the benefits to your sponsor of being associated with your event. You should promise publicity in terms of newspaper coverage or programme mentions. Think of racing drivers, for example, who have their sponsors' names and logos all over their vehicles. Beware of promising anything you can't do!

Ticket sales

Depending on the type of event you are organising you can charge an entry fee. This is acceptable for any type of entertainment or sports event. However, you may not be able to charge people who come to see an exhibition of your work.

Although a lot of money can be raised in ticket sales, you run the risk of not breaking even. This is because you commit yourself to paying money out before being certain of your revenue. You need to carry out some market research to establish how much you can charge and how many people are likely to participate.

Co-operative

If you are sure that your event will eventually make money you might raise some cash by forming a co-operative. Each member of your team is asked to contribute a set amount. You all agree that each person's money will be refunded at the close of the event plus a share of any profit. It is a good idea to put this in writing and obtain everyone's signatures. Of course, if the event fails your money is lost.

Raffle

If you hold a raffle at the event itself, you can raise some extra funds very easily. However, if you want to hold a raffle in advance of the event as a fund raiser you will have to be sure that you meet the current legal requirements on gaming laws. Check these requirements with your city council legal department.

Non-financial resources
People

People are an important resource. It is likely that you will need experts in one area or another to help you make your event a success.

Think about the party you were planning in the earlier activity. Were skilled people needed? Sociable guests, certainly, but also caterers or friends who are skilled at preparing food. Perhaps you would like to hire a disc jockey? Whatever event is planned a variety of skilled people will be called for.

Materials and equipment

Don't forget that special equipment may be needed for your event: a bus if you are going on a trip, lighting for a stage show or sports equipment for a sports event.

Information

You may need to find out some special pieces of information. This might concern legislation, for example what kind of licence do you need to sell drink , or is a public entertainment licence necessary?

If you are planning to travel you will need information on fares and timetables.

Making a resource plan

A jumble sale is being organised by the parent-teacher association (PTA) at a village school.

The parents are very efficient and have many other matters besides the sale to discuss at their meeting. They have therefore asked in advance for a resource plan to be produced for the jumble sale. The plan (Figure 41) is presented at the meeting.

	Details	Source	Action
Finance	Change float	Treasurer	Provide on day
Venue	Saturday 25/4 12–5 p.m.	School Hall	Booked
People	Collectors: Thurs 23/4 Fri 24/4 Sorters: Sat 25/4 10–12 a.m. Sellers: 2–4.30 p.m. Clearing up: 4.30–5 p.m.	Parents	Mrs Jones to ask parents and draw up a rota
Materials/ Equipment	letter to parents 2 weeks before the sale	PTA Secretary	Mr Allen to write and distribute
	Tables	School	PTA parents to lay out prior to sale
	Tills	?	Use boxes instead
	Bags for packaging	All parents to bring used plastic bags	Mrs Raines to collect bags
	Goods to sell	From collection	Mrs Jones's rota

FIGURE 41 An example of a resource plan

You will see from this chart that a lot of preparation is needed for a fairly simple event.

Consider what will happen at 5.00 p.m. when the sale is over. What other activities will be necessary at the end of the sale?

Activity   Your group has decided to hold a raffle to support a local charity.

a   Produce a resource chart for this event.
b   Present your chart to the group and compare notes.

Working with constraints

When you plan your event you must consider the constraints which are likely to affect the event and plan with these in mind. What is a constraint? It is a limit within which you must work.

The most obvious constraint is the budget. Very few people or companies have unlimited budgets for event planning.

You may also be constrained by the availability of places or people. If the band you set your heart on has another gig you need to change your party date. If your venue is already booked you need to change your date or location.

Licensing and insurance requirements

The size of the venue you choose will affect the size of your audience and also how much you need to charge. The number of people a venue will hold (its capacity) is limited by health and safety considerations, for instance everyone must be able to escape easily in case of fire. You should find out what kind of safety legislation applies to your event.

If you are opening up a hall to the public you will need a public entertainment licence. This licence is issued by the legal department of a city or district council. Cost depends upon council policy and the size of the venue. Expect a minimum of £100. Check first that it has not already been licensed; you will save yourself money. The emergency services will come and examine exits and safety procedures before granting this licence.

You are not allowed to sell alcohol at your event without a licence. This is available through your local court for a one-off fee. Allow plenty of time to arrange licences – it is very disappointing to find you are too late.

If your venue is a public building it probably has insurance against accidents to members of the public. If not, this is something else you have to consider. Public liability insurance is not the remit of the council; it is acquired through an insurance company.

All these constraints should be considered: it is important for the success of an event that they are observed. They also cost money which should be taken into account in the budget.

Contingency plans

You should try to think of everything that might go wrong at your event.

These are some likely problems.

- The bus doesn't turn up.
  Make sure you have the telephone number of the bus company. If your college has many sites the bus may be waiting in the wrong place. A telephone call to suppliers and helpers the day before the event to confirm all details is a good idea.
- You don't sell enough tickets for a show.
  You need 'rent a crowd', that is classes of students who will come to anything for free. You might not make so much money but you will ensure a good atmosphere. A half-full venue looks poor.
- It pours with rain.
  Make sure you have an alternative inside venue. This applies to any outdoor event arranged in the UK!
- Someone – the presenter or the make-up team – doesn't arrive at all.
  Have an understudy ready – in the case of make-up, get some willing students to improvise.

Allocating roles

It is vital to allocate specific responsibilities for 'getting things done' to individuals, otherwise nothing will be done with the best of intentions.

At every event meeting, when a decision is made to take action, for example a letter, you must always allocate a task and set a deadline.

Deciding on the role for each person involved in organising an event is a priority as soon as you have your objectives sorted out. You will first need someone in overall charge. It is a good idea to elect this chairperson so that everyone is happy to accept their authority.

Other roles may vary according to the event, but you will probably need at least the following.

- Secretary – to document meetings and all decisions.
- Finance manager – to look after income and spending.
- Marketing manager – to publicise your event.
- Sales manager – to oversee selling of tickets.

Once you have decided on the necessary roles, consider each individual's skills and preferences before deciding who should do what.

Activity

1 Look at Part 2 of the case study on the next page. Produce an organisation chart showing all the roles that have been adopted for the fashion show in the case study. All roles should report to the chairperson.

   Are there any roles which have been left out by Jocelyn's students? If so, add them.

2 Imagine your own class group is to produce a fashion show. Assign the roles from your chart to the group members according to their strengths and weaknesses.

   Discuss your proposals with the group.

Managing administrative records

It will be extremely helpful to everyone involved in the planning and running of an event if a proper record is kept of all the organisational activities that are going on. You may think someone will remember what you have asked them to do verbally but all arguments later can be resolved if a simple written request was made at the same time.

A variety of useful written records will be discussed.

Job description

A job description is a useful means of summing up someone's responsibilities. It need not be formal or all-inclusive (or exclusive!) but it often helps that people have agreed what responsibilities a job title actually carries.

Figure 42 on page 112 gives a sample job description for the fashion event's publicity officer, Carole.

Action plan

Figure 43 on page 112 shows you an example of the publicity officer's action plan.

Case study

A student event – Part 2

Jocelyn's group of students meet to determine the roles and responsibilities they will each take on to produce their fashion show.

First they decide on the tasks to be done. Lots of ideas emerge: decide on venue, get clothes, arrange for models, and we need lights and music. Where will this money come from? Tickets, programmes, publicity – somehow the public must know its on – who will design, set, print and distribute? The list seems endless, and has to be brought into some kind of order so that roles can be assigned within the group.

Matthew volunteers to be responsible for raising money and for finance. He has achieved good grades in financial assignments, so the group are pleased to let him take this on.

Vera wants to be in charge of administration. This means looking after the taking of minutes at meetings, writing any letters needed, talking to personnel within the college and making any telephone calls deemed necessary by the group. Vera is very confident communicating with people, so the group is happy with this choice of role for her.

A chairperson is needed. This role goes to Suki. She is a fairly quiet group member, but has grown in confidence through the year, and is not afraid to voice her opinions. She is also well respected by her classmates.

The publicity officer is Carole. She already has some good ideas for contacting local newspapers and television stations. Two of the other girls, Sonia and Chloe, volunteer to help. Jocelyn points out that they will have to organise posters, programmes and tickets as well.

Douglas hasn't thought of anything he could do, so Suki suggests he takes on responsibility for technical needs, like lighting, music and so on. Douglas accepts this role, but looks a bit bewildered at the prospect.

Kevin and Gloria want to organise the actual show, that is choreograph the models and decide what music to use. Kevin has a good CD system at home which will help with this.

Julia and Sindy say they will be responsible for choosing clothes and finding shops to lend them.

Everyone now has a job, lots has been agreed and Jocelyn is pleased with progress to date. Next time they meet they can act on their decisions.

Job description	Publicity officer: Fashion Show
Responsible to	Group chairperson
Responsible for	Marketing assistants (2)
Responsibilities	To secure publicity for the event To write and send out press releases To oversee the production of posters, tickets and programmes To advertise the event internally To produce posters for the advertising of auditions

FIGURE 42 Carole's job description

Action plan	Publicity officer: Fashion show
8 weeks prior to event	Design posters for auditions
4 weeks prior to event	Compose press release, send to local television stations, local radio, local newspapers Write programme with acknowledgements Get quotes for ticket and programme printing Print posters
3 weeks prior to event	Finalise ticket design, get it printed, arrange programme printing Put up posters around building, advertising the event
2 weeks prior to event	Visit all personnel in all departments, inform them of event Check proofs of programme
1 week prior to event	Telephone all press, ask if they are covering the event
2 days prior to event	Receive programmes back from printer
1 day prior to event	Telephone all press, ask if they are covering the event
The event	Welcome press, distribute programmes, do anything else needed

FIGURE 43 Carole's action plan

Agendas

Once roles have been established and job descriptions agreed the chairperson will call regular meetings to ensure that team planning is taking place and action taken as agreed.

For each meeting the chairperson will draw up an agenda. It may look like the sample in Figure 44.

The typed minutes of the previous meeting must be given to everyone present and agreed as a true representation of what happened. The chairperson will then read or announce anyone's apologies for absence which the secretary should note.

AGENDA

Five-a-Side Event Meeting April 1996

(i)   Minutes of previous meeting
(ii) Apologies for absence
(iii) Matters arising
(iv) Feedback on availability of Sports Hall
(v) Applications of entry received
(vi) A.O.B.

(vii) Date of next meeting

FIGURE 44 A meeting agenda

Matters arising is the time the meeting allots to reporting the completion or otherwise of any action that was promised at the previous meeting.

The rest of the agenda relates to new or further matters for discussion. A.O.B. stands for any other business.

Tips for agendas
- Don't try to deal with too many items at one meeting.
- Set a time limit on the meeting – make sure you deal with all the business in this time.
- One of the secretary's tasks is to keep minutes of meetings. A copy of the minutes is distributed to each team member as soon as possible after the meeting. Thus, they know what has been agreed and can keep a record of progress for the event.

Minutes
Figure 45 gives the minutes of the Five-a-Side Event meeting.

Note the action points in the minute. Each person knows what they have to do and will be expected to report back at the next meeting.

Memoranda
You may be assigned the task of finding out information from someone within your organisation. If you cannot do this in person, write a memorandum, or memo.

MINUTES of the Five-a-Side Event Meeting, April 1996

Present   A. Hill, J. Singh, M. Matthews, K. McHugh
Apologies S. Sarendon

(i)   The minutes of the previous meeting were agreed.
(ii) J. Singh reported that the Sports Hall is available on 6th June
      1996. It was agreed that this should be booked (no cost).

   Action: JS

   M. Matthews, Sales Manager, agreed to organise a sales
   drive with posters and visits to classes.

   Action: Posters AH
              Visits MM

Under Any Other Business, M. Matthews raised the question of
refreshments. The team agreed to approach the canteen in the first
instance.

   Action: JS

The date of the next meeting was fixed for 10 May 1996

FIGURE 45 Minutes of a meeting

Your organisation may have pre-printed memos – they will
start something like this

MEMORANDUM
To:
From:
Date:
Ref:

Make up a pre-printed memo following the above layout and
then write your message as briefly as possible. Remember to
say how you can be contacted.

Figure 46 shows an example.

Case study

A student event – Part 3

Jocelyn's student group are gathered for an event meeting. It is 5th May 199-. Jocelyn took the minutes of the last meeting and has circulated copies to the group. They now all check and agree the minutes, and there are no matters arising.

Jocelyn is therefore able to move quickly to agenda item 3 – resources

Some fundamental decisions must be made, and discussion is energetic. They need:

- a venue;
- a date;
- money;
- clothes;
- models.

These are only the basics – they might also need lighting, music system, props and an infinite list of other things…they put their minds to the basics first.

Money first – well, they haven't any so they need sponsorship.

Matthew, as finance manager, agrees to come up with a list of organisations, including banks that they might contact. He is also supposed to write the actual letter but Vera agrees to help with this. Jocelyn asks him for a deadline. He says that the letter will go out in a week's time. Jocelyn points out that it should not take a week to write a letter and look up a few addresses. Two days is agreed as the deadline.

The group all think the library should be used as a venue. It is convenient, spacious, has a wonderful central stairway to show off the models and holds a host of people. Other possibilities are 'The Rockhouse', a local club venue suggested by Kevin. He agrees to find out how much it is to hire, and what facilities it can offer. Sonia says they should approach hotels and is assigned to do this. All of these venues will be approached within two days.

The group agrees that their show should take place in June. Friday 23rd June is agreed as the best date. This gives over two months of planning and preparation – not long really!

Suki remembers that they need models and suggests that an audition be held one lunchtime. After some argument about who should attend, it is agreed that Gloria and Kevin will run this as they are the show directors.

The group is excited; they feel they have achieved a lot in their meeting. They agree to meet again in three days' time.

MEMORANDUM

To: Mr Jeffries, Sports Hall Manager
From: M. Matthews, GNVQ Int Leisure and Tourism

Date: 17.4.96
Ref: Sports Hall Insurance

We have booked the Sports Hall for 6.6.9- for a Five-a-Side
competition. Please let me know if any extra insurance is
required.

I can be contacted via Mr Hussein, my course tutor.

FIGURE 46 A
memorandum

There is no need to sign a memo.

Activities   Re-read the account of the Fashion Show meeting on page
115. Now produce a set of minutes for it with action points.

Write a memo to Jenny Hughes, the Canteen Manager, asking
her whether refreshments can be provided at your Five-a-Side
competition.

Business letters

Earlier on in this unit sponsorship was suggested as a means
of raising finance or providing goods for an event. You might
ask for finance from an organisation such as a bank. They will
always look more favourably on your request if your event is
for charity.

You should always write when asking for sponsorship. Write
to as many organisations as you can and do not be too
disappointed when they do not all reply.

The letter you send out must follow a business layout. The
simplest one is shown below. Find out who to write to in each
organisation (normally the Manager) by telephoning and
asking for the name. This makes your request more personal.

Your letter should be on your college or organisation's headed paper. Figure 47 shows an example.

Mrs R Franklyn
Manager
Lloyds Bank
18 Percival Street
LONDON
W16 5LS

**Anytown College
of Further Education
Anytown
Northamptonshire
PE8 1TP**

14th April 1996

Dear Mrs Franklyn

The students of the GNVQ Int Leisure and Tourism course at Anytown college are organising a Five-a-Side football competition on 6th June 199-. The event is to be held in the college sports hall. The purpose of the event is to raise funds for the NSPCC and to help us achieve our GNVQ unit 'Contributing to the Running of an Event'.

We invite you to sponsor the event. We need about £100 to provide refreshments for participants and to cover essential costs.

We expect the local press to cover our event and if you sponsor us we will be pleased to include Lloyds Bank on our programme.

We look forward to hearing from you.

Yours sincerely

Michael Matthews

M. Matthews (student)
c/o Mr A. Hussein (Course Tutor)

FIGURE 47 A business letter

Activity   The canteen manager at Anytown College has said that she is unable to provide refreshments for the Five-a-Side contest.

Using the business letter format, compose a letter to your local supermarket asking them to provide refreshments.

Safety considerations

Activity   The extract from a magazine article in Figure 48 is from *Which?* magazine, March 1995. The magazine conducted an investigation into crowd safety. Although the Health and Safety Commission issue guidelines on safety at pop concerts, clubs and dances these guidelines are voluntary. *Which?* is calling for mandatory rules.

Read the reports made by the inspectors.

1 Which safety factors could have been planned for and which are out of the organiser's control?

2 What were the strengths at the UB40 concert?

3 What were the weaknesses at the Bucks County Show?

FIGURE 48 Safety assessed at two major public events

4 Make recommendations for safety measures at future events at both these locations.

FIRE FOLLY A small bonfire of uncollected rubbish, started by some of the crowd, was quickly extinguished by security staff

UB40 CONCERT AT NATIONAL BOWL, MILTON KEYNES
13 AUGUST 1994

SAFETY RATING GOOD

The National Bowl was opened in 1993 and can hold up to 60,000 spectators. The stage is a permanent structure and the crowd occupies a semi-circular, grassed area which slopes upwards away from the stage towards the seven entrances to the Bowl. Around 45,000 people attended.

Our inspector was generally very impressed by the professional approach adopted by the management of the venue and the emergency services to organisation and liaison. The only problem he found occurred when some spectators set fire to piles of rubbish. Security staff dealt with these incidences quickly. This could have caused more serious problems had the grass been longer and dry.

ELECTRIC SHOCKS Left, a sub-station door left open; right, poorly-protected cables, joined by tape, lie in wet grass

BUCKS COUNTY SHOW, NEAR AYLESBURY
1 SEPTEMBER 1994

SAFETY RATING POOR

Bad weather meant a low turn-out, which was just as well. We found serious deficiencies in electrical safety, fire safety provisions and marquee layout, all evidence that the consultation process to ensure safety had failed.

The electrical installations caused most concern (see left). And virtually all of the portable generators being used were not properly earthed. We found no fire extinguishers on any stand or in any tent. The only fire engine on site was there as an exhibit – ironically promoting fire safety. The layout of the marquee fell well short of fire safety requirements, too (see right). The organisers said they would take our findings seriously and ensure safety requirements were met for the next show.

Element 4.2 Undertake a Role in a Team Event

About this element

This element looks at undertaking a role in a team event. By the end of this element you should be able to:

1 contribute to the team event according to the agreed role (performance criterion 4.2.1);
2 use available resources effectively (performance criterion 4.2.2);
3 contribute to the team event with due regard to health, safety and security (performance criterion 4.2.3);
4 co-operate effectively with others during the team event, as required by the plan (performance criterion 4.2.4);
5 explain any changes to the agreed role (performance criterion 4.2.5);
6 react promptly to any disruptions to the event, and inform others of any changes that affect them (performance criterion 4.2.6);
7 keep a log of your own contribution to the event (performance criterion 4.2.7).

Assignment activity Unit 4

The group task for this assignment is to organise an event. Individually, you must undertake a role in the planning of the event. Your contribution will be monitored by other members of your group and by your tutor.

It is essential that you keep a diary or 'log' of all activities you undertake, together with minutes of meetings and any other documentation, for instance copies of memos or letters that you have written together with replies.

Figure 49 shows an example of a log. It is part of Gloria's log – for the day of the fashion show itself.

a As a group, determine the type of event you wish to hold. You may do this by means of a brainstorming session.
b As a group, draw up a list of the objectives of the event.
c As a group, determine the roles required and assign them within the group. Draw up an organisation chart.
d Individually, draw up a job description for your own role and write an individual action plan leading up to the event.

e Draw up a resource plan for your own role. Present this to your group so that a 'team resource plan' can be made.

f Attend and participate in all meetings. Take action as agreed at meetings. Keep a log, amending your action plan as necessary according to the decisions taken.

g Attend and participate in the event, taking any role necessary.

FIGURE 49 One day of Gloria's fashion show event log

Friday 14th June

Show time

Today is either the end of the world or a start of a new career. Today we all met early and weren't able to get into the hall until 11.30 because of an exam, so I went to a meeting then had to go back to Sawston to pick up the masks. When I got back it was rehearsal after rehearsal. The group were all excited and worried. The next rehearsal was dress rehearsal – I hardly had time to get myself ready because the models needed dressing and constantly telling what scene they were in etc. The whole thing was mayhem. The makeup ladies from Debenhams arrived at 3.00. I finished talking through scenes with Kevin and Julia and went and had a shower. (This is it Gloria I now really have to get on stage with people staring at me –OHHHH NOOOO !!!!)

Well I went and had my makeup done and a lot of the girls were constantly moaning about their nerves. Well we all went and had something to eat and the next thing it was 7.15 and people were arriving.

The changing rooms were now just buzzing with excitement. I was next on stage and I looked in the mirror and felt sick. My god have I really got to go on stage looking like this.

I can now hear the music starting.

Element 4.3 Evaluate the Team Event

About this element

This element looks at how to evaluate a team event. By the end of this element you should be able to:

1 agree with the team the criteria for evaluating the event (performance criterion 4.3.1);
2 devise with the team an evaluation form and complete it individually during evaluation (performance criterion 4.3.2);
3 gather evaluation feedback from the appropriate sources and record it on the form (performance criterion 4.3.3);
4 exchange evaluation feedback with the team constructively and positively (performance criterion 4.3.4);
5 summarise the overall findings of the team's evaluation (performance criterion 4.3.5);
6 make and record suggestions for improvements to the way in which similar events are staged in the future (performance criterion 4.3.6).

Activity Evaluate the event by drawing up a list of its strengths and weaknesses. Make recommendations for changes if the event were to be held again. Use the notes below to help you. Submit task 8 in the form of a report, together with log, minutes and other documents from previous tasks.

You may be asked to participate in a group, oral evaluation session.

Notes
In order to evaluate your event, that is decide whether it was a success or not, you need to gather together all the information you have collected in the form of memos, minutes, letters and log diary entries.

- Look back at your original objectives. Take each one in turn and decide whether it has been met – did you use resources efficiently? Did you raise any funds you planned? How well did the team work together?
- Consider the strengths and weaknesses of the planning and the event itself. Draw up a list of each. Think about why the

strengths and weaknesses occurred and note them down.

- If your event has an audience, ensure some members of your group are in among them, listening to reactions and comments. This will provide helpful feedback.
- If your event is an exhibition or participative event, ask customers to complete an evaluation form which you design.
- Consider carefully any recommendations for improvements.
- Evaluate your own performance. Be honest about how well you contributed. Write a list of things you could do better next time.
- Design a form which can be used when evaluating other members of your group. Include the following headings. How well did they perform in their role? Did they attend all the meetings, produce results to deadlines, communicate well? Did they participate in the event?
- Discuss these evaluations of each other as a group.

Your course assessor will do the final evaluation of everyone's performance.

Unit ⑤ The Sport and Fitness Business

Introduction to the unit
This unit comprises the following elements required by the course and gives you practice in all the performance criteria that provide your understanding of each of these elements.

Element 5.1   Investigate the products, activities and services associated with sport and fitness provision

Element 5.2   Describe the types of ownership, funding and regulation of sport and fitness provision

Element 5.3   Explore trends and influences in sport and fitness provision

⊞ Element 5.1 Investigate the products, activities and services associated with sport and fitness provision

This element looks at products, activities and services in the sport and fitness industry. By the end of this element you should be able to:

1 describe types and give examples of sport and recreation activities (performance criterion 5.1.1);
2 describe types and give examples of health and fitness activities (performance criterion 5.1.2);
3 describe the products and services used to deliver sports and fitness activities (performance criterion 5.1.3);
4 explain the main benefits of participation in sports and fitness provision (performance criterion 5.1.4);
5 describe factors affecting take up of activities by different types of participant (performance criterion 5.1.5);
6 explain the appeal of selected sports and fitness activities (performance criterion 5.1.6).

What are sport, health and fitness activities?

Sports activities

The wide range of sporting activities available in the UK can be categorised as either indoor or outdoor, although some activities like swimming fall under both headings.

Figure 50 gives examples of the different types of sport that come under each category.

Activity

1 Make a list of the activities you have participated in under each of the two categories (Indoor sport and Outdoor sport) and sub-headings in Figure 50 and briefly describe the kind of activity it is (e.g. individual, group, competitive or non-competitive, popular reasons for participating).

2 Now make a list of the activities you would like to participate in, stating your reasons. What might prevent you from trying any of the activities you have listed?

3 Share your lists with other members of your group. What are the most popular activities? Why do you think they are popular?

Indoor sport		Outdoor sport		
Dry	Wet	On land	In the water	In the air
Basketball	Swimming/	Horse riding	Sailing	Parachuting
Indoor football	synchronised swimming	Hunting	Canoeing	Hang gliding
Ice hockey	Diving	Polo	Wind surfing	Flying
Indoor hockey	Water aerobics	Mountaineering	Surfing	Para sailing
Badminton	Aqua push	Rock climbing	Swimming	Kite flying
Squash	Water polo	Abseiling	Water skiing	
Indoor tennis		Caving	Rowing	
Martial arts		Mountain biking	Punting	
e.g. karate		Running	Fishing	
Trampolining		Football		
Gymnastics		Rugby		
Yoga		Hockey		
Ice skating		Cricket		
Tenpin bowling		Athletics		
		American football		
		Tennis		
		Bowls		
		Skiing		
		Golf		
		Baseball		
		Rounders		

FIGURE 50 Types of sport and recreation activities

Health and fitness activities

Although these activities are certainly part of sport (and recreation) they need to be considered separately because they place particular emphasis on personal health and development.

Here are some examples of the health and fitness activities which are available in gymnasia and fitness suites around the UK.

In the gym, using weights:

- body building;
- weight training;
- stamina training.

In fitness suites:

- circuit training;
- exercise to music (e.g. aerobics, step aerobics, slide aerobics, body sculpting);
- dance.

Activity   1   In pairs, list the health and fitness activities in which you have participated and those which you have not yet experienced.

2   Individually, prepare a short presentation describing at least one activity which you would like to encourage other people to try. Remember to say why you find the activity so personally satisfying.

The benefits of health and fitness activities

Campaigns by the Sports Council and Health Education Authority have aimed to raise public awareness of the health benefits of getting some exercise. These include:

- a reduction in the risk of heart disease;
- improved muscle tone and improved stamina.

Aerobic exercise can also burn fat, contribute to a reduction in high blood pressure and improved cholesterol levels. Aerobic exercise is a controlled duration of exercise at the right level, for the right amount of time, in order to include a training effect (i.e. when the body is working at between 60 to 80 per cent of its maximum). Examples include swimming, jogging, cycling, running, dancing and exercise to music.

The mental benefits include reduction in stress levels and increased feelings of well-being. People who exercise regularly also benefit in their daily lives because everyday tasks such as gardening, house-cleaning or running for a bus become easier.

Taking part in both sports and fitness activities offers people an important further benefit; the opportunity to socialise with others. If the venue used has a bar or café socialising is made simple!

Finding a challenge

For some people the challenge of acquiring a new skill is enough to fuel their interest. It is important to realise, however, that what is challenging for one person may be very unappealing to others. The highly skilled and physically demanding sport of rock climbing is an exciting challenge to those who relish testing themselves to the limit under difficult conditions but others may feel very threatened by this type of activity.

Many people are motivated to take part in team sports because of the camaraderie of being a 'team-mate' and the excitement of competition when playing against other teams.

Activities such as weight training often appeal to those who like to set their own targets and work for them single-mindedly. When you take part in body-development sports you are effectively competing against yourself.

Products and services

Where products and services are offered

Private sector venues may offer you a high standard of facility, such as better equipment, more luxurious showers and easier access to instructors. However, they are often expensive.

Venues in the public and voluntary sectors may offer less luxurious facilities and more limited access to instructors but the prices charged are cheaper.

Local authorities

Local authorities have a legal duty to provide sports and recreation facilities for the whole community. Some local authority leisure centres and swimming pools are run by private organisations who are legally obliged to operate their facilities according to guidelines in the contract issued by the local authority.

Private organisations

As we have seen, private health and fitness clubs may offer a more exclusive service and better facilities. Golf and country clubs, for example, cater for members who are willing to pay significant charges in return for a more exclusive package of services.

FIGURE 51 Types of providers and venues for sports and fitness activities

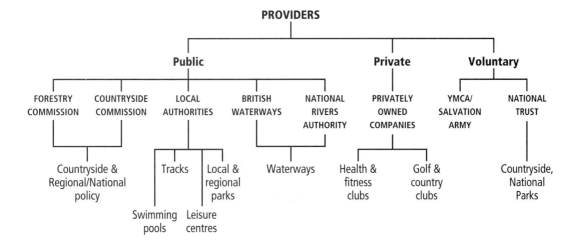

Voluntary organisations

The YMCA and the Salvation Army both offer sporting facilities and activities to the public. They are particularly keen to serve the needs of the wider community and may offer childcare facilities so that young mothers can participate in an exercise class.

Who the providers are

Figure 51 summarises the types of providers and venues for sport and fitness

How programmes are offered

The sports and fitness programmes on offer in all sectors have been carefully planned and will reflect their differing aims. Public sector venues have a duty to provide for the whole community including senior citizens and disabled people. Their programmes will therefore contain specific activities for these groups, for example '50-plus' exercise classes or swimming for people with special needs.

Private sector organisations, however, aim to make a profit and tend to feature only the most profitable (often the most fashionable) activities or classes on their programmes. This may exclude activities for disabled groups or ante and post-natal exercise classes, for example.

For more information on programming you should refer to Unit 7.1, page 186 (schedules).

Finding advice

Giving advice is considered to be an integral part of any sports and fitness instructors job: an exercise-to-music instructor may be asked about dieting, other forms of exercising or sports injuries. Gym instructors expect to advise on appropriate training programmes and will provide one which is tailor-made for you.

Modern research has shown that the motivation to eat a healthy diet is strongly linked with the taking of regular exercise. Many health and fitness clubs therefore offer a complete package of advisory services including dieticians, sports injuries clinics, massage and beauty treatments.

Some private sector organisations specialise in giving specific health advice and guidance. Weight-watchers, which monitors and encourages people who are trying to lose weight by dieting, is an example.

GP referral

Rather than resort to prescribing drugs, GPs are increasingly referring patients with certain medical conditions to sports centres for a programme of exercises. Results have been encouraging and for some people this type of treatment may be more effective in the long term than medication.

Assessing cost and access problems

If people are being advised to take up fitness or sport activities on health grounds they will then have to consider the cost. Prices are likely to be lower in public and voluntary sector organisations, who may charge minimal rates for the unemployed, for example. Many local authorities now offer leisurecards to local residents: for a small annual fee, people who live locally can purchase a leisurecard which gives them discounted rates for swimming and other recreation activities within their own town.

Some activities such as windsurfing or mountaineering involve a high initial outlay on equipment and this can prevent people on lower incomes from participating. Gaining access to these activities may also be difficult if you do not live near a lake, the sea or mountains.

People who live in areas where there are mountains, on the other hand, may find access to certain activities such as ice skating difficult as rinks are located only in large towns and cities which may be many miles away.

The influence of 'image'

Purchasing clothing and equipment

Sports clothing has become a fashion accessory for many sports enthusiasts and is part of the 'feel-good' factor of taking part. Many non-sports participants buy sports clothing to wear on a casual basis as it projects an image of fitness and vitality.

Whenever a top sports personality is seen on television the audience is taking in details of his or her appearance. Major sports manufacturers like Nike and Adidas stress the style and fashion appeal of their sports clothing by sponsoring high-profile, glamorous sports personalities like tennis stars and professional footballers. These athletes then endorse the clothes by wearing them at major competitions. The fact that this costs manufacturers very large sums of money is an indication of the importance they attach to association with sporting success and glamour.

The equipment you purchase, from the most unassuming cricket bat to the most sophisticated gymnasium air machine for low-impact resistance while weight training is now painstakingly researched and tested.

The purchase of sports clothing and equipment of every description is now a significant and lucrative part of the sport and fitness industry. Ask for a trip round your local gym and fitness suite and you will see sophisticated electronic equipment. Climb Mount Everest and you will be protected by clothing that has been specially invented to keep out the cold.

Overcoming image problems

The image portrayed by different sport and fitness activities does not always encourage new people to participate. You may feel that aerobics, for example, is an activity only for the slim, fit person who looks good in clingy sports wear. If you do not see yourself as slim and fit, you may well find that image off-putting when you consider joining a class. Similarly, dance classes may not attract people who feel that they are unco-ordinated. A solution sometimes used to solve the image problem is to target these groups specifically by offering special activities such as the 'Can't Dance' class!

Weight training sometimes suffers from a rather 'macho' image and can deter women from using gyms because they feel intimidated in a very male-dominated environment. This is often overcome by having 'ladies only' sessions to encourage women to try out the gym.

In order to encourage you to try different activities some local authorities offer 'community sport' schemes where anyone can 'come and try it'.

Activity   Write down the list of activities given below.

For each activity, note down a few words which you feel best describe the image it conveys to people who are unfamiliar with what is involved.

What sort of people do you think are attracted to each activity?

Polo	Fishing
Rugby	Yoga
Surfing	Bungy-jumping
Water aerobics	In-line skating

Providing for different participants

The range of people participating in sports and fitness activities is very broad. In order to encourage new participants, it is important to provide sufficient classes or sessions for beginners. Some of these beginners will then progress and become enthusiasts who regularly participate. Some people do not have the time, or the inclination, to participate regularly in activities: they may enjoy an occasional game of badminton for example. These people are known as 'casual' users.

The commitment of the talented minority who climb to the top of their sport in competition must be total. They have to be prepared to sacrifice much of their social life to rigorous training schedules.

Disabled people may have physical or mental disabilities, but with help (from able-bodied carers) and encouragement, they can enjoy a wide range of physical activities.

Women often find it more difficult to participate in sports because of the other demands on their time. Childcare facilities in sports centres would encourage more of them to participate, but there is still insufficient provision in the UK.

The UK is a multi-cultural society and the needs of different cultures must be recognised.

The need for modesty among Asian women, for example, means that many will only play sport in an all-women environment (see Racial Equality Policy Statement – Sports Council 1992). Asian definitions of work and leisure (Sports Council 1991) mean that there is a tendency to relegate the importance of sport to the background behind male education, religious duties and family life.

 Activity

As participants get older their pattern of participation in sports and fitness activities also tends to change.

Look at Figure 52 and compare the participation rates for 16–19 year olds with 45–59 year olds. List the activities in which a higher percentage of the younger age group take part. Why is this? Now list the activities where there is little difference in the rate of participation. Suggest some reasons for this.

Persons aged 16 and over   United Kingdom: 1993

Active sports, games and physical activities*	16–19	20–24	25–29	30–44	45–59	60–69	70 and over	Total	Median age of adults
				Age					
	Percentage participating in the 4 weeks before interview								
Walking	43	44	44	44	44	40	25	41	43
Any swimming	25	22	20	22	13	8	3	15	35
Snooker/pool/ billiards	41	31	19	13	8	4	1	12	29
Keep fit/yoga	17	19	19	165	10	6	5	12	35
Cycling	25	15	14	12	9	5	3	10	35
Darts	13	14	8	6	4	2	1	6	32
Weight lifting /training	20	15	11	6	2	0	0	5	27
Golf	9	7	6	6	5	5	2	5	39
Running (jogging etc.)	14	11	9	6	3	0	0	5	28
Any soccer	23	14	9	4	1	0	0	4	24
Tenpin bowls/ skittles	10	12	6	5	3	1	0	4	30
Badminton	11	4	4	3	2	1	0	3	30
Tennis	11	3	2	2	1	0	0	0	29
Fishing	3	2	2	3	2	1	1	2	38
Any bowls	1	1	0	1	2	5	3	2	60
Squash	4	5	4	3	1	0	0	2	29
Table tennis	9	2	2	2	1	0	0	2	30
Horse riding	3	2	2	1	1	0	0	1	31
Cricket	4	2	1	1	1	0	0	1	27
At least one activity (exc. walking)†	81	71	65	58	43	28	16	47	36
At least one activity†	86	80	77	73	64	51	33	64	40
Base = 100%	899	1379	1649	4768	3959	2301	2597	17552	

* Includes only activities in which more than 1.0% of all adults participated in the 4 weeks before interview.
† Total includes those activities not separately listed.
Source: Household Survey 1993

FIGURE 52 Sports, games and physical activities, participation rates in the 4 weeks before interview by age

Case study

Urban parks

For people who live in towns, the park may be one of the few venues where they can exercise outdoors. This case study is based on a newspaper article which highlights the problems of parks and suggests some measures which need to be taken to improve them.

Parks allowed to sink into decline

Urban parks were created in Victorian times when they were considered to be at the forefront of urban development! It was felt that they made a vital contribution to public health, social unity and local identity.

Yet many parks today are in a condition of desperate decline as a result of budget cuts by the government, resulting in staff redundancies and general neglect.

Neglect
Britain's parks are characterised by neglect, vandalism, dog excretia, boring landscapes and undesirables. In the United States, some parks have declined so much that they are now 'no go' areas. In McArthur Park in Los Angeles, drugs gangs have taken control; 30 people were murdered there in 1990.

However, in spite of the fact that most people have access to cars and the countryside, parks in the UK are still valued locally.

In inner city areas such as Southwark in South London, 43 per cent of park users have never visited the countryside and 70 per cent do not have access to a car. About 70 per cent walk to parks and 40 per cent visit them every day. Only 28 per cent of people never visit parks. Parks remain important to urban communities because they offer a sense of freedom and thus play an important role in physical and mental health.

Without them, life in towns and cities could be unbearable for many people.

One solution to the problem of decline might be for local authorities to sell off surplus open space to pay for improvements to parks.

If more activities and buildings, such as childcare and health centres were allowed in parks, more people would be encouraged to use them. Local authorities could also fund grants to local groups to build and create different types of parks, such as city farms, wildlife gardens, health-parks and specialist children's parks.

Financial support
The government supports rural areas through the Countryside Commission, and some people believe that urban parks should be given similar financial support. Recently, financial help has been made available from the Millenium Commission, (funded through the National Lottery), which has allocated funds to revitalise parks throughout the country in an attempt to restore them to their former glory.

FIGURE 53 The decline of parks

Activity   Read the article in Figure 53 and answer the questions which
follow.

1   In your own words, explain why urban parks were
    originally created?

2   Why do people go to parks?

3   Why are parks in a position of 'desperate decline'?

4   What do you think is meant by the idea of 'health' parks?

5   Why have some parks in the USA become 'no go zones'?

6   What problems do UK parks suffer from?

7   Why are urban parks vital to the health of local
    communities?

8   When did you last go to a park? For what reason?

9   How does your local park compare with those in the case
    study? Write an article for your local newspaper entitled
    'At Leisure in the Park'. The article should include a
    description of the park with a sketch map. Make a list of
    the good and bad points (e.g. evidence of vandalism,
    condition of the toilets and play facilities). Briefly describe
    the types of people who use the park and the type of
    recreation activities which take place there. Conclude your
    article with ideas on how the park could be improved, with
    suggestions for attracting more people and different
    activities.

10 Design a poster which focuses on one or two target
    groups, promoting the park as a recreation venue.

Element 5.2 Describe the Types of Ownership, Funding and Regulation of Sports and Fitness Provision

About this element This element describes ownership, funding and regulation of sport and fitness provision. By the end of this element you should be able to:

1 describe the providers, and types of venues for sports and fitness activities (performance criterion 5.2.1);
2 explain how sports and fitness provision is funded (performance criterion 5.2.2);
3 explain, with examples, the roles of regulatory bodies for sports and fitness provision (performance criterion 5.2.3);
4 describe, with examples, the role of manufacturers of equipment and clothing in sports and fitness provision (performance criterion 5.2.4).

Types and sources of funding

As we have already seen, private sector organisations need to make a profit in order to provide the people who have invested in the venture with some return on their money. Therefore prices of activities, and membership fees, tend to be higher in these private facilities.

Voluntary organisations, however, rely heavily on fundraising to subsidise their services. The YMCA is an example of this: they manage to keep prices lower through fundraising and obtaining grants.

Public sector organisations used to be subsidised by local authorities, but increasingly the emphasis is on self-funding. The prices charged will therefore reflect this, although membership fees tend to be lower than in private sector venues.

Sponsorship
Many professional teams, tennis players and top athletes are sponsored by major companies who often provide a large part of their income. Local, amateur teams also rely on occasional sponsorship in the form of a donation of money or equipment. In both cases the sponsoring company gains valuable publicity; their 'image' in the community also benefits.

Grants

Grants can be obtained from providers such as the Countryside Commission or regulatory bodies such as the Sports Council. Local authorities also allocate grants to local schemes and clubs.

The National Lottery

Part of the profits from the Lottery are allocated for investment in sports projects. Beneficiaries of this include a projected new National Sporting Centre of Excellence, which will train talented young people in their chosen sport. Other examples of projects which have benefited from the lottery include a new sports centre for the University of East Anglia, a community hall for badminton and bowls and a rowing facility of international quality at the Royal Albert Dock in Liverpool.

Activity

In small groups, decide on a local sporting facility which either needs expansion, refurbishment or a new building.

a Make brief notes on why your proposal should receive money from the National Lottery

b Choose a chairperson to direct the discussion. Appoint a spokesperson to present your views to the rest of the group. When each group has shared their proposals, choose (by voting individually) which scheme should be given priority.

Regulating sport and fitness provision

The following organisations are known as 'regulatory bodies'.

The Forestry Commission

This is a government department which is responsible for forest policy in the UK. In addition to advising the government, it provides advice to the forestry industry and sets standards of forest management and business practice. It has a duty to balance the needs of successful forest exploitation and the environment; it also controls the timing and extent of tree felling and undertakes forest research. Public access to Commission-owned forests has been encouraged by the government in recent years through the development of footpaths and cycleways, picnic areas and designated car parks.

The Countryside Commission

This is an independent organisation funded by the Department of the Environment. Its role is as follows:

1 to promote conservation and maintain landscape beauty in England
2 to encourage the provision and improvement of facilities in the countryside. The Commission often gets involved with the development of country parks, for example.

The Commission also works to secure public access to the countryside for open air recreation. Many public footpaths in the UK cross private land and the Commission tries to ensure that these paths remain open and accessible to walkers.

The British Waterways Board

This is the navigational authority for rivers and canals in England, Scotland and Wales. It is responsible for developing 1,200 miles of inland waterways for boating, fishing, walking and related leisure activities.

The National Rivers Authority

This independent organisation (it is not under the direct control of government) was set up under the 1989 Water Act, when water authorities were privatised. It has nine regional units. It is responsible for monitoring the quality of the water in our rivers and lakes and controlling pollution. In addition, it manages water resources, flood defence and fisheries.

The Central Council of Physical Recreation

The CCPR is an independent voluntary body. It was established in 1935 and consists of 240 governing and representative bodies of a wide variety of sport and recreative activities.

The aims of the Council are to improve and develop sport and recreation by providing courses and supporting the work of all local sports-governing bodies.

It also acts as a forum in which all the national governing bodies of sport are represented. It is officially consulted by the Sports Council.

The Sports Council

Funded by the Department of Heritage, the Sports Council has an overall responsibility for sports in England. Scotland and Wales have different Councils with different aims.

The Council has its headquarters in London and regional sports councils have the responsibility of putting the policies into practice locally.

How the Sports Council is administered

Figure 54 shows how the council is administered.

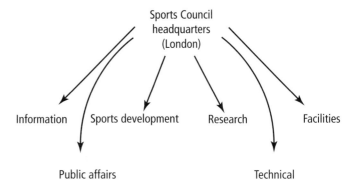

FIGURE 54 Organisation structure for the Sports Council

The aims of the Sports Council are as follows.

1 To promote a general understanding of the social importance of sport and recreation.
2 To increase the provision of new sports facilities and stimulate existing use.
3 To encourage wider participation in sports and physical recreation as a means of enjoying leisure. Here are some examples of former promotional campaigns.

  • 50-plus and all to play for
  • Sport For All
  • Ever Thought of Sport? (for 13 to 24 year olds)]
  • What's Your Sport? (for women)

4 To raise standards of performance. It administers national residential sports centres such as Bisham Abbey and Lilleshall, where top athletes train.

Governing bodies

Most sports have their own 'governing bodies'. They set out the rules of their sport, organise training and establish health and safety practices. The governing body also acts as a representative for the sport nationally and actively promotes its image. To qualify for recognition by the Sports Council, certain conditions have to be met. These conditions demand that a governing body:

  • is non-profit making;
  • promotes equal opportunities;
  • is financially independent;

- has been established for a minimum of one year's duration;
- holds an Annual General Meeting.

Examples of governing bodies include: the Squash Racquets Association, the Lawn Tennis Association, the Football Association, the Mountain Leadership Training Board, the Royal Yachting Association, the British Canoe Union, the International Amateur Athletic Association, and The Exercise Association.

Focus on The Exercise Association
This voluntary organisation is the governing body for exercise and fitness and is recognised by the Sports Council.

It aims to:

- promote and develop public participation in health related exercise and fitness activities;
- safeguard consumer interests;
- promote and monitor standards of quality;
- provide information, advice and membership services to the public and professionals.

FIGURE 55 Promoting the Exercise Association

Professional members of the Exercise Association (qualified instructors) benefit from receiving public liability insurance, access to seminars and workshops and a bi-monthly magazine.

The influence of clothing and equipment manufacturers

The manufacturers of sports clothing and equipment Reebok, Adidas and Nike are dominant names in the sports and fitness industry. They set trends, sponsor training and promote images in order to maintain and create markets for their products.

Activity

1 Look at the case study on the next page. Why do you think Reebok discounts shoes to instructors?

2 Look at the Step Reebok advertisement in Figure 56 and list the health and safety points about the product which would particularly appeal to the customer.

3 Read the Reebok seminars advertisement in Figure 57. Given the choice, which seminar would you choose to attend? Why?

4 Conduct a small survey amongst your group to find out the following information.
   a Which brand of sports clothing they are most likely to buy? Why?
   b Which brand is the most popular in the group? Why?
   c For what purpose do they buy sports clothing – for leisure or specific sports?

Case study

Reebok

Reebok produce a wide range of sports shoes and clothing in addition to new exercise equipment. They were the first company to develop the 'Step', followed by the 'Slide', aerobics programme. Both developments were rigorously tested for safety prior to being publicly launched. The 'Walk Reebok' programme is a flexible walking programme which can be adjusted to suit everyone's level of fitness. This has enjoyed great success in the USA and the UK is likely to follow suit. Special fitness walking shoes have been developed by Reebok and participants are encouraged to wear them, with clothing from the 'Freestyle' or 'Classic' ranges.

Reebok's promotional activities are broad. Television advertising is used and 'fitness conventions' are sponsored. The Reebok University unit which is responsible for education and development runs workshops and issues professional exercise teachers with a free Reebok magazine at regular issues. It contains information on all their new products and includes discount vouchers for the purchase of instructor footwear.

FIGURE 56 The Step system

Additional Reebok Products

THE STEP REEBOK SYSTEM

SAFE - A mat set into the top of the System ensures no slippage whilst exercising. The Step Reebok System is 36" long and 14" wide which gives a large area for exercising.

LIGHTWEIGHT - At only 7.5Kg for the complete Step Reebok System, including the feet, it is easily transportable.

STABLE - The feet are an integral part of the construction of the Step Reebok System, providing an extremely stable base.

ADJUSTABLE - The Step Reebok System can be set at 3 separate levels - 6", 8" and 10". No separate blocks are necessary to adjust the height of the System. Adjustments are made by changing the position of the legs.

PORTABLE - The Step Reebok System incorporates a grip which can be used when the System is in its' 6" position.

Reebok University - Reebok's educational programming arm - acts as an umbrella for all of Reebok's fitness programmes and products, and is a development body for future fitness innovations.

SEMINARS

Reebok University seminars offer you:- training with the best presenters... a full support package of materials and a comprehensive instructional manual... ongoing marketing and promotional support... membership of the Reebok Professional Instructor Alliance... can you afford to miss out?

The most popular aerobic programme in the country, **Step Reebok** has had an unrivalled impact on the fitness movement since it was first introduced in 1990. An average of 250,000 people enjoy **Step Reebok** classes every week.

Turn up the power of your **Step Reebok** classes! **Step Reebok Power** gives you the opportunity to increase the intensity and variety of your step classes. **Note** - for advanced enthusiasts only!

Walk Reebok is a formally developed fitness walking programme, and is a fun fitness activity for all ages and all levels of ability. Using a three-level goal orientated approach, the seminar teaches you how to add this revolutionary workout to your existing repertoire.

Slide Reebok is an athletically inspired, lateral-movement training programme suitable for every one from the conditioned fitness enthusiast to the Olympic athlete.

WORKSHOPS

Already completed an RU Seminar?... Looking for new inspiration?... Wanting to add new ideas to your existing classes?... **Reebok University Workshops** offer you the ideal opportunity to extend the scope of your classes. These half-day speciality workshops include:
Step Reebok Dance Mixes, Step Reebok Circuit, Step Reebok Power Combinations, Step Reebok Interval, Slide Reebok Endurance, Slide Reebok Interval, Walk Reebok Distance, Reebok City Jam.

MASTERCLASSES

Are you planning a special event or activity day at your club?... Don't forget the availability of a wide range of **RU Masterclasses** individually organised to suit your requirements and presented by our RU Team.

For further details please contact
REEBOK UNIVERSITY BOOKING OFFICE
0113 236 0066

FIGURE 57 Reebok seminars advertisement

Element 5.3 Explore Trends and Influences in Sport and Fitness Provision

About this element

This element explores trends and influences in sport and fitness. By the end of this element you should be able to:

1 examine trends in sport and fitness provision (performance criterion 5.3.1);
2 explain the influences on development of sport, health and fitness (performance criterion 5.3.2);
3 explain the factors influencing the sport and fitness business (performance criterion 5.3.3).

New activities

The 1980s were boom years for high-impact aerobics. High-impact aerobics involve the foot or feet leaving the ground, as in hopping, skipping, jumping and running movements. More impact is imposed on the joints than in low-impact aerobics. It has since become evident that too much high-impact aerobics eventually causes knee and shin stress injuries and as a result a modified form of aerobics has now become popular. The use of a step offers low-impact form of exercise to music. Slide aerobics became popular in the early 1990s, but this popularity was short-lived.

Research in the early 1990s has shown that exercise with some form of resistance (weight) training should form part of everybody's exercise programme. Not only does working against this resistance tone the muscles, it also helps to reduce the rate at which bone density is lost as people get older. This is particularly applicable to women, who tend to suffer more from brittle bones than do men. As a result of these findings, classes such as 'body conditioning using hand weights' have appeared and proved popular.

Fitness walking has grown in popularity in the USA in the 1990s because it is safe, cheap and easily incorporated into busy lifestyles. The sight of people walking to work in their trainers and formal suits is common in cities like New York. There are now signs that fitness walking is coming to the UK. Walking is the number one sporting activity in the UK; there are already some qualified fitness walking instructors working here and fitness walking classes are available in some areas.

Another activity which is one of the fastest-growing UK sports of the 1990s is 'off-road cycling' (mountain biking). Mountain bikes have become widely used as a form of transport, and they enable enthusiasts to cycle on tracks in areas which were previously inaccessible to conventional bicycles.

In-line skating originally saw a boom in the USA and then transferred to the UK. In-line skates were used first by ice hockey players and skiers for summer training. Now a wide range of recreational skaters are attracted to this high aerobic, low impact form of exercise which has the additional benefit of being good fun. Parks are the most popular venues for in-line skaters but there have been some dangerous collisions as people are moving at high speeds. The In-line Skating Association has therefore tried to encourage skaters to 'bear up' with protective clothing and to learn the rules of the road.

FIGURE 58 A growing leisure activity – in-line skating

Established activities

There are many influences on established sporting activities like football, cricket, tennis and golf which cause participation rates to vary. In the 1980s squash saw a growth in participation because it was viewed as a sport which was compatible with the 'yuppy' lifestyle (competitive, fast-moving and financially successful) which many people aspired to. The yuppy lifestyle has now become less fashionable, however, and as a result squash has shown a decline in participation rates.

Education

In recent years people have been made more aware of the benefits of exercise through advertising campaigns organised by the Sports Council, the Health Education Authority and various governing bodies of sport.

In the early 1990s, the government produced a report, 'The Health of the Nation', which indicated that although the public is more aware of the health benefits of exercise many adults still take little or no regular physical exercise. There are proven links between a sedentary lifestyle (that is physical inactivity) and an increased risk of heart disease. The government wants to reduce heart disease and therefore a 'Physical Activity Task Force' was set up in 1993. The aim is to create new, realistic exercise targets to current non-exercisers. People are being encouraged to go to school or work on foot or by bicycle rather than by car.

The influence of the media

Media coverage of sport in the 1990s has increased with the widespread availability of satellite and cable television; a global network, which enables the same programme to be broadcast world-wide is now in existence.

Some sports have enjoyed increased spectator numbers because of wider ranging television coverage as we have already seen in Unit 1, page 11. Some of these spectators feed their new-found enthusiasm from home and their armchairs, while others are inspired to go out and attend a 'live' performance of a sporting event first seen on television.

Daily newspapers all have a sports section and sports news stories are subject to the same sensationalising treatment as other newsworthy subjects, particularly by the tabloid press. For example items on drug abuse in sport may distort the truth or exaggerate stories to create more reader interest.

Many sports have their own magazines which keep enthusiasts up-to-date on news, issues and the latest developments.

Merchandising

Sports organisations are exploring new trends in merchandising all the time. Football clubs, for example, earn a great deal of additional revenue from selling football kit in club colours to their supporters. Items such as ties, scarves, pens, bags, clocks and sweatshirts are all produced in the same colours to attract supporters to buy. Some clubs have even been accused of changing their club colours (known as 'strip') too often in order to increase profits by selling the resulting new merchandise. During the Euro 96 football tournament in England, sales of the England strip soared, and items such as Euro 96 towels and mugs were sold as souvenirs to fans.

Diet, exercise and fashion

The fashion industry has developed a very powerful influence on young people, and the fitness industry benefits; glossy magazines focus on pictures of perfectly-shaped models, sending many women and some men to the gym. Articles on new body-shaping exercises and diets are often included in beauty features, raising their readers' awareness of the benefits of eating sensibly and exercising. Thus fashion and health issues combine to fuel the demand for health and fitness activities. Some people, however, are vulnerable to suggestions that 'slim' is the only way of being beautiful and damage their health with obsessive dieting.

Drugs and sport

During the Second World War, amphetamine-like substance (stimulants) were developed and administered to combat troops to enhance their mental awareness and to delay the onset of fatigue.

Athletes soon realised that their performance in sport could benefit from these stimulants. Cyclists were some of the first athletes to use drugs, but deaths of sportsmen from amphetamine abuse in the 1960s demonstrated how widespread drug abuse had become. In 1967, the death of Tommy Simpson during the Tour de France was linked to amphetamine abuse. More recently, Ben Johnson was stripped of his gold medal in the 100 metre final of the 1988 Seoul Olympics after failing a drug test. He was also banned from competing for two years.

The increase in drug abuse in sport could also be linked to the more liberal approach to experimentation in drug taking in society in the 1960s. This was particularly notable amongst followers of pop music. Additionally, the pharmaceutical revolution began in the 1960s, when pharmaceutical (drug) companies competed to produce more powerful, selective and non-toxic drugs. Some athletes saw these as a means of improving their performance beyond anything that they could achieve by hard work and rigorous training.

Performance-enhancing drugs (PEDs) have become a major sports issue in the 1990s. As a result of universal drug screening, all athletes found to be taking PEDs are now discredited and banned from competition.

The rise of professionalism

If you have professional status in a sport it means that you are paid officially for competing because you have achieved a high enough standard for your sport to be, in effect, your occupation. Amateurs are not paid and take part in sport because of the enjoyment and satisfaction they get from the activity.

The distinction between a professional and a top amateur is not always clearcut. Athletes, for example, are all officially amateurs, yet some of the most successful ones command large sums of money for appearing in events. Torvill and Dean, who became professional ice skaters after winning all the major competitions, were able to return briefly to amateur status in order to compete in another Olympic competition. International governing bodies of each sport draw up rules to decide who is an amateur and they decide if professionals may compete with amateurs. How, then, can professional sports be defined?

Professional occupations in sport tend to possess the following characteristics.

1 Journals on the sport are published, containing information and research, news, views and discussion.
2 The sport's governing body, or other source, provides continuous education and training.
3 Society accepts that the sport is a profession.
4 The sport has a published a code of practice containing rules, professional dress, appropriate behaviour and advertising fees.

Activity Decide which of the sports below have professional or amateur status. Discuss your answers with other members of your group and together consider the reasons for the choice you make in each case.

- Netball
- Basketball
- Hockey
- Karate
- Gymnastics
- Squash
- Showjumping
- Swimming

Assignment activity Unit 5

You should keep all your assignment activity work, clearly labelled, in your Portfolio of Evidence. This work provides evidence of coverage of all the elements and performance criteria covered in Unit 5.

1   Choose one health and fitness activity and two sports and recreation activities.

Produce an information booklet containing information on your three chosen activities. Use plain paper and either print or wordprocess your text. Here are some notes to help you.

- The cover should be attractive (perhaps showing the logo of the sport's governing body), and have a suitable title.
- Give the names and addresses of a variety of local venues.
- Identify which sector the activity is in and indicate what the sources of funding are, giving specific examples.
- Find out the name of the regulatory body for the activity and include a brief summary of its role.
- Choose one sports manufacturer. Visit a shop where their clothing and equipment for the activities is sold. Look at the range of equipment in the shop, (particularly for the activities you are researching) and list it in your booklet with sample prices. Look out for new or improved products and briefly describe them, stating their benefits to the consumer. Include pictures or illustrations if possible.
- Note any promotional materials for your activities which are available to the public, including catalogues, displays, posters or videos. Give a short summary of each and indicate how effective you think they are.

2   You are required to carry out a mini-survey and will need to find four people who participate in different sports and recreation activities and three people who participate in different health and fitness activities.

Now compile a questionnaire which covers all of the following points and devise a table to record the answers. Here are some notes to help you.

- Description of the activity (including its image), cost, clothing and equipment.
- Details of the venue including access and additional services connected with the activity, for instance, coaching, sports injuries clinic.
- Make a note of male or female, age and socio-economic group for each person. How typical are they as participants in their activity?
- What are the benefits to the person taking part?

Write a report which summarises your findings.

3 Look at the table of participation rates in established sports from 1987 to 1993 and examine the trends for each activity.
  a Decide whether the trend in participation is increasing, declining, or showing little change (stable).

Persons aged 16 and over

Active sports, games and physical activities*	Percentage participating in the 4 weeks before interview			Percentage participating in the 12 months before interview		
	1987	1990	1993	1987	1990	1993
Walking	37.9	40.7	40.8	60.1	65.3	65.5
Swimming	13.1	14.8	15.4	34.6	42.4	42.6
Snooker/pool/ billiards	15.1	13.6	12.2	22.9	21.7	19.5
Keep fit/yoga	8.6	11.6	12.1	14.3	18.8	19.9
Cycling	8.4	9.3	10.2	14.8	17.0	18.7
Darts	8.8	7.1	5.6	15.4	13.1	10.4
Weight lifting /training	4.5	4.8	5.5	8.2	9.1	9.6
Golf	3.9	5.0	5.3	9.2	12.2	12.0
Running (jogging etc.)	5.2	5.0	4.6	10.5	9.5	8.2
Soccer	4.8	4.6	4.5	8.9	8.5	8.1
Tenpin bowls/ skittles	1.8	3.8	4.0	5.7	11.4	14.9
Badminton	3.4	3.3	2.7	8.2	8.5	7.1
Tennis	1.8	2.0	2.1	6.6	7.4	7.2
Fishing	1.9	2.0	2.0	5.8	6.1	5.8
Lawn/carpet bowls	1.7	2.1	2.0	3.7	5.3	4.5
Squash	2.6	2.5	1.9	6.7	6.2	4.7
Table tennis	2.4	2.0	1.7	6.3	5.4	4.7
Horse riding	0.9	1.0	1.0	2.6	3.1	3.0
Cricket	1.2	1.1	1.0	4.2	3.8	3.5
At least one activity (exc. walking)†	44.7	47.8	47.3	61.9	67.3	67.9
At least one activity†	60.7	64.5	63.7	77.6	81.9	82.1
Base = 100%	19529	17574	17552	19529	17574	17552

* Activities are listed in descending order of 4 week participation rate for all adults in 1993. Includes only activities in which more than 1.0% of all participated in 4 weeks before interview in 1993 and sports for which results are available for all years.
† Total includes those activities not separately listed.

FIGURE 59 Participation rates

Then make up a table using the headings shown below to summarise the trends.

Declining participation	Increasing participation	Stable participation
e.g. squash	e.g. walking	

   b Now write a brief paragraph which summarises the reasons for the trends in activities under each of the three headings.

4 Look at the table on spectator sports below and answer the following questions.
   a Which 'armchair' sport has the biggest total number of viewers? Why do you think this is?
   b Of the remaining armchair sports listed, what are the attractions for the spectators?
   c Which sports do you judge to be poor spectating events? State your reasons.

ARMCHAIR SPECTATORS
Top ten sports programmes, 1993

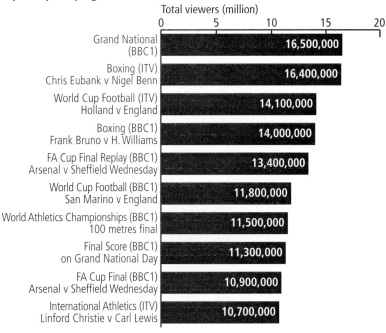

FIGURE 60 Spectator sports

Source: Daily Telegraph, 13.12.93

5 Read the article 'Drugs, Sport and Young People' and answer the following questions.
   a What is the link between social drugs and PEDs?
   b Why might a young sports performer turn to drugs?
   c What is meant by the phrase 'the use of drugs can become a vicious circle'?

d The article lists a number of preventative measures which can be taken. Briefly summarise what you understand by 'good nutritional advice and the opportunity to play sport as well as compete'.

e Design a poster aimed at young athletes to raise their awareness of addiction to PEDs.

FIGURE 61 Drugs in sport

DRUGS, SPORT AND YOUNG PEOPLE

Sport used to be regarded as an alternative activity for young people which might distract them from involvement in drugs or other substances of abuse. In today's society this notion now seems unlikely: drugs seem to be more freely available, offered more frequently and experimented with more often. Furthermore, there are potential 'danger' areas and opportunities for drug misuse by young people, particularly those aspiring to performance excellence standard, of which sports organisations, parents, coaches and teachers should be aware.

The drugs which may be used include Performance Enhancing Drugs (PEDs), therapeutic medications, Social Drugs (SDs) or a combination of any or all of these. The categorisation of drugs in this way is not exclusive: drugs such as amphetamines are regarded both as social and performance enhancing. Beta-blockers may also be used therapeutically or an an aid to performance. Similarly, narcotics can be therapeutic and addictive.

There are many reasons why a young sports performer may turn to any of the above drugs.

As a young athlete begins to show performance potential, the pressures can build. The young performer may seek to maintain and improve achievements (particularly as the age group in which they compete changes); parents and/or coaches might seek to 'assist per-

formance' by offering 'performance enhancing drugs', and some would argue that targets and expectations have been set at such a high level that the use of drugs is encouraged either actively or passively by parents, coaches and others.

Therapeutic medications may be taken in an attempt to sustain, or return to, performance. Such medications may be for the (self) treatment of injuries or for asthma conditions which may be exercise-induced.

Finally, the lifestyle (perceived and actual) of elite sportsmen and women can influence drug behaviour, as can peer-group pressure. The media-reported relationship between drug use and success in certain sports also has much to answer for.

A Vicious Circle

The use of drugs can become a vicious circle. PEDs may be alternated with other drugs to aid relaxation, (stimulants and steroids with other mood-changing substances). PEDs may also be regarded as a 'short-cut' to maintaining performance when social drugs have left the athlete debilitated. Some injuries may be difficult to deal with psychologically, leading to PED or SD use, whilst psychological and physiological dependence (especially with the highly addictive stimulants and narcotics) is a major factor in continued use, even when athletes have tested positive for doping offences.

Prevention

Early prevention strategies, which combine the support of parents, peers, governing body officials and coaches are necessary to prevent drug misuse occurring, including:

good nutritional advice and the opportunity to play sport as well as compete

reduced parental/coach pressure through ethical behaviour examples

reduced personal pressure through realistic targets

monitored training programmes, with open discussion of preparation, relaxation and injuries

realistic approaches to medical conditions, particularly when returning to training following injury or illness

suitable, positive role models and the emphasis of the healthy lifestyle required to maintain performance

the development of coping skills to face failure and success

a stable support base for the young athlete

an awareness of the dangers of addiction

a clear policy with respect to the image of the sport, the club and the athlete, including the means to deal with those who break the rules (not only punishment, but rehabilitation).

6 For a period of two weeks, sample a number of major sports stories which appear on the television and in the tabloid press.

   a Keep a daily diary of any current newspaper articles, television reports or radio items.

   b Summarise the stories and make a note of any conflicting facts given by the different media.

   c Decide whether the coverage of each story is sympathetic or hostile? Do you think that the coverage given is fair? Why?

7 Conduct a survey in your class to find out about people's experience of school sport.

   a What did they like or dislike? Why?

   b Do you feel that the views of your group are typical?

   c Devise a table to record the replies.

8 Produce a leaflet which briefly summarises what is meant by 'a healthy diet'.

   a Using all the information you can find, produce your leaflet.

   b Now keep a daily diary of all the food and drink you consume in a week.

   c Compare this to your healthy-eating leaflet and list the changes you need to make in order to eat more healthily.

   d Report your findings to the rest of the group.

Unit 6 Researching Tourist Destinations

Introduction to the unit

This unit comprises the following elements required by the course and gives you practice in all the performance criteria that prove your understanding of each of these elements.

Element 6.1   Investigate major tourist destinations in the UK and in Europe

Element 6.2   Investigate principal travel routes within the UK and to Europe

Element 6.1 Investigate Major Tourist Destinations in the UK and Europe

This element looks at the major tourist destinations in the UK and Europe. By the end of this element you should be able to:

1 identify and use recognised sources of information on tourist destinations (performance criterion 6.1.1);
2 locate major tourist destinations in the UK and Europe (performance criterion 6.1.2);
3 classify major tourist destinations in the UK and Europe according to type of travel product (performance criterion 6.1.3);
4 describe the key features of major tourist destinations in the UK (performance criterion 6.1.4);
5 describe the key features of major tourist destinations in Europe (performance criterion 6.1.5).

If you work in the travel and tourism industry, particularly in the holiday market, you will be expected to develop a thorough knowledge of tourist destinations.

In this unit we will look briefly at some of the more popular destinations but, more importantly, you will be guided to sources of information so that you understand how to find out about destinations yourself.

Tourist destinations in the UK

How do we know which areas or cities are major tourist destinations?

If you worked in a travel agency you would see which destinations received most bookings. However, this method of judging popularity is not entirely accurate as the location of the agency affects bookings. For example, if the agency is situated in the North West, there will be more bookings for Blackpool and Morecambe than for Brighton because many people choose to go to their nearest resort. A more accurate way of determining the most popular destinations on a national basis is needed.

Major sources of information on destinations

The British Tourist Authority (BTA), the English Tourist Board (ETB), the Scottish Tourist Board (STB), the Wales Tourist Board (WTB) and the Northern Ireland Tourist Board all conduct research and publish the information they gather. The BTA in particular publishes many statistics and reports which are available for sale to individuals, companies or libraries. The Digest of Tourist Statistics, for example, is a comprehensive guide showing where people go, who they are, what they do there, how much they spend and other information. The United Kingdom Tourist Survey measures tourism by UK residents. Visits to the UK by tourists from abroad are measured by the International Passenger Survey. From these figures and reports it is easy to see where the major destinations in the UK and Europe lie.

FIGURE 62 Volume and value of tourism in English regions 1993

Tourism Fact Sheets are also available from the BTA or from the Regional Tourist Boards. These give similar information to the UK Tourist Survey but are broken down into regions.

	All tourism			Holiday tourism		
	Trips m	Nights m	Expenditure £m	Trips m	Nights m	Expenditure £m
Cumbria	2.5	10.2	350	2.0	8.8	280
Northumbria	2.8	9.7	310	1.6	6.4	170
North West	6.9	21.6	860	3.9	14.6	535
Yorkshire and Humberside	6.6	25.7	825	4.2	19.2	530
Heart of England	7.1	21.4	740	3.1	11.4	320
East Midlands	6.0	22.2	715	3.4	15.3	440
East Anglia	8.4	23.6	1,035	4.8	23.5	725
London	7.2	18.7	875	2.9	8.8	340
West Country	13.0	67.8	2,195	9.6	58.7	1,810
Southern	8.9	33.9	1,070	5.3	23.5	735
South East	6.0	23.6	685	3.5	15.6	460
Total	**73.0**	**288.2**	**9,650**	**42.7**	**205.8**	**6,340**

Source: United Kingdom Tourism Survey (English Tourist Board, Scottish Tourist Board, Northern Ireland Tourist Board, Wales Tourist Board)
Note: Trips and nights are rounded to 100,000, expenditure to £5 million. The counties which previously formed the Thames and Chilterns region were allocated to neighbouring regions from 1992 onward

Activity   Look at Figure 62 above. Then answer the following questions through group discussion.

a Which two UK regions attract most tourists? Why do you think this is?

b Which two regions attract the least tourists? Why do you think this is?

c London has 2.9 million holiday trips per year but 7.2 tourist trips altogether. Can you account for the difference?

Other sources of information on destinations
Tourist organisations

Each tourist region has a tourist board which will provide free information on its resorts, attractions and accommodation. Figure 63 shows where these regions are.

FIGURE 63 The regions covered by tourist boards

Many other countries have tourist offices based in the UK. The function of these organisations is to provide information designed to attract people from the UK to travel abroad to their country. Similarly, the BTA has offices in many countries abroad, from Argentina to the USA, to attract overseas visitors to become tourists in the UK.

A full list of addresses and telephone numbers for tourism organisations is available in the *Travel Trade Gazette Directory* which you will find in your library.

Holiday brochures

These are very useful sources of information on resorts and accommodation. It is important to remember that their purpose is to sell holidays and any unattractive features about a destination will probably go unmentioned.

Videos and television travel programmes

Videos are sometimes made by tour operators to show off destinations. You can borrow these as a potential customer. Again, remember that the information will be biased in the resort's favour.

Tourist offices also provide videos on their country's attractions. These, too, can usually be borrowed.

Television programmes are a more objective source of information as they give the advantages and the drawbacks of a resort. Many holiday programmes are broadcast each season.

Gazetteers

Gazetteers are collections of geographical information. They give information on resorts and are usually designed for reading by the trade only. Examples include the *Worldwide Travel Guide* which gives objective (unbiased) information on destinations. You can obtain copies of these gazetteers if you work in the industry or they are available from the library.

CD ROM

If you have access to CD ROM on a home, school or college computer, you have some very useful CD packages at your disposal. *World Atlas* is one, offering facts and figures as well as maps; *Europe in the Round* is another, giving information on European resorts and attractions.

Atlases and maps

Make full use of a good atlas to familiarise yourself with the location of destinations.

Guide books

There is a comprehensive range of guide books covering almost every tourist destination world-wide available in most bookshops. You should ensure that you read these: friends who have been on holiday will be able to lend their guides or your library will provide them.

Travel press

All the Sunday newspapers and some of the dailies and magazines have travel sections. These are useful sources of information as they carry advertisements on travel availability and prices as well as articles on different resorts.

The trade press also has regular features with information on destinations. A good example is the *Travel Trade Gazette*, which has resort features in each edition.

Summary of major destinations in the UK

Cities

London

London is the most popular choice for UK residents and overseas visitors. It attracts tourists for both residential stays and day trips.

Its attractions are described in detail in many guide books. Briefly, they include the following activities.

- Sightseeing – historic buildings, for instance the Tower of London, Buckingham Palace, St Paul's Cathedral and Westminster; museums, for instance the Natural History, the Science and the Victoria and Albert.
- Shopping – Oxford Street, Kings Road, Kensington, Knightsbridge and many famous markets like the Portobello Road.
- Entertainment – theatres, cinemas and nightclubs abound.
- Parks and heaths – walking in St James' Park, Hampstead Heath, Blackheath and Hyde Park.

York

York is also a popular choice, particularly for visitors from the USA. It has many attractions on offer including the famous Jordvik Centre, which recreates life in Viking times.

Not only is York a beautiful, historic city, but it offers a base giving easy access to equally beautiful countryside and stately homes such as Castle Howard.

Stratford, Cambridge and Oxford

These cities are included as they are very popular with overseas visitors doing a tour of the UK or Europe. They are heavily promoted by the BTA as they have many attractions to offer. Tourists can go punting in Oxford and Cambridge, seeing the historic college buildings. Both cities are important shopping centres too. Stratford is a cultural centre, being the home of the Royal Shakespeare Company. It is also close to attractive countryside.

Edinburgh

Although further afield, this Scottish city is of interest to many overseas visitors. It has the historic palaces of Holyrood

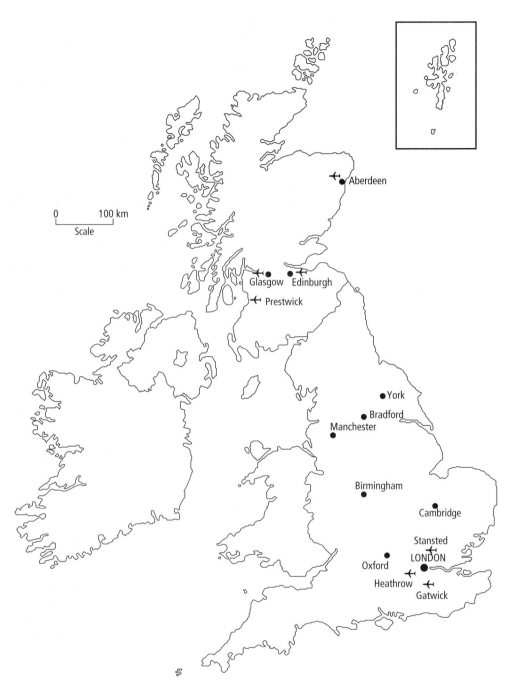

FIGURE 64 The major tourist city destinations in the UK

and Edinburgh Castle, museums, parks and shops on offer. It is often used as an interesting stopping off point on the way to a holiday in the Highlands of Scotland.

Manchester, Birmingham and Bradford

These are industrial cities, but still have attractions for tourists. Manchester and Birmingham attract business tourists particularly, who visit the trade exhibitions held at the Gmex Centre and the National Exhibition Centre respectively. Bradford offers tours of its mills and industrial heritage while the National Museum of Photography, Film and Television attracts many visitors.

Seaside resorts

The most popular resorts with UK residents are in the West Country, that is Devon and Cornwall. These areas include Torquay, Ilfracombe, St Ives, Newquay and Penzance. There are two main reasons why people choose this part of the country: the climate is warmer and more temperate and the beaches and countryside are renowned for their beauty.

Seaside resorts in the South of England include Bournemouth, Brighton, Eastbourne and the Isle of Wight.

Again, the climate is favourable in these resorts and a lot of visitors are attracted in the summer months. Many attractions are promoted by local business to encourage tourists. These include the HMS *Victory* and the *Mary Rose* in Portsmouth, Marwell Zoo in Hampshire and Osborne House on the Isle of Wight.

On the East Coast resorts are less popular as the climate is less favourable to beach activities than that in the South – cold east winds often prevail. However, there are still traditional seaside resorts on this often unspoilt coastline, offering many facilities. Resorts in the East include Southend and Clacton, popular with Londoners for easy day trip access, Great Yarmouth, Scarborough and Bridlington. The countryside varies greatly as you travel from South to North up the coast, with Scarborough benefiting from memorable cliff walks and a renowned theatre.

The beaches in the North East of England are very attractive, but do not attract many seaside visitors from outside the area as it is often cold and windy and people are unwilling to travel 'away from the sun'. Blackpool, Southport and Morecambe, the North West's famous seaside resorts, similarly attract mostly local tourism.

Countryside, lakes and mountain areas

The Countryside Commission has designated certain areas of the UK as protected countryside. Visitors are attracted to enjoy the unspoilt beauty of mountains, dales, cliffs and coastline. There are two main categories of protected countryside, which are given on page 162.

FIGURE 65 The major seaside tourist destinations in the UK

SEE THE WORLD ... VISIT

Blackpool Pleasure Beach

Fleetwood Harbour

SEASIDE FUN

Some of Britain's most famous seaside resorts can be found in the North West, along its stretch of beautiful, sandy coastline. Blackpool is renowned for its Pleasure Beach and spectacular autumn Illuminations and is a great holiday destination for kids of all ages. All the traditional seaside entertainments, and a whole lot more, can be found on the resort's three piers, within the tower and at Blackpool Pleasure Beach. Among the many exciting rides is "The Pepsi Max Big One" - the world's fastest and tallest roller coaster.

You can try a taste of tropical fun at The Sandcastle with its waves, waterslides and flumes, or continue down the Prom to the Sea Life Centre on the Golden Mile and have a glimpse of underwater sea-life at close quarters. The resort's night-life is equally spectacular, with the Grand Theatre, three Piers and the Winter Gardens all hosting an exciting variety of live entertainment.

Take a tram ride along the coast, for this is Britain's last remaining stretch of coast which still uses this traditional mode of transport and a ride to the north of Blackpool takes you to Fleetwood, calling at Cleveleys which is an excellent shopping centre, to cosy pubs and restaurants, and lovely sandy beaches along the way whose hidden creeks invite exploration.

The bustling fishing port of Fleetwood is another place where trams are a common sight as they weave their way between the town's splendid Victorian architecture. The Maritime Museum tells the port's varied history as it developed and grew to rival Liverpool, handling cargoes of cotton and grain from America, before fishing took over and it gradually became the country's third largest fishing port. Although fishing still plays an important role here, there is a wealth of other nautical activity too, with fishing vessels, yachts, power boats and windsurfers making up a colourful floating display and you can even catch a SEACAT to the Isle of Man from here.

18

FIGURE 66 What is on in England's North West?

National parks
National parks include Dartmoor, the Lake District, Snowdonia and the Yorkshire Dales. These parks are particularly popular with walkers and climbers.

Areas of outstanding natural beauty
This designation includes 'Heritage Coastline', that is areas of particularly beautiful coastline, including Anglesey. Another area of Outstanding Natural Beauty is the Cotswolds in central England.

Scottish National Heritage has similarly designated Areas of Outstanding Natural Beauty in Scotland.

Besides walking and climbing, visitors can participate in outdoor activities such as sailing, bird watching, fishing, riding and cycling. The Countryside Commission publishes information leaflets on all these areas.

Activity   Read Figure 66 carefully. Now answer the following questions.

1   Classify the activities and facilities the North West is offering in this promotional leaflet. Use the following headings.

- Natural attractions
- Purpose built attractions
- Entertainment
- Shopping
- Sports
- Sightseeing
- Eating and drinking

2   Locate Blackpool on a detailed map. State how you would get there from your home:
   a   by car;
   b   by rail.

Purpose-built attractions
Holiday camps
Holiday camps have been popular in the UK since the 1950s and Butlins is probably still the most famous one. These camps aim to provide all the facilities a family needs for a holiday on one site. They aim to offer good value for money to ordinary families.

Centerparcs, a holiday resort 'village' development, is a fairly recent addition to this market but the products and services

FIGURE 67 National Parks and Areas of Outstanding Natural Beauty in the UK

are more sophisticated. The target market is mainly families. Self-catering accommodation is provided in beautiful surroundings with the aim of blending the camp into the countryside. Extensive sports facilities, both indoor and outdoor are provided.

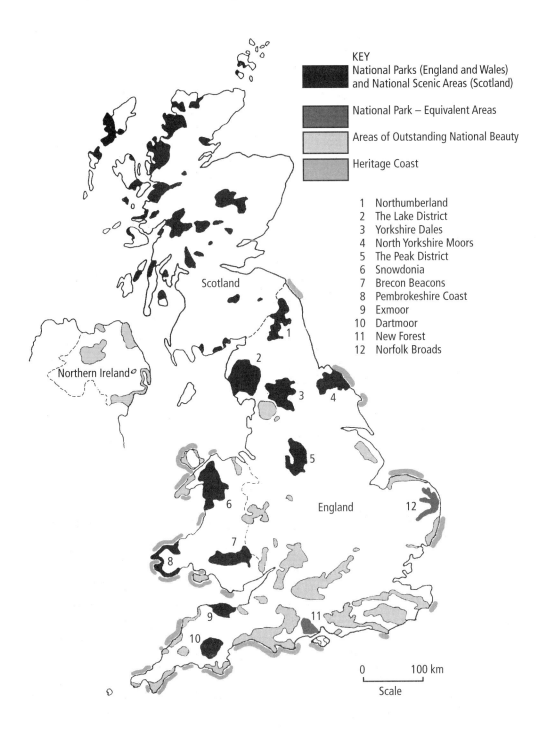

KEY

National Parks (England and Wales) and National Scenic Areas (Scotland)

National Park – Equivalent Areas

Areas of Outstanding National Beauty

Heritage Coast

1   Northumberland
2   The Lake District
3   Yorkshire Dales
4   North Yorkshire Moors
5   The Peak District
6   Snowdonia
7   Brecon Beacons
8   Pembrokeshire Coast
9   Exmoor
10 Dartmoor
11 New Forest
12 Norfolk Broads

Scotland

Northern Ireland

England

0   100 km

Scale

FIGURE 68 Guides to natural landscape areas published by the Countryside Commission

Theme parks

Theme parks are day visitor attractions which have collections of thrilling rides, shows and other entertainments for all ages. The most famous are the Disney theme parks in the United States. Alton Towers is the UK's biggest theme park and is consistently the leader of the top twenty attractions in the UK. In 1993 Alton Towers had over two and a half million visitors. You should, however, bear in mind that Blackpool Pleasure Beach was estimated to attract over six million visitors in 1993. As admission is free, accurate figures are not available.

Other theme parks in the UK are Chessington and Thorpe Park in Surrey, American Adventure in the Midlands and Camelot in the North West.

Areas of historical and cultural interest

We have already mentioned the UK's historic cities. Royal Palaces such as Windsor, Balmoral and Sandringham are also very popular with tourists both from the UK and abroad.

The UK is rich in historical sites going back thousands of years; these are particularly attractive to visitors from the USA whose own national history is either undocumented or very much more recent. Particularly important sites are Roman – spa towns such as Bath still have the Roman pump rooms and baths to visit – mediaeval, such as the castles of the Welsh borders, or even pre-historic, such as Stonehenge on Salisbury Plain, a major attraction with its mysterious circle of monumental stones.

East, West, Home's Best

At last the British seaside is recovering from the impact of cheap holidays on the continent.

In 1994, there were 24.5 million holidays taken at home and 110 million day trips. Is it because Victoriana is back in fashion? Resorts, like Blackpool, are smartening up their seafronts. Bandstands, railings and kiosks are decked out in Victorian style. Weston-super-Mare has revived grand British traditions of donkeys, ice cream, deck chairs and seafood sold on the prom.

Councils have poured money into redevelopment. Bridlington has spent £5 million on its promenades, Eastbourne is building a new harbour, Blackpool is refurbishing its famous tram-tracks and illuminations. Besides all this memorabilia, tourists demand clean beaches and promenades. Measures taken include banning dogs from sands, sweeping beaches clean and ensuring wheelchair access.

The message is clear: there's no place like the British seaside for family holidays.

FIGURE 69

Activity   Read the article in Figure 69 entitled 'East, West, Home's Best'. Now answer the following questions.

1 How many holidays were taken at home in 1994?
2 Why do you think holidaymakers are choosing to stay in the UK?
3 Give three examples of refurbishment which have taken place to attract tourists.
4 What environmental measures are being taken to attract tourists?

Tourists destinations in Europe   The top ten European holiday resorts for people from the UK are as follows:

- Majorca
- Ibiza
- Minorca
- Corfu
- Tenerife
- Benidorm
- Costa Del Sol
- Gran Canaria
- Rhodes
- Algarve

The common factors are sun, sea, sand and cheap!

Most of these resorts are in Spain, a country which has reigned over all others with UK holidaymakers since the 1970s and the advent of mass tourism.

Activity   Figure 70 shows the destinations chosen for a holiday by people from the UK between 1970 and 1993. Study it carefully and then answer the following questions.

1 Although Spain is still the most popular destination overall, it has decreased in market share. Why do you think this is so?

2 What destinations might be popular in the 'rest of the world' category?

3 What types of holiday are popular in Austria and Switzerland?

4 Why are there no early 1990s figures for Yugoslavia?

5 The Greek category includes islands. Name five Greek islands.

6 Name two Italian islands in the Mediterranean.

Destination of long holidays (1+ nights) taken abroad

Country	1984 %	1993 %	1994 %
Spain, inc. islands	36	25	30
France, inc. Monaco	10	11	12
Greece, inc. islands	7	8	10
Italy, inc. islands	6	3	3
Portugal	3	4	3
Germany	5	3	2
Yugoslavia	3	–	–
Austria	4	2	1
Republic of Ireland	2	3	3
Malta	2	2	2
Netherlands	2	2	1
Switzerland	2	1	1
All Europe*	85	74	77
USA	3	9	8
Canada	2	2	2
All rest of world	10	19	17

FIGURE 70 Countries stayed in for 4 nights or more on holidays abroad 1984 to 1994

*Including Northern and Southern Ireland
Note: Some 1+ night holidays are not included in this table because they lasted less than 4 nights in total and could not therefore include a 4 night stay in any country. Also excluded are holidays lasting 4+ nights which did not include a stay of 4 nights or more in any one country. For these reasons 'All Europe' and 'All rest of world' do not sum up to 100%.
Source: The British National Travel Survey (British Tourist Authority)

European cities

Cities do not feature in the list of most popular European resorts given above as most tourists visit cities only for short-break holidays of two or three nights. However, these trips are an important and growing market among UK holiday-makers.

Paris

Paris is often chosen for short breaks, as it is easy to reach by air, sea and now rail, in only a few hours from London.

FIGURE 71 Major European tourist destinations

Paris, like London, offers a very wide range of attractions. The city is attractive with the River Seine, on which boat trips can be taken, flowing through it. There are extensive shopping and entertainment facilities, with the Boulevard Haussman's department stores and the famous Moulin Rouge nightclub in Pigalle. It has many historic buildings including Notre

Dame, Paris's famous mediaeval cathedral and the Eiffel Tower, built in 1889, once the highest metal construction in the world.

A recently-added attraction is the Paris Disneyland, which opened in 1992. It has had many teething problems: the unreliability of European summer weather, combined with very high entrance fees, meant that many people left feeling disappointed. Cheaper entry and investment in high-tech rides like 'Space Mountain', improved admissions and took the park into profit in 1995.

Rome

Rome is an important destination for those interested in the cultural history of Europe. Visitors are able to visit ancient ruins such as the Colosseum, a vast amphitheatre built by the Romans, and the Roman Forum. Churches and museums house treasures and many tourists visit the Vatican, the Pope's residence. Rome is most easily reached by air from the UK.

Madrid

Madrid, the capital of Spain, is a very beautiful city. The architecture is a great attraction, including a preserved mediaeval village around Plaza de la Paja. There are interesting treasures from the 19th and 20th centuries to be seen, and many parks and gardens. It is important for business tourism as well as for holidays: Madrid is Spain's centre of commercial activity and has excellent air connections throughout Europe.

Brussels

Brussels deserves to be mentioned as a major business tourism destination; it is home to the European Economic Commission and seat of the European Parliament.

Other European destinations

Resorts lying on or near the Mediterranean coast are the most popular with UK tourists as they provide a hot climate within a comfortable flying time from home. They are also, mostly, relatively cheap. Our fellow Europeans from Germany and the Netherlands are attracted for the same reasons.

Spain

The resorts in Spain are to be found on the coast as follows.

- Costa Dorada – Calella, Sitges, Calafell
- Costa Brava – Estartit, Palafrugell
- Costa Blanca – Benidorm

- Costa Del Sol – Marbella, Torremolinos
- Costa Almeria – Roquetas de Mar

Other areas are less popular with UK tourists.

FIGURE 72 Mediterranean Spain

Greece

The larger Greek islands, particularly Corfu and Rhodes, are popular destinations for families. Again, the attraction is that they are hot and fairly cheap, with good beaches. Other popular islands include Crete, Kos, Cephallonia and Zante. Younger tourists with no family ties go to Greece in search of beaches on the smaller islands like Paxos and Santorini where accommodation and food are very cheap.

France

France is not as cheap as some other tourist destinations in Europe, but it is a land rich in heritage, culture, picturesque landscapes and of course food and wine. Many people from the UK visit regularly.

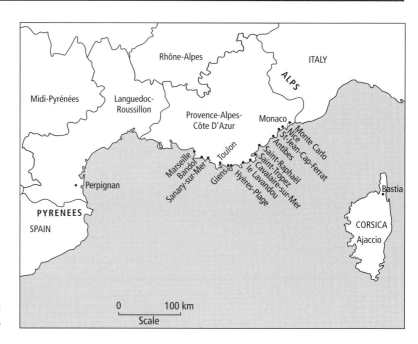

FIGURE 73 Mediterranean France

The south coast is very popular and has attractive beaches from Nice to St Tropez (the Côte d'Azur). It is easy to fly to Nice by scheduled services, but there are few package holidays available. Most UK tourists in France choose to camp or take a caravan, either driving to their destinations or boarding the Motorail (a train service carrying cars). Self-catering holidays in apartments or cottages are also popular, particularly in the areas of Brittany and Normandy which are nearer to the UK and have beautiful countryside as well as seaside. A type of holiday cottage is known as a 'gîte' from the French for 'resting place'.

Italy
Italy, like France, offers a rich heritage of architecture, art and culture, food and wine. It also possesses lakes and coastal resorts which attract many people from the UK who want sun and watersports. The lakes, particularly Lake Garda, the largest, and Lakes Maggiore and Como, are set in beautiful countryside; tourists who enjoy walking are particularly attracted to this area of Italy.

The Adriatic Riviera, where Rimini is perhaps the most famous resort, and the Neapolitan Riviera around Naples, particularly the resorts of Amalfi and Sorrento, attract many people wanting a hotel holiday.

The Mediterranean islands of Sicily and Sardinia are popular for beach holidays although more expensive than those in Greece.

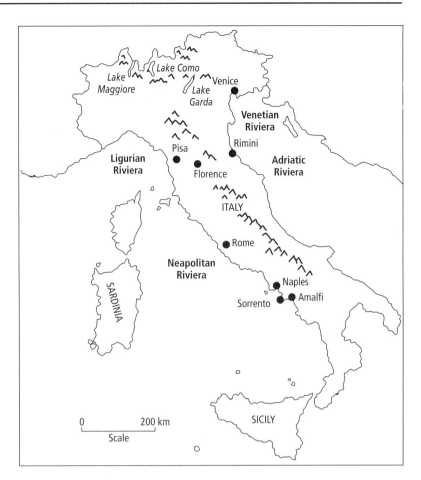

FIGURE 74 Tourist destinations in Italy

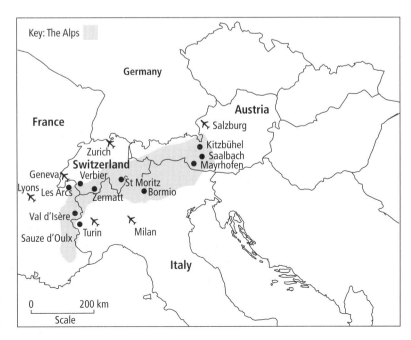

FIGURE 75 The location of the Alps

The Alps

The Alps, a great mountain range, cover areas of France, Switzerland, Austria and Italy.

Their main attractions to tourists are the skiing facilities in winter. February is the peak time, but Christmas is also popular. Some skiing resorts have been built up around traditional villages, for instance Westendorf in Austria. Others are purpose built, for instance Val d'Isère in France. These regions are also used for summer walking holidays and more specialised sports like rock-climbing.

Activity

1 For each of the following types of holiday give at least two examples of destinations. One must be in the UK and one in Europe. Then locate all your choices on a copy of the maps given in Figures 76A and 76B.

- City breaks
- Beach holidays
- Farm holidays
- Activity holidays
- Wintersports
- Watersports
- Winter sun
- Sightseeing

2 **a** Interview a friend and an older relative about their last holiday. Draw up a comparative chart showing:

- destination features;
- type of holiday;
- cost;
- season;
- activities undertaken.

Here is an example.

	Mary	Tim
Destination	Corfu	Algarve
Attractions	sea, sun, beach	sea, sun, beach
Entertainment	nightclubs, waterparks	restaurants
Weather	hot	warm, sunny
Season	August	January
Activities	sunbathing, nightclubbing	walking, sightseeing, driving, sunbathing

b Draw conclusions about their choice of holidays. What are the differences and similarities? Are they what you would expect?

FIGURE 76 A Map of
Europe

0   100 km
Scale

FIGURE 76 B Map of the UK

Investigate Principal Travel Routes within the UK and to Europe

This element looks at the principal travel routes within the UK and to Europe. By the end of this element you should be able to:

1 describe the principal routes to major tourist destinations in the UK and to Europe (performance criterion 6.2.1);
2 identify and locate the major UK gateways for the principal routes to tourist destinations in Europe (performance criterion 6.2.2);
3 explain the advantages and disadvantages of principal routes used to arrive at a tourist destination in the UK (performance criterion 6.2.3);
4 explain the advantages and disadvantages of principal routes used to arrive at a tourist destination in Europe (performance criterion 6.2.4).

Routes by road within the UK and to Europe

When travelling to tourist destinations within the UK, many visitors choose to go by car because it is both more convenient (door to door travel) and cheaper than travelling by public transport. The large increase in car ownership in the UK in recent years, however, has meant that a journey by car in holiday periods is often prolonged by frustrating traffic jams. Despite this, people continue to prefer the car as a means of travelling to tourist destinations as they then have the use of the car throughout their holiday to visit attractions or go shopping.

Motorways
The map in Figure 77 shows the principal motorways and A roads within the UK.

Tolls
French autoroutes tend to be less congested than UK motorways, but drivers are charged a 'toll' or payment for using the roads. Tourists need to budget for the autoroute tolls when planning a journey through France. Organisations in the UK such as the AA (Automobile Association) and the

RAC (Royal Automobile Association) give information on current French toll charges.

In the UK, road travellers do not yet have to pay motorway tolls. This may change in future, the argument being that people who use motorways should pay for them as they are very costly to maintain. The counter-argument is that car drivers will simply divert to toll-free A roads to avoid paying tolls, causing even more congestion among local traffic.

FIGURE 77 Trunk roads and motorways in Great Britain

Activity   Study Figure 78 carefully. Now answer the following questions.

1   What can you say about the percentages of people choosing to travel by car? What environmental problems will persist if this trend continues? What measures can be undertaken to discourage this trend?

2   Describe the trends for travelling by train. Why do you think this is the case? What needs to be done to change this situation?

FIGURE 78 Methods of transport

3   Give examples of what you think is meant by 'other' forms of transport.

Main methods of transport used to reach destination on holidays of 4+ nights in Great Britain 1971 to 1993

	All holidays									
	1971 %	1974 %	1976 %	1978 %	1980 %	1981 %	1982 %	1983 %	1984 %	1985 %
Car	69	69	69	72	71	69	68	72	69	71
Bus/coach	15	14	13	11	12	12	15	12	15	14
Train	13	13	11	11	13	13	12	10	11	10
Other	3	4	4	4	4	5	3	5	4	4

	All holidays								Main holidays	Additional holidays
	1986 %	1987 %	1988 %	1989 %	1990 %	1991 %	1992 %	1993 %	1993 %	1993 %
Car	72	73	74	74	76	78	75	76	76	76
Bus/coach	15	14	13	13	12	12	11	12	13	11
Train	8	8	8	8	7	6	8	7	7	7
Other	4	5	4	4	4	4	5	3	4	2

Source: British National Travel Survey (British Tourist Authority)
Note: Figures may not add up to 100% because of rounding and because a proportion of people could not recall method of transport used.

Railways

British Rail has a large network of inter-city lines which connect the main towns and cities in the UK. Figure 79 gives a map showing these routes.

Travelling by train can be comfortable: there are buffet-cars serving food and drinks, toilets and room for young children to move about during the journey. Sleeper trains offer carriages with bunks and washing facilities for overnight journeys, so that travellers can arrive at their destination feeling refreshed.

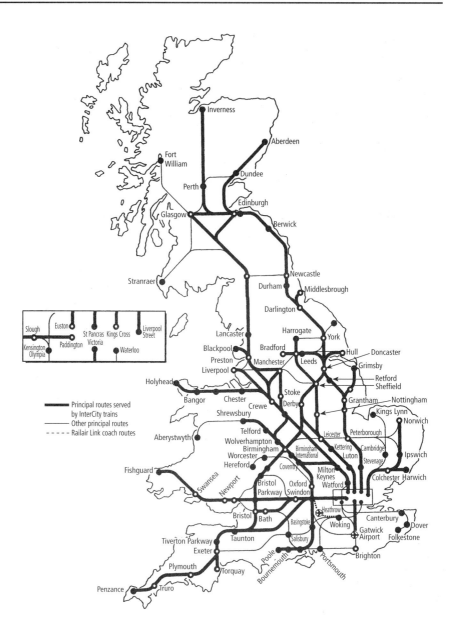

FIGURE 79 The InterCity rail network

However, there are still congestion problems at peak times; unless seats are reserved, travellers can find themselves without anywhere to sit during the journey. The prospect of having to stand in the aisles for a long period of time can be very off-putting to potential travellers, especially the elderly and people with young children.

Journey times between main cities may be faster than by car, but the overall travel time can be longer if a traveller has to wait for connections to his or her final destination. There is also the added inconvenience of having to move luggage on and off trains when changing connections.

British Rail offers special discount cards to certain groups of people such as students and senior citizens. Discounts are sometimes available for travel within a local region, which can benefit local people. Off-peak travel (outside travel to and from work periods) is always cheaper. This can suit the holiday traveller who, unlike the business traveller, does not have specific deadlines to meet.

The future of rail travel within the UK depends very much on the plans of the political party in power. Currently, the rail network is being sold off on a regional basis to private companies. Whilst some argue that this will make the network more competitive and therefore bring prices down for customers, others feel that privatisation will decrease the services available because less profitable rail routes will be taken out of service. There may also be difficulties in offering through routes when the regions are owned by different private companies.

Domestic and European air routes

Air travel within the UK is the fastest way of travelling between destinations which are far apart, such as London and Edinburgh. Air UK, for example, operates mainly from Stansted near London and offers scheduled flights to Aberdeen, Belfast, Edinburgh, Glasgow and Newcastle. Other regional routes, such as London to Manchester, are operated by airlines like British Airways and British Midland.

Travelling by air within the UK is often popular with business travellers: the cost over longer routes compares favourably with train fares and travelling time is reduced to less than an hour for many domestic routes. Flying within the UK is still one of the least used forms of tourist travel, however, because the car is still by far the cheapest form of travel for families, the distances between destinations are relatively small and most people require a car when on holiday anyway.

Air travel to Europe is fast and cheap when obtained as part of an all-inclusive package holiday. Charter flights are also popular with holiday travellers, who can be more flexible about departure times and dates. Charter flights operate for a specific purpose, usually to transport holiday makers. They run like private coach hire companies and if a charter flight company cannot sell enough seats on a particular flight it can cancel, or combine it with another.

Air routes are the most convenient and popular way of reaching traditional Mediterranean destinations such as Spain, the Balearic islands and Greece. The most important airports in the UK for international tourist departures are London's Heathrow, Stansted and Gatwick, Manchester Airport and Birmingham Airport. Different airlines will be able to supply you with maps of their domestic and international flight routes. Travel agencies can also supply this information.

Crossing the Channel

Tourists travelling from the UK to Europe by train or car cross the English Channel by using the Channel Tunnel route (train only or car on train), the ferry or hovercraft. These routes are useful for people who wish to go camping or touring in France or other European countries. There are several major ferry companies which offer services from major UK gateways such as Dover, Hull, Harwich, Holyhead, Folkestone and Portsmouth.

Hovercraft offer a quicker alternative to ferry routes, but they are very vulnerable to unfavourable weather conditions and are likely to be the most threatened form of cross-Channel transport against the increased competition offered by the Channel Tunnel.

Case study

Ferries compete with Le Shuttle and Eurostar

Le Shuttle
The Channel Tunnel went into operation on 2nd January 1992. Le Shuttle is the drive-on drive-off car train which operates from Folkestone to Calais. The tunnel train takes 35 minutes to cross the Channel; the same time as a hovercraft but quicker than a ferry. However, as cars have to arrive 20 minutes before departure and take ten minutes to disembark, the total journey time by hovercraft is 105 minutes from motorway to motorway, compared with one hour by Le Shuttle and over two hours by ferry.

When you cross to France with your car by Le Shuttle, fares are calculated on a flat rate for the car; there are no additional fares for passengers. Cross-Channel ferries charge for the passengers in addition to the vehicle.

Passengers travelling by Le Shuttle do not have to book in advance: they can pay at tollbooths before embarking. The Channel Tunnel can therefore be regarded as a 'rolling motorway' between the UK and France – the French motorway links conveniently to the French tunnel terminal in Calais.

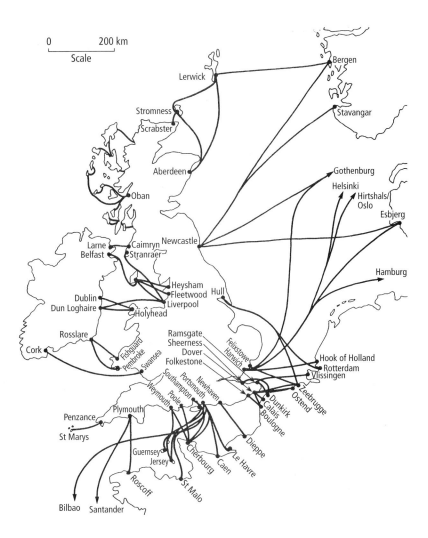

FIGURE 80 Major passenger car-ferry services from the UK

Ferry companies claim that UK tourists like to have the security of a ticket which guarantees them travel, even though a high proportion of people do not travel on the actual ferry for which they have booked.

Once on Le Shuttle, passengers stay with their car in a separate air-conditioned compartment. This can be advantageous for families travelling with young children. Passengers who wish to eat or buy duty-free goods must do so before boarding the train as there are no facilities apart from toilets and a radio service. The 35 minute journey is too short to make the provision of buffet cars worthwhile.

Ferry companies have invested large sums in improving their passenger services, including refurbished restaurants, shops and leisure facilities with children's play areas. For some, this 'supermarket' like atmosphere may be unappealing, but for others using the restaurants and shops is a part of their holiday. A further appeal of travelling by boat for families is the fact that children can actually see the boat leaving the UK. Travelling by tunnel gives them no sense of leaving the shores of England and arriving at the coast of France.

Promotions of Le Shuttle stress that, unlike ferries, the service it offers is not subject to delays or cancellations due to fog, rough seas or high winds.

Ferries claim that trains are subject to delays from strikes and ice or snow on the tracks in winter. They point out that stabilisers on their boats ensure that crossings are reasonably comfortable and that, generally, they have a high safety record. Many people fear travelling through the tunnel and it will need to maintain a very high safety record to convince certain groups of people that they should use it.

Eurostar
Eurostar is a three-country train service, jointly run by the railways of the UK, France and Belgium. It takes foot passengers only and is operated from London by the UK partner European Passenger Services. Since November 1994 passengers have been able to travel from London via the Channel Tunnel to Paris or Brussels. It is then possible to board connecting trains to destinations all over Europe. The advantage for travellers is that they can move from city centre to city centre without the inconvenience of having to travel to and from airports. This is particularly appealing to regular business travellers. Eurostar promotes its service as an attractive alternative to air travel: it is cheaper and convenient. Where a comparably cheap ticket is available on an airline it is often for inconvenient dates and times.

The modern Eurostar train has a comprehensive catering service and business travellers can take advantage of being able to work on the train. The journey time from London to Paris is three hours and from London to Brussels three and a quarter. These times are likely to be reduced when the Belgian and UK high-speed rail links have been completed.

Activity

1   Summarise the list of advantages and disadvantages to visitors travelling across the English Channel by ferry service.

2   Summarise the list of advantages and disadvantages of travelling through the Channel Tunnel by Le Shuttle and Eurostar.

3   Which form of Channel crossing (tunnel, ferry or hovercraft) would you choose for the following people? Give reasons.

   a   A group of day trippers on a shopping trip to France.
   b   A business traveller who regularly travels to Europe. She needs to take a car in order to visit a variety of clients in Europe.
   c   A couple going on a weekend trip to France.
   d   A family going on a camping holiday to Brittany with their children aged one and three.
   e   Yourself and a group of friends going on a short break to Amsterdam.

4   Discuss all your answers with the rest of your group.

Assignment activity Unit 6

You should keep all your assignment activity work, clearly labelled, in your Portfolio of Evidence. This work provides evidence of coverage of all the elements and performance criteria covered in Unit 6.

1   You work as an assistant in the operations department of a relatively new tour operator which offers tailormade all-inclusive holidays to destinations in the UK and Europe for people who are physically disabled. You have been asked to do some research into possible travel routes and make recommendations to the department manager in the form of a written report. Use maps to illustrate your information.

When reporting on each route, you also need to comment on the following:

   • costs (giving specific prices);
   • the accessibility of the route;
   • services offered, such as catering or shopping;
   • how long the journey takes;
   • an indication of how convenient and comfortable the route is.

Bear in mind the type of customer your company serves.

a You are first required to report on rail, road and (where applicable), air routes from Birmingham to the following destinations.

- Brighton
- Great Yarmouth
- Scarborough
- Edinburgh
- Anglesey
- London

b You are now asked to cover routes from Manchester to the following destinations.

- Paris
- Rome
- Amsterdam
- Benidorm
- Lake Garda
- Val D'Isère

2 You work for a large tour operator and have been asked to give an educational, promotional talk to a group of travel agents. The aim of your presentation is to increase the agent's knowledge of two destinations so that they can sell them effectively. You will make the presentation with a colleague.

Choose a partner. To prepare for your presentation you must together research and produce a file of information for each of your two destinations. One must be in Europe and one in the UK.

Each file should include the following information:

- location (include maps);
- how to get there;
- types of holidays available;
- attractions – natural and man-made;
- physical features;
- climatic information – when to go;
- general tourist information, for instance currency, local customs, health precautions.

You should prepare a suitable five-minute presentation, supported by visual aids, on each destination. Remember who your audience is and why you have been asked to give them a presentation.

Unit  Operational Practices in the Leisure and Tourism Industries

● ●

Introduction to the unit   This unit comprises the following elements required by the course and gives you practice in all the performance criteria that prove your understanding of each of these elements.

Element 7.1   Investigate operational practices in a selected leisure or tourism facility

Element 7.2   Investigate the maintenance, security and health and safety procedures within a selected facility

Element 7.3   Examine the administrative procedures used in the operation of leisure and tourism facilities

▣ Element 7.1 Investigate Operational Activities in a Selected Leisure or Tourism Facility

About this element This element looks at operational practices in a selected leisure or tourism facility. By the end of this element you should be able to:

1 describe the objectives of a selected leisure or tourism facility (performance criterion 7.1.1);
2 explain the relationship between key operational activities and the objectives of a selected leisure or tourism facility (performance criterion 7.1.2);
3 explain how schedules are used to plan uses of resources in a selected leisure or tourism facility (performance criterion 7.1.3);
4 describe the requirements of key operational activities in a selected leisure or tourism facility (performance criterion 7.1.4);
5 describe the evaluation criteria for key operational activities in a selected leisure or tourism facility (performance criterion 7.1.5).

The need for schedules

When you visit a sports centre you expect to find a timetable of activities from which you can choose the activities you want to participate in. Venues such as cinemas and theatres publish their programmes of events and publicise them. If no timetables or programmes were made available no-one would know what was happening or when.

Figures 81 and 82 show examples of a health club schedule and a published concert programme.

These programmes are both important sources of information for the customer and the means by which the facility advertises its services thus achieving its aim, to attract custom.

A tourism facility, such as a National Trust property, also has a programme of special events. The purpose of special events may be to spread the number of visitors into less busy times or to increase the number of visitors (and therefore revenue), but without the published programme the National Trust could not achieve its objective.

Daily class schedule

Times	Monday	Tuesday	Wednesday
7.30–8.00	Aqua Tone	Aqua Aerobics	Aqua Tone
7.30–11.30	Gym Instruction	Gym Instruction	Gym Instruction
8.00–8.30	Morning Jog	Morning Jog	Morning Jog
8.30–9.00	Wakeup Workout	Wakeup Workout	Wakeup Workout
9.30–10.45	Bodyshaping	Country Walk	Bodyshaping
9.30–10.30	Yoga	Yoga	Yoga
10.30–11.30	Relaxation	Relaxation	Relaxation
10.30–11.15	Step	Hi/Lo Aerobics	Step
11.00–11.30	Aqua Aerobics	Aqua Tone	Aqua Aerobics
11.30–12.30	Diet & Exercise Talk	Body Alignment	Diet & Exercise Talk
11.30–12.00	Sit & Be Fit		Sit & Be Fit
	LUNCH	LUNCH	LUNCH
	LUNCH	LUNCH	LUNCH
2.00–2.45	Jazz Class	Bodyshaping	Jazz Class
3.00–3.30	Intro To Step	Backs & Tums	Intro To Step
3.00–3.30	Aqua Tone	Aqua Tone	Aqua Tone
3.30–4.15	Step	Step	Step
4.30–5.00	Stretch Class	Stretch Class	Stretch Class
4.30–6.00	Yoga & Relaxation		
5.00–9.30	Gym Instruction	Gym Instruction	Gym Instruction
5.15–6.00	Gentle Tone		Circuit W'Out
6.15–7.00			
7.00–7.30		Aqua Tone	
7.15–8.00			
8.30–9.15			

FIGURE 81 Part of a health club timetable

Objectives: public facilities

The objectives of a public facility must include providing a service to the community as well as generating profit and its schedules will reflect this. As an example, we will look at the objectives of a local authority sports centre as it demonstrates very well the complexities and restraints of running a public service facility.

Activity   Read the Case Study on page 189. Figure 83 shows the programme for St Mulvo's swimming pool. Look at the key and you will see how different groups are catered for to ensure that a service is provided in the locality. Some of the activities will generate income, some will not. Study the timetable carefully and then answer the following questions.

FIGURE 82 An advertisement for a concert programme

1 Calculate the number of hours the pool is operational each week.

2 Draw a bar graph showing how many hours are devoted to each group.

3 Calculate the percentage of total hours allocated to each group.

4 Which sessions do you think will generate most income, and which the least?

5 How would you expect the sessions marked 'special' to be used? Give your ideas for promoting these sessions.

Case study

St Mulvo Sports Centre

The objectives of St Mulvo are as follows.

1 Maximise the use of the sports centre.
2 Provide leisure and recreational activities for the local community within a three mile radius.
3 Provide a venue for local sports clubs to meet.
4 Provide facilities for disabled clients.
5 Provide recreational activities for 14 to 16 year olds.
6 Gain the maximum income possible.
7 Promote a corporate image.

Public money is invested in the facility and the centre management must justify the use of this money; aims 1 and 2 are therefore essential. Aim 3 is to provide a public service and encourage sport in the community. Aim 4 is to cater for disabled people; public centres are in fact obliged to cater for special needs on their schedules. Aim 5 is to provide activities for young people, particularly in the summer holidays.

Figure 83 shows St Mulvo's timetable of swimming classes and services. You can see that whoever designed this programme has had to fit in a great deal in order to fulfil the centre's objectives.

Objectives: private facilities

A private facility also has objectives, but there is a greater emphasis on profit-making than community service. Disabled people's needs are sometimes expensive to cater for and private facilities may ignore them. Young people's needs may also be ignored as not many are able to afford expensive membership fees. Of course, the facility must still offer a high level of customer service, as dissatisfied customers will not return and therefore the facility would not make a profit.

Figure 84 shows part of the leaflet from a health farm called Springs Hydro. The leaflet itself is a marketing tool to show what the facility has to offer. Many services are on offer to attract customers or guests. Customers who enjoy their stay will return regularly and contribute to the revenue of the Hydro. The services in this private facility are targeted at those who can afford to pay relatively high prices, rather than being offered cheaply to all sections of the community. This is a vital difference between the public and private sectors.

FIGURE 83 St Mulvo's timetable

	Mon	*Tues*	*Wed*	*Thu*	*Fri*	*Sat*	*Sun*
07.00–08.00	EMC	EMC	EMC	EMC	EMC	EMC	EMC
08.00–09.00						LIFSAV	LIFSAV
09.00–10.00	P&T	FIF	P&T	FIF	P&T	SL	FAM
10.00–11.00	SN	SCH	SN	SCH	SCH	SL	FAM
11.00–12.00	SN	SCH	SN	SCH	SCH	FAM	FAM
12.00–13.00	ADU	LANE	GEN	WOMEN	AQUAFIT	FAM	GEN
13.00–14.00	LANE	ADU	LANE	ADU	LANE	GEN	GEN
14.00–15.00	SCH	P&T	SCH	P&T	SCH	GEN	GEN
15.00–16.00	SCH	WOMEN	SCH	FIF	SCH	GEN	GEN
16.00–17.00	SL	SL	SL	SL	GEN	LANE	CLUB
17.00–18.00	AQUAFIT	SL	LANE	SL	GEN	SPECIAL	CLUB
18.00–19.00	GEN	CLUB	LIFSAV	SL	GEN	SPECIAL	CLUB
19.00–20.00	CLUB	CLUB	LIFSAV	GEN	CLUB	SPECIAL	LANE
20.00–21.00	CLUB	ADU	AQUAFIT	ADU	CLUB	SPECIAL	LANE
21.00–22.00	ADU	LANE	ADU	LANE	ADU	SPECIAL	

KEY TO TIMETABLE

ADU	Adults only	AQUAFIT	Keep Fit
CLUB	Swimming Club	EMC	Early Morning Club
FAM	Family Time	FIF	Over Fifties
GEN	General Sessions	LANE	Lane Sessions
LIFSAV	Life Saving Courses	P&T	Parents & Toddlers
SCH	Schools	SL	Swimming Lessons
SN	Special Needs	SPECIAL	Special Events
WOMEN	Women Only		

Activity   Study the leaflet in Figure 84 on the next page carefully. Now complete the following tasks.

1   Make a list of all the services available at the Hydro. These are evident from the photograph and the text.

2   The emphasis at this Hydro is on individual customer service. Plan a programme for a guest at the Hydro: Samantha West, age 29. Samantha manages a hair salon and is spending two days at the Hydro for a break from work. She wants to fit as much as possible into her stay. She will arrive at 11 a.m. on Tuesday and will leave at 5 p.m. on Wednesday. Give times and activities in your programme.

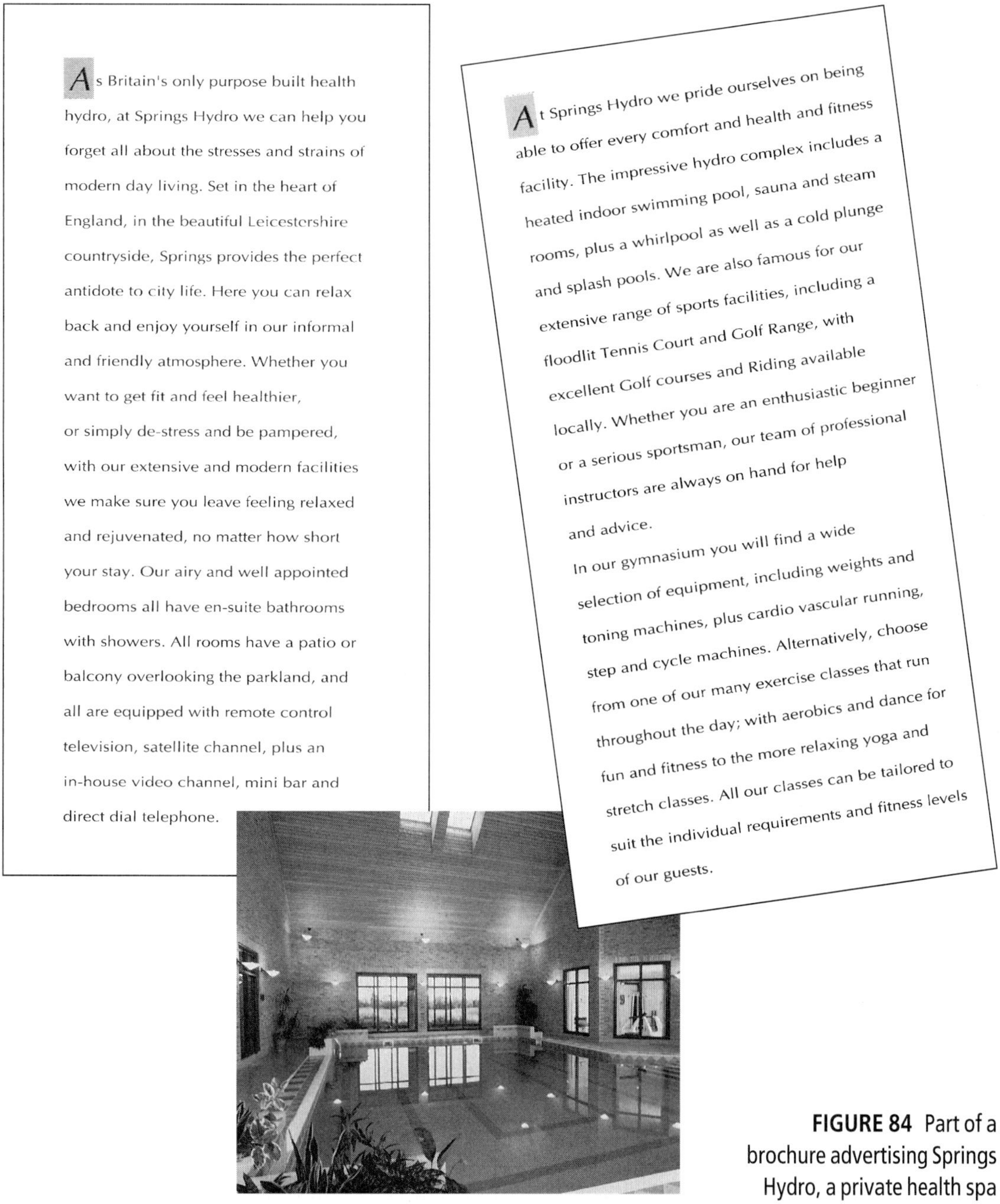

As Britain's only purpose built health hydro, at Springs Hydro we can help you forget all about the stresses and strains of modern day living. Set in the heart of England, in the beautiful Leicestershire countryside, Springs provides the perfect antidote to city life. Here you can relax back and enjoy yourself in our informal and friendly atmosphere. Whether you want to get fit and feel healthier, or simply de-stress and be pampered, with our extensive and modern facilities we make sure you leave feeling relaxed and rejuvenated, no matter how short your stay. Our airy and well appointed bedrooms all have en-suite bathrooms with showers. All rooms have a patio or balcony overlooking the parkland, and all are equipped with remote control television, satellite channel, plus an in-house video channel, mini bar and direct dial telephone.

At Springs Hydro we pride ourselves on being able to offer every comfort and health and fitness facility. The impressive hydro complex includes a heated indoor swimming pool, sauna and steam rooms, plus a whirlpool as well as a cold plunge and splash pools. We are also famous for our extensive range of sports facilities, including a floodlit Tennis Court and Golf Range, with excellent Golf courses and Riding available locally. Whether you are an enthusiastic beginner or a serious sportsman, our team of professional instructors are always on hand for help and advice.

In our gymnasium you will find a wide selection of equipment, including weights and toning machines, plus cardio vascular running, step and cycle machines. Alternatively, choose from one of our many exercise classes that run throughout the day; with aerobics and dance for fun and fitness to the more relaxing yoga and stretch classes. All our classes can be tailored to suit the individual requirements and fitness levels of our guests.

FIGURE 84 Part of a brochure advertising Springs Hydro, a private health spa

Meeting financial targets

Every organisation, in both public and private sectors, must set a budget before the start of the financial year on 1st April. The budget lays down all the estimated expenditure for the year and all the estimated income. The local council or private owner will set a financial target which managers must then try to meet. Programmes must therefore be

designed to generate income to meet the financial targets as
well as achieving any other objectives. At the same time,
managers will try to keep expenditure low.

Expenditure may include:

- heating and lighting;
- new equipment;
- repair of equipment;
- servicing of equipment;
- cleaning;
- printing for programmes and posters;
- publicity;
- licences;
- caretaking;
- sundries.

Salaries are included in expenditure, but may be paid by the
local authority in the case of a public facility.

Income may include:

- block bookings (e.g. sports hall booked for 30 weeks for a 2
  hour weekly slot for five-a-side);
- exercise classes (30 weeks at £3 per head);
- casual use of hall (e.g. for parties);
- sales of sundries (e.g. small sports equipment);
- equipment hire;
- tuition on gym equipment;
- sponsorship of events;
- advertising (e.g. in halls, on lockers, on squash court
  walls);
- membership fees.

In a public facility a contribution will also be given from
council tax funds.

Membership fees
Leisure organisations
The most important source of income for a private sports
centre is its membership fees. These will be very expensive
but once paid the customer will not expect to pay many extras
although the centre may generate a little income from sales
of equipment and, for instance, solarium hire.

Figure 85 shows an example of membership fees for a private
sports centre.

In a public organisation the sources of income are much
more varied as we have seen and membership fees are

relatively unimportant. Here is an example of the kind of membership offered in a public facility.

Membership

Adult (over 18):

per annum £10.20

This entitles adults to a reduction of 35p per visit on swimming or hire of a squash court or any other centre activity.

Adult members also receive by post advance notice of courses and events.

 Activity   Study Figure 85 carefully and then answer the following questions.

1 Calculate the cost of membership for a family of five, joining for the first time, and requiring full membership.

Membership is offered on an annual basis.
All prices are inclusive of VAT.
Please tick relevant boxes.

FULL MEMBERSHIP		Joining Fee
Single	£415.00☐	£35.00☐
Husband and Wife	£620.00☐	£70.00☐
Each child	£120.00☐	

MID-WEEK (off-peak)		
Single	£255.00☐	£35.00☐
Husband and Wife	£395.00☐	£70.00☐
Each Child	£120.00☐	
(Child 15 years or under)		

CORPORATE	
6 named persons	£2300.00☐
10 named persons	£3500.00☐

TOTAL FEE PAYABLE   £ _____

Full membership is 7 days a week Monday to Sunday 7.00am-10.00pm.

Mid-Week off-peak Membership is Monday to Friday 8.00am-4.00pm excluding Public Holidays.

Please note that children only qualify for Membership if their parents have taken out the Husband and Wife Membership. CHILDREN MUST BE ACCOMPANIED BY AN ADULT AT ALL TIMES.

Children under 14 years of age are not allowed to use the spa bath.

Towels are not included in the cost of your Membership but may be hired at a charge of 50p per towel per session.

FIGURE 85 An example of membership fees for a private sports centre

2 If the family visits the centre twice a week for the first year, what is the cost of each visit?

3 Why is off-peak membership cheaper? What kind of customers will take up this membership?

4 What is meant by corporate membership?

Tourism

In a tourist facility income will be determined by the number of visitors and admission prices.

The prices must be very carefully calculated. They must be high enough for the attraction to make a profit, but low enough to represent value for money to visitors.

The example in Figure 86 shows an example of the kind of simple pricing structure used for entry to a family farm park.

1996 ADMISSION PRICES		
Adults **£3.50**	OAP's **£3.20**	Children **£2.50** (3-14 inc)
SAVER TICKETS		
2 children and 1 adult		**£7.00**
2 children and 2 adults		**£10.50**
PARTIES (minimum 15 persons)		
Adults **£3.20**	OAP's **£2.90**	Children **£1.00** (3-14 inc)
		Children **£2.20** (5-14 inc)
OPEN DAILY 10am to 5pm **25 March to 31 Oct 1996**		

FIGURE 86 An example of entry fees for a tourist and leisure attraction

The use of resources

Any sports and leisure programme must be designed to make best use of the physical space available.

If a local sports centre has a large hall the management must make maximum use of it. They have to consider that, if classes such as aerobics are to be offered, they will not need the whole hall: the rest can be used for another activity such as badminton. On the other hand activities such as korfball may need the entire hall.

Squash courts and tennis courts are easier to deal with on the schedule as they have only one function and can be available at all times.

A purpose-built venue such as the Barbican in London has many different physical resources available for events. These include the art gallery, the foyer, stalls gallery and the library, as well as the main hall, the Pit Theatre and the cinema. The centre is owned by the Corporation of London and aims to provide a home base for the Royal Shakespeare Company and the London Symphony Orchestra.

As with the local sports centre, extensive planning is needed to ensure that all the available space in the building is fully used both to provide an arts facility and to generate income.

Figure 87 shows a few of the Barbican's space-using range of events advertised in an information leaflet.

Activity   You have seen several examples of programmes. Now try to design a programme for your own school or college sports hall.

Here are the facilities and constraints.

- The programme is for evenings only – from 4.00 to 10.00 p.m., Monday to Friday.
- Squash courts are always available.
- There is a large hall, which can be divided and used for aerobics, badminton or large space activities.
- There is a separate fitness suite.
- You are committed to community sports provision as follows.

  Wednesday 6 to 8 p.m.:   staff and student sports
  Tuesday 7 to 8 p.m.:   special needs

- You wish to keep five hours free for hall hire during the week. This is to allow for one-off, non-scheduled bookings.

Here are the activities that you must fit into your programme.

- Circuit training   1 hour per week
- Boxaerobics   1 hour per week
- Step aerobics   1 hour per week
- Short tennis for primary
  school children   5 hours per week
- Five-a-side football league   2 hours block per week
- Korfball   2 hours block per week
- Karate class   2 hours block per week
- Stretch class   1 hour per week

Badminton courts are available in the hall whenever it is not in use for another activity.

Plan your programme and design a leaflet which includes all the details.

BARBICAN CONFERENCES AND EXHIBITIONS

BARBICAN HALL - IDEAL FOR AGMs
Call the Conference Sales Team now for more information on 0171-638 4141.

For further information on how your Public or Trade Event can benefit from being held at the Barbican Exhibition Halls or for details on forthcoming shows telephone the Exhibition Sales Team on 0171 382 7053.

MPRC STUDIO

Sir Colin Davis conducting *The Trojans* 'live' at the Barbican Centre, and Leiferkus and Gorchakova in *Eugene Onegin* 'live' at Covent Garden - just two of hundreds of unique archive recordings of live performances from the 1930s to the present day, exclusively available for listening at the **Music Performance Research Centre** studio in the Barbican Music Library, and now you can watch video archive recordings of historic *live* performances by legendary artists. Open 9.30am-5.30pm Mon-Fri; 9.30am-7.30pm Tue; 9.30am-12.30pm Sat. Closed Sun and Bank Holidays. To book a listening or viewing appointment telephone 01932 860472.

BARBICAN CHESS CLUB

Meetings every Thursday at 6.00pm
JUNIOR COACHING SESSION
Saturday 8 and 22 July 2-6pm
Full details from John McAllister, 27 Cambrian Green, Snowdon Drive, London NW9. Tel: 081 200 6683.

BARBICAN CENTRE TOURS

Barbican Centre tours offer a fascinating insight into how the Barbican operates. We can do tours for groups of 10 or more at a cost of only £3.50 (or £2.50 concession) per person. For further details and booking information, please phone the **Tour Organiser** on 0171-638 4141.

INFORMATION

Advance Box Office, Silk Street Entrance 9.00am - 8.00pm Library Information Desk open during Library hours (see page 10) General telephone 0171-638 4141 ext 7538 Box Office enquiries: 0171-638 8891 (9.00am - 8.00pm every day) 24 Hour Recorded Information Service: 0171-628 2295 or 0171-628 9760.

FACILITIES FOR THE DISABLED

Details about the facilities provided are available in a special leaflet which can be obtained from the Information Desk (tel: 0171-638 4141 ext 7538) Minicom 0171-382 7927 for deaf patrons. Disabled patrons can obtain a voucher permitting free exit from our car park on presentation of their disabled care registration certificate (orange badge) at the Box Office/Ticket Desks.

The best place to park for the disabled is in Car Park 3 off Silk Street. Spaces are limited in the car parks generally and early arrival is recommended. There is level access to the Centre from Car Park 3.

A frequency induction loop system operates in the Barbican Hall. Patrons should set their hearing aids to 'T'. Please mention that you require this service when booking your tickets. Infra-red headsets (£5 returnable deposit required) are available for the Barbican Theatre.

FIGURE 87 An extract from the Barbican's information leaflet

Getting the best from a programme

Marketing

Marketing activities can be carried out using the leaflets and posters setting out the timetables, programmes and facilities available. Most organisations keep a database of customers and send out mailshots enclosing up-to-date information on events and special notices. The database can be very sophisticated: for example, if you have booked tickets for three ballets in the last year at a multi-event venue like the Barbican, the computer can pick this up and send you a leaflet about a forthcoming ballet. Mailshots always include vital information on how to book tickets or classes and aim to make it as easy as possible for the customer to do so.

Organisations will also advertise events in local or national press and possibly on local radio. The extent to which they advertise is governed by the budget they have.

Staff training

In order for a programme to be a success, you must have friendly, well-trained staff waiting to welcome customers.

Staff should be trained in customer care, but they will also need specific training depending on their role. In a sports centre you expect staff to be trained in First Aid and in gym instruction, and to know about health and safety legislation through updates from the Sports Council. Supervisors may be expected to take additional management courses such as those run by the Institute of Supervisory Management.

Only sports centres where staff are trained on the NHS Gym Rehabilitation Course are eligible to take patients sent by 'GP referral' (see Unit 5, page 129).

Other types of training must be given in, for example, computer skills and telephone technique in a box office or basic life-saving for people working near a swimming pool.

All the equipment involved must be properly used and regularly serviced. In a gym logbooks and service certificates should be available for inspection.

Reviewing and evaluating

There are various means of determining a programme's success.

First, if the venue has met its financial target then the programme has achieved an important objective. In this case managers are often expected to review their financial target and aim for a greater profit the next year.

Analysis of customer numbers

Visitor or customer numbers should always be analysed. This is usually fairly easy to carry out if all data has been kept. It can then be seen whether there is a rise in visitor numbers or membership numbers, and by what percentage. If there is a rise or fall in numbers within certain categories of people, for instance families at a weekend attraction, student numbers at a concert or disabled visitors on a walk, then appropriate action can be taken.

Discussion with staff

Discussions, both informal and formal, should take place with the staff. They are the people with most customer contact and can best pass on suggestions or complaints from customers. Where there are gaps in a programme, perhaps a hall available but not hired in a sports centre, then ideas can be put forward on how to fill these gaps next year.

Questionnaires

Formal questionnaires are sometimes used to ask visitors or customers their opinions of a facility. These must be carefully designed and analysed so that the results can be used for effective future planning. You can see an example of a questionnaire on page 58.

Press album

Every organisation should keep a press album. This is where cuttings are kept of all reviews of events and articles about the facility. Careful, regular analysis of these cuttings will show what kind of image the organisation has in the public eye and reflect the success, or otherwise, of programmes.

Element 7.2 Investigate the Maintenance, Security, Health and Safety Procedures within a Facility

About this element

This element looks at the maintenance, security, health and safety procedures within a facility. By the end of this element you should be able to:

1 describe the physical features of a selected leisure or tourism facility (performance criterion 7.2.1);
2 explain the maintenance requirements of a selected facility (performance criterion 7.2.2);
3 explain the importance of using a maintenance checklist for a selected facility (performance criterion 7.2.3);
4 explain the need for security procedures in a selected facility (performance criterion 7.2.4);
5 explain the security procedures in a selected facility (performance criterion 7.2.5);
6 explain how the selected facility meets health and safety requirements (performance criterion 7.2.6).

Maintenance

The Health and Safety at Work Act 1974

The provisions of this Act set out very important guidelines for working practices in the field of both maintenance and security (see pages 201 and 204).

Briefly, the aims of the Act are as follows.

- To ensure the health, safety and welfare of people at work.
- To protect other people against risks to health or safety arising from the activities of people at work.
- To control the keeping and use of dangerous substances, for instance toxic cleaning materials.
- To control the emission into the atmosphere of noxious or offensive substances from premises.

Whatever the organisation you work for from a travel agency to an outdoor pursuits training centre it is always necessary for staff to ensure the safety of both clients and themselves to comply with the Health and Safety at Work Act.

In a sports centre

In a sports centre, wrong use or abuse of equipment can mean that someone's personal safety is endangered. Clients must be taught how to use exercise equipment properly and many centres insist that you follow an induction course if you are a new client. However, it is thorough maintenance of equipment that is of key importance to ensuring safety. The constant use to which it is subjected means that regular repair and service is essential. Most leisure facilities therefore employ a maintenance manager.

Activity   Study the photographs of a health and fitness centre in Figure 88.

1   Make a list of the physical features of the two rooms. Include any fittings, fixtures, furnishings and equipment that are evident.

2   Consider the basic maintenance requirements necessary to maintain standards in each room. List these and state whether they should be carried out daily, weekly, monthly or annually.

FIGURE 88 A well-equipped fitness centre

Maintenance

The maintenance requirements of the buildings and furnishings of an organisation range from cleanliness to repairs, from routine checks to emergency procedures.

The minimum working standards of maintenance should be laid down by management and must adhere to the provisions of the Health and Safety at Work Act. These minimum standards are often laid out in an internally distributed manual, perhaps prepared by staff in head office for the use of relevant people in branch offices.

To outline the maintenance requirements of all the facilities that might be owned by an organisation would take a full manual, but we will consider some examples using a hotel as illustration.

Case study

Glebe Hotel

The maintenance manager at the Glebe Hotel is Mr Pacino. He has two staff helping him and one youth training scheme (YTS) trainee.

Mr Pacino is also the Glebe's health and safety officer and as such he must implement the rules and regulations of the Act.

The maintenance manual

Mr Pacino has two important documents to aid him in his work. Firstly, a maintenance manual lists all the necessary checks for all areas of the hotel including fixtures and fittings. These lists (or 'matrices') indicate how often the tasks must be carried out. Figure 89 gives an example of the matrix for exterior and grounds checks.

All the pages in the manual cover routine tasks. Even though some checks may be made only once a year, they are still routine.

Although the lists of checks to be made are extensive and many of the checks are daily, they are not always time consuming to carry out as different section heads will take responsibility for their areas of the hotel. For example, the head chef will carry out checks in the kitchen, the housekeeper will cover bedrooms. In our example, it can be seen that problems with the grounds of the Glebe would immediately be apparent and action could be quickly taken.

The maintenance book

The other document that is important to Mr Pacino is the maintenance book which he refers to constantly. If a member of staff notices that a repair is necessary, for instance a lamp is not working, she enters this in the maintenance book with details and the date. Mr Pacino then allocates these jobs to his team on a daily basis. Also entered in this book are jobs which are not urgent, for instance putting up new shelves. These will be allocated to the maintenance team as the schedule allows. All these jobs are non-routine tasks.

Inspection

The maintenance manager must also be prepared to meet various inspectors who visit the premises.

Most leisure premises require a fire certificate to comply with the Fire Precaution Act 1971. The fire inspector will visit once a year and check all fire precautions. The inspector may make requirements which have to be implemented within a given period, or recommendations which the inspector considers should be carried out, but will not insist upon in the short term.

Working in a hotel, Mr Pacino also meets health inspectors who will examine the kitchens.

EXTERIOR & GROUNDS	Daily	Weekly	Monthly	3 Monthly	6 Monthly	Annually
General The following actions must be implemented at all times unless otherwise stated						
Gardens Well Tended	✓					
Car Park Entrances Lit	✓					
Hotel Entrances Well Signposted	✓					
Exterior Paintwork, etc.	✓				✓	
Disposal of Rubbish	✓					
External Areas Checked		✓				
Group Flag Flown Where Applicable	✓					
Car Parks/Pavements, etc.						
Well Maintained	✓					
Clean and Tidy	✓					
Sound Surfaces	✓					
Well Lit	✓					
Adequate Markings	✓					
Disclaimer Notices Displayed	✓					
Check on Above		✓				
Hotel Signage						
Maintained in Full Working Order	✓					
High Level Servicing (as required)	✓					
Low Level Servicing	✓					

FIGURE 89 An at a glance job matrix for the buildings and grounds of the Glebe Hotel

Health hazards
He must be aware of health problems which can occur, such as Legionnaires Disease which can break out in the water supply. This is carefully checked for: water is tested every six months and even more frequently in swimming pools; showerheads are bleached and descaled every six months to ensure hygiene.

Preventative maintenance
The aim of preventative maintenance is to avoid, as far as possible, the need for emergency repairs.

At the Glebe there are 40 bedrooms and the contents of each are given a thorough check every six months and a copy of the result kept on file. Any jobs required are entered in the maintenance book. The kind of items that are checked in a bedroom would include the following.

- Door lock
- Room number
- Door closer
- Door stopper
- Door hinges
- Door appearance
- Drawers – appearance and operation
- Kettle
- Long mirror
- Dressing table
- Luggage rack
- Electricity sockets
- Table lamps

These preventative checks are usually carried out on a six-monthly basis. If every area of a facility is checked in this way then high standards are more easily upheld.

High standards of maintenance encourage customer confidence and loyalty; it also increases the motivation and job-satisfaction of staff to feel that they work with well-cared for equipment in a well-presented building.

 Activity

Draw up a maintenance checklist form for either your classroom or your work environment. Use the following headings.

Item	Date checked	Comment	Action	Date of action	Signature

Now list all the items that should be checked. Remember to indicate how often the checks should be carried out – should your check be daily, monthly, six-monthly or annual?

Once your checklist is finished, ask another member of your group to check the room against your list for any repairs required and complete the form accordingly.

Discuss your findings together and decide whether any further action should be taken, for instance reporting any electrical damage uncovered – for example, the wiring of a plug may be loose and in need of attention.

Security

Effective security arrangements are essential in any organisation for the following reasons.

- To protect property within a facility.
- To protect the property of clients.
- To preserve the personal safety of staff and clients.
- To prevent unauthorised use of a facility.

Management and staff, in whatever capacity they work, should be constantly aware of security procedures.

In a sports centre

Most sports centres are designed to be easily accessible and welcoming to the public and this means that a vigilant and efficient reception system is essential. The usual procedure is as follows.

1 Clients are met at reception, thus preventing unauthorised use of the facilities.
2 Clients sign in at reception, so it is known who is on the premises.
3 Clients are requested verbally and by prominent notices to use the lockers provided in changing rooms to keep their personal belongings safe.

The personal safety of people using the centre is important and, as we have already noted, effective safety procedures for the use of equipment are essential. In swimming pools lifeguards are usually in attendance and notices warn of other safety procedures that the centre wishes their clients to observe.

In a hotel

Most hotels are, like sports centres, easily accessible to the public and it is therefore possible for anyone to walk in and out without authorisation.

There are a number of measures which can be taken to help staff know exactly who people in the hotel are and why they are there.

- Physical car park barriers – opened by remote control operated by the receptionist.

- A signing-in book, for guests, and one for casual visitors or workers at the reception. Part of a receptionist's duties is to ensure that everyone who comes in signs one of these books.
- A policy of stopping people at random in the hotel if it is suspected that they are not residents (this is difficult to put into practice in a tactful manner).
- The employment of night porters, who keep a watchful eye on exits and entrances.
- A duty manager who patrols around the hotel and its grounds.

Again, the safety of guests is important and the measures outlined above will help to ensure that they feel personally secure. Many hotels now use key cards for hotel rooms, rather than keys. If a card is lost it can then be invalidated quickly and a new one issued.

Security responsibilities

When putting security procedures into place the management of an organisation should ensure, as with maintenance procedures, that they are complying with the Health and Safety at Work Act 1974 (see page 199).

The employer and the employee both have duties under the Act.

Employer's duties

- To provide and maintain safe plant and equipment.
- To provide information and instruction to staff on health and safety.
- To provide a written safety policy and bring it to the notice of employees.
- To provide safe storage for harmful substances.
- To provide a safe working environment which is regularly monitored.
- To ensure that systems and practices are safe.
- To ensure that the public is not exposed to risk.

A health and safety officer is appointed in the workplace to ensure that these policies are implemented.

Employee's duties

- To take reasonable care for themselves and others.
- To co-operate with the employer to ensure that the requirements of the Act are adhered to.
- To refrain from interfering with anything provided to protect their health, safety or welfare.

Element 7.3 Examine the Administrative Procedures used in the Operation of Leisure and Tourism Facilities

This element looks at administrative procedures used in the operation of leisure and tourism facilities. By the end of this element you should be able to:

1 explain the purposes of administrative procedures in leisure and tourism facilities (performance criterion 7.3.1);
2 identify and give examples of the administrative systems used in the operation of leisure and tourism facilities (performance criterion 7.3.2);
3 explain the procedure for making bookings and reservations in leisure and tourism facilities (performance criterion 7.3.3);
4 explain the procedure for handling incoming payments in leisure and tourism facilities (performance criterion 7.3.4).

Administration procedures

Administration procedures are the systems used by an organisation to record and act on a wide variety of information. Examples include administrative procedures for recording bookings and payments in a sports centre and one for paying the telephone bill in a travel agency.

Sometimes, particularly in large organisations, people find administrative procedures tedious and over-complex. It is important that everyone is made aware of the reasons for these procedures, so that they carry them out efficiently and effectively. This is often done when you first start a job, as part of your induction training.

Providing management information
Properly kept administrative records provide vital business information. Management must know how facilities are being used, whether they are used to capacity and what revenue is being made. Without this and other information they cannot plan for the future or adjust services to suit demand.

There must be information on standards achieved so that weaknesses can be recognised and acted upon. In service

The management and staff of the Northshire Hotel trust that you have enjoyed your stay. To assist us in maintaining high standards we would appreciate your comments on our performance.
Thank you.
George Othersun
General Manager

Reception	YES	NO
Did you receive a courteous and efficient welcome?	☐	☐
Did you receive your early morning call on time?	☐	☐
Did you receive your newspaper?	☐	☐
Were any room services requested to your satisfaction?	☐	☐
Did you find the telephone service courteous and efficient?	☐	☐

Your Bedroom
Did you like the following aspects of your bedroom?

– Cleanliness	☐	☐
– Decor	☐	☐
– Heating/Ventilation	☐	☐
– Bathroom	☐	☐
– Lighting	☐	☐
– Beds and Furniture	☐	☐

The Restaurant

Did you like the decor and general atmosphere?	☐	☐
Was the quality and choice of breakfast to your satisfaction?	☐	☐
Was the dinner menu selection to your satisfaction?	☐	☐
Was the quality of the food to your satisfaction?	☐	☐
Was the service friendly and efficient?	☐	☐

Gallery Bar

Did you like the decor and general atmosphere?	☐	☐
Was the choice of beverages to your satisfaction?	☐	☐
Was the service friendly and efficient?	☐	☐

Leisure Club
Did you like the following aspects of the club?

– Golf Course	☐	☐
– Swimming Pool	☐	☐
– Squash	☐	☐
– Spa Bath/Solarium	☐	☐
– Gymnasium	☐	☐
– Changing Facilities	☐	☐
– Service from Staff	☐	☐

How did you find out about us?
Your Company ☐   Travel Agent ☐   Conference ☐
Friends ☐   Advertising ☐   By Chance ☐   Other ☐

Do you have any requirements for
Conference and Banqueting?   ☐   ☐

Do you have any other comments to make about any aspect of the Hotel?

_____

_____

Name_____ Room No._____

Company_____ Date of arrival_____

Address_____

Telephone No. _____

FIGURE 90 An example of a hotel questionnaire

industries like leisure and tourism it is particularly important that there is information on the standards of customer care an organisation actually achieves.

Figure 90 shows an example of a questionnaire which collects information on customer service. If every guest in the hotel over a one year period fills it in, a great deal of very valuable information about customer likes and dislikes is available to be analysed by management. The use of standardised forms for recording information allows everyone to keep to the same procedure and standard of reporting.

Booking and reservation systems.
In a sports centre

In a sports centre a simple manual system of recording information is usually used for taking bookings. A book or file with times and names for each class or piece of equipment entered on a separate page is all that is needed to create accurate lists of the people booked. In larger centres, the swimming pool, fitness suite and gym may each keep their own manual booking system along these lines.

In a hotel

In a hotel booking and reservation systems may be manual or computerised. Large hotels always have a fully computerised system designed to make all the information it holds as easy as possible to understand. For instance, when an enquiry is made, the bookings clerk must be able to see from the reservation system on the computer screen what rooms are available. These will be categorised into smoking and non-smoking, twins, doubles, family rooms and suites so that queries can be answered quickly and accurately.

The clerk will take details of the reservation on a reservation form (see the example in Figure 91), and then enter the details into the computer. Sometimes a letter of confirmation is requested from the client, confirming the details of date of arrival and number of guests. This will be filed for reference when it is received.

A credit card number is often taken to guarantee bookings, however, as this allows the customer to book by telephone call only. Reservations made by telephone are now common in a hotel. The procedure for dealing with these is very strict so that high standards both of customer care and of administration are maintained.

Study the reservations procedures in Figure 92.

```
┌─────────────────────────────────────────────────────────────────────┐
│                                                      Reservation  ☐   │
│                   **Enquiry/Reservation**            Enquiry      ☐   │
│                                                                       │
│  Arrival Date:_____ No. of nights___ETA:_____RLS:_____ │
│                                                                       │
│  Contact _____ Telephone No: _____    │
│                                                                       │
│  Company:_____  │
│                                                                       │
│  Accommodation Required: _____   │
│                                                                       │
│  Rate:_____Persons/Children:_____   │
│                                                                       │
│  Guest Name: _____  │
│                                                                       │
│  Address:_____  │
│                                                                       │
│  _____  │
│                                                                       │
│  _____ Postcode:_____   │
│                                                                       │
│  Account Details:  Cash☐ Cheque☐ Deposit_____Account to Company____ │
│                                                                       │
│                    Credit Card:_____Number:_____   │
│                                                                       │
│                    Expiry Date:_____Cardholder's Name:_____   │
│                                                                       │
│  Special Instructions:_____  │
│                                                                       │
│  Dinner Reservation: _____  │
│                                                                       │
│  Why? (Over 3 rooms)_____ What Else?_____   │
│                                                                       │
│  Who books Meetings/Training in your Company?                         │
│                                                                       │
│  Name:_____ Telephone Number: _____    │
│                                                                       │
│  Taken by: _____ Date: _____                             │
└─────────────────────────────────────────────────────────────────────┘
```

FIGURE 91 A sample reservation form

Finally, when the guest arrives they will complete a registration card like the example given in Figure 93.

Activity

Choose a partner. You are going to do some role play as client and booking clerk. Take a copy of Figures 91 and 92, the reservations procedure and the reservations form.

One person, as the client, should now telephone to make a booking. The other person answers as booking clerk, taking the details in line with the procedure given in Figure 92.

Practise this role play a few times, changing roles when you are ready, until you are both confident with the procedure.

Travel agency reservations

When a client wishes to book a holiday, or travel, the travel agent must first confirm that the holiday or flight they want is available. This is done by means of a computer system which links up with tour operators. The 'Galileo' system is widely used.

In the unlikely event that the agent does not operate a computer system they will have to telephone the tour operator to check availability.

Once availability is confirmed the agent will complete the tour operator's booking form, found in the back of the brochure.

RESERVATIONS		Telephone reservations
Answering the call	You should pause to allow time for the call to connect, and your manner should be: CLEAR PRECISE WITH WARMTH (SMILE) UNHURRIED	Saying, 'Good morning/Good afternoon/Good evening, (your name*)... speaking. When would you like to stay?'
Speed of answering	All calls must be answered immediately, if the response time exceeds 15 seconds or 5 rings the operator must apologise.	Good morning/Good afternoon/Good evening, (your name*)... speaking. When would you like to stay?'
Listen to the callers needs	Ask for and take note of their name and telephone number. This then allows you to use the callers name frequently, during the taking of details.	'Whilst I'm checking the availability, can I take your name and telephone number?' (If you are asked why, then say 'Because I would like to call you by your name.' or similar)
Taking the reservation	The following details must be recorded: – Date of arrival – No. of nights – Number and type of rooms required – Company name – Estimated arrival time and agreed release time – Payment details	Selling points – Refer to the guest often by name – Check the Go-go chart – Check selling strategy for period – Hotel availability – Match package to guest needs – Up sell/Sell High – Quote package before price – Offer alternatives/Referrals
Reason for guest staying	In addition to the basic reservation details, if the guest or the reason the guest is staying is not known, then Reception/Reservations must also find out why they are coming to the area.	Sales Lead – Ask the Five W's Why? Who else? Where else? When is he coming back? What other business?
Close the call	Use the guests name, summarise the booking details, and confirm who is taking the next step i.e. confirm from guest or deposit taken from credit card by hotel.	'Thank you for your booking Mr. ... I look forward to welcoming you to our hotel.'

REMEMBER – The more often you ask the more business you'll discover.

FIGURE 92 The procedure to follow for telephone reservations

NORTHSHIRE HOTEL
Registration Card

Name _____

Address _____

_____

Postcode _____

Tel No. _____

Car Reg No.

Arrival Date

Departure Date

No. of Nights   Room No.

No. of Guests   Room Rate

Dinner   Call   Paper

Company

How will the account be settled?

Cash ☐

Cheque (with bankers card) ☐

Credit Card ☐

Account to Company ☐

Would you like to use our

Express Check Out Service? ☐

Overseas Visitors

Nationality

Passport No.

Issued at

Next Destination

Guest Signature

FIGURE 93 A sample registration card

Activity You work in a travel agent and have just confirmed that a holiday to Barbados is available. Copy and complete the booking form in Figure 94. Details of the booking are as follows.

> Travel agent:
> R M Major, High Street, Melbourn-on-Sea, Zedshire
> ABTA No 82142
> Mr J Sims and Mr H Emerson accompanied by Master L Sims
> (23.07.88)

They will be travelling to Crystal Cove, Barbados, Tour Ref. CCB630, departing on 2nd February next for 13 nights, from Heathrow. They will take half board, and require a superior room. The emergency contact is Mrs R Emerson, business telephone: 01234 5678910.

Once the booking has been made the travel agent must telephone the booking to the tour operator so that the holiday is removed from the availability list. The form is then forwarded to the tour operator. The travel agent also takes the customer's deposit and forwards this to the tour operator. The tour operator will then send a confirmation invoice to the client who must pay within six to eight weeks of departure. They can pay this invoice through the travel agent as well if they so wish.

BOOKING FORM

Send to: Travel Ltd.,
Travel House, Kington, Abshire AZ1 2BC

Member of ABTA No. 1234
ATOL Licence No78
Travel Ltd. is a bonded tour operaor with a
licence granted by the Civil Aviation Authority)

BOOKING REFERENCE							

ADDRESS to which all correspondence and documents wil be sent
or Travel Agents stamp

ABTA No.					YOUR REF	

LEAD BOOKING NAME	HOTEL OR TOUR NAME

TOUR REFERENCE	NUMBER OF NIGHTS	MEAL PLAN	ROOM GRADE

DEPARTURE DATE	DEPARTURE AIRPORT

PLEASE LIST OPTIONAL EXCURSIONS AND TOURS	PLEASE LIST OPTIONAL PRIVATE TRANSFERS

EMERGENCY CONTACT FOR NEXT OF KIN:
IMPORTANT IN CASE OF EMERGENCY
Name _____
☎ Private _____
☎ Business _____

PLEASE SUBMIT ANY SPECIAL REQUESTS IN WRITING TO OUR CLIENT SERVICES DEPARTMENT.

SURNAME (as shown on passport)	INITIALS	MR/MRS/ MISS	INSURANCE (delete if not required)	Tick and give child's date of birth for discount
FIRST ROOM:			YES	
			YES	
			YES	
SECOND ROOM			YES	
			YES	
			YES	

INSURANCE
We strongly recommend that travel insurance with full cancellation cover is taken out. You will automatically be covered by specially arranged insurance (see below for details) unless you delete 'YES' in the space opposite. The appropriate premium should be enclosed with your deposit cheque see 'Remittance' below.

I have read, understand and accept on behalf of all persons listed, the Code of Conduct Important Holiday Information and Insurance details as shown on pages 120 -123. I also accept that all persons listed are themselves responsible for seeing that immigration and health requirements are fulfilled

*Signed	Date

*must be signed by person travelling (18 years plus), not travel agent

REMITTANCE
Please reserve holiday as detailed above, for all passengers listed, on behalf of whom I enclose a cheque for the following:

DEPOSIT ☐ x passengers @ £100 per person = £ _____   **INSURANCE** ☐ x passengers @ £44 per person = £ _____

Total amount enclosed = £ _____

TRAVEL INSURANCE

All persons are automatically covered for insurance unless they indicate otherwise on the booking form.

We summarise below cover under a speciai holiday insurance scheme arranged by Wards Ltd., through IBS Ltd., underwritten by Insurance Company SA, a member of the Association of British Insurers and the Insurance Ombudsman Bureau. A detailed copy of the cover will be forwarded with your confirmation invoice. A specimen pdicy is also available on request shouid you require further information before booking. Children under two years of age at the date of departure are fully covered when travelling with an insured adult.
Premium: £44 for up to 61 days cover. Thereafter a further premium of £12 per person per week will be charged.
SUMMARY OF COVER:
Cancellation
Up To The Holiday Cost (Excess = £50 except loss of deposit £10)

Medical and Repatriation Expenses
Up to £2,000,000 (Excess = £50)
Hospital Benefit/Miscellaneous Expenses
Up to £900 (Excess = NIL)
Curtailment
Up To The Holiday Cost (Excess = £50)
Personal Accident
Up to £10,000 (Excess = NIL)
Personal Baggage
Up to £1,000 (Excess = £25)
Personal Money
Up to £200 (Excess = £25)
Personal Liability
Up to £1,000,000 (Excess = NIL)
Departure Delay
Up to £150 (Excess = NIL)
Missed Departure
Up to £500 (Excess = NIL)

24-HOUR MEDICAL EMERGENCY COVER
Emergency assistance service with Europ Assistance.
SCUBA DIVING
Applicabie when diving with a qualified and approved instructor.
MAIN EXCLUSIONS
(a) Excesses on claims as detailed above.
(b) Holidays booked against medical advice or for the purpose of obtaining treatment.
(c) Loss or damage not reported within 24 hours of discovery.
CLAIMS
Claims must be made in writing within one month of the event to Claims Ltd.
ADDITIONAL COVER
If you wish to increase any of the benefits provided please contact Wards Ltd.

FIGURE 94 A sample booking form

Special bookings

Hotels do not only take bookings for rooms, they also book for conference facilities, weddings, parties and so on. Larger hotels have a specialist conference manager to deal with the facilities, booking and organisation required by these events.

An enquiry form is often used for such bookings. The form is designed to ensure that all the correct details are taken.

 Activity

You work in a large hotel reception. You have received a booking for a training day from a local company. Copy and complete the enquiry/booking form in Figure 95. Details of the booking are as follows.

A training day is to be held for Dyson Electronics of Newhaven, Oxfordshire, telephone 01523 58143. It has been planned by Ms M Ridgeon who will be running the programme. She will have 20 delegates, who will require dinner, bed and breakfast for one night, plus a buffet lunch. They need one large room for the training session with video playback and flipchart facilities. You have quoted a rate of £120 per person for accommodation and food, plus £950 for the conference room. The date of the conference is 12th August next. Guests will arrive for dinner on 11th August.

Payments

Payments may be made in various ways.

- Cash   Change is given and a receipt issued.
- Cheque   This should be supported by a cheque guarantee card which will be for £50 or £100. Details on the cheque should be carefully checked, and the clerk should write the card number on the back. If the amount is for more than £100 it can still be taken but there is no guarantee of payment.
- Credit or debit card   The card should be swiped. The voucher will be given to the customer to sign and they will retain a copy. The money will then be debited from their bank account or, in the case of a credit card, added to their credit card account for future payment.
- Traveller's cheques   Hotels and travel agents will usually accept traveller's cheques or foreign currency for payment as they have facilities for currency exchange.

In all cases a receipt must be given.

ENQUIRY FORM		BOOKING REF 1047 / 1203	
ORGANISATION		EVENT DATE/TIMES	
CONTACT		NUMBERS	
POSITION		TYPE OF EVENT	
		AGENT	
ADDRESS		ADDRESS	
		TEL NO. COMMISSION %	
		FAX NO.	
POSTCODE		RATES QUOTED	
TELEPHONE NUMBER			
MOBILE/CAR			
FAX NO.			
CONTACT ON DAY			
EVENT NAME		VALUE OF BOOKING	SOURCE
		ESTIMATED ACTUAL	
ACCOMMODATION – DATE, TYPE, NUMBERS			
MEETING REQUIREMENTS – MAIN ROOM, LAYOUTS, SYNDICATES, AV AIDS			
PROGRAMME TIMINGS – INCLUDING FOOD & BEVERAGE		ACCOUNT/CREDIT	

		F/U DATE	F/U DATE
		F/U DATE	F/U DATE
		F/U DATE	F/U DATE
		F/U DATE	F/U DATE
INFORMATION REQUESTED	SENT	F/U DATE	F/U DATE
	CONFIRMED	REGRETTED	INVITE TO VIEW
	CONTRACT SENT	UNWANTED	VISIT DATE
PROVISIONAL MADE	CONTRACT DUE	REFERRED TO	VISIT DIARY
DIARY ENTRY	CONTRACT RETURNED		NAT SALES

CONF REF: .... ACCOM REF: .... DATE OF ENQUIRY: .... TAKEN BY: ....

REF EF/94/1

FIGURE 95 A sample enquiry form

Payments must be recorded as they are taken. Normally this is done automatically on the till roll, and the transaction may be recorded on a computer or manual system as well. Figure 96 shows an example of the simplest manual system of recording payments used by a hotel.

INITS	DATE FROM	RECEIVED No.	ROOM No.	RECEIPT	AMOUNT
GD	26/2/96	MR Z.W. BAKER	92	2430	56 94
GD	26/2/96	MISS E FINN	67	2431	106.32
SP	27/2/96	MR A DALE	31	2436	71.35

FIGURE 96 A manual system of recording payments

All payments, particularly cash, must be securely kept. Any organisation that requires you to take money will have a safe and the money will be regularly removed and taken to the bank. Where a lot of cash is involved, a firm such as Securicor will be employed to collect the money.

Other administrative procedures

In any organisation, large or small, there will be systems for producing staff rotas, procedures for staff recruitment and forms for keeping staff records. Where there is a personnel department confidential staff records will be kept there.

Accountants are often employed to list and total payments once they have been received and to arrange payment for goods and services bought by the organisation. Formal accounts will be kept of all these payments.

Assignment activity Unit 7

You should keep all your assignment activity work, clearly labelled, in your Portfolio of Evidence. This work provides evidence of coverage of all the elements and performance criteria covered in Unit 7.

1 In small groups, you are going to find out about the administration systems used by a leisure or tourism facility. Choose one for each group from your local area.

   a Contact the administration manager of the facility chosen for your group. Arrange a meeting, explaining who you are and what you are doing. Before the meeting, prepare a list of questions to ensure that you find out:

- the purpose of the administration procedures;
- the kinds of administration systems in place;
- how bookings are made;
- how payments are received.

b Now assume that a new manager has been appointed to the facility. Write a report explaining the systems to her and present it, wordprocessed if possible, as a booklet with a table of contents. Put any examples of forms or documents in appendices.

2 Riverside premises have just become available in Marshtown. Josephine Hunter has recently been made redundant from her job as assistant leisure centre manager in the town, due to reorganisation. With her savings and a bank loan she has leased the premises and had them refurbished as follows.

Top floor   – bar with terrace overlooking the river
             – small dance area
             – kitchen suitable for preparation of light meals and snacks

Ground floor – fitness suite with cardiovascular and weights equipment
             – men's and women's showers
             – exercise studio

Basement   storeroom

In order to secure her bank loan, Josephine must write a report for the bank manager explaining the following.

- The objectives of the facility.
- The resources that will be needed – human, physical and financial. (Try to estimate the costs of staff and equipment.)
- How these resources will be used.
- How scheduling will help achieve the company objectives (attach your planned schedule as an appendix).
- How she will review the effectiveness of the operation.

Write the report on Josephine's behalf.

3 You must now find out about the security procedures used at your workplace or college.

a As a member of the organisation, you will be aware of many procedures and you can ask about others. You should make notes on all the following areas in which security and safety must be taken into account:

- people entering the building;
- students and/or workers;
- visitors;
- car park;
- night time;
- staff room;
- class or work room;
- property;
- information (e.g. student files and grades, confidential reports, health and safety hazards).

b Once you have made your notes write a report for the attention of the health and safety officer. Present it, wordprocessed if possible, as a booklet with a table of contents.

Your report should cover all your findings, including any breaches of security of safety that you have noted. You should conclude your report by making recommendations for any improvements in procedures that you feel are necessary.

Unit 8 The Environmental Impact of Leisure and Tourism in the UK

Introduction to the unit This unit comprises the following elements required by the course and gives you practice in all the performance criteria that prove your understanding of each of these elements.

Element 8.1   Explore the environmental impact of leisure and tourism facilities and activities

Element 8.2   Investigate environmental initiatives in leisure and tourism

Element 8.1 Explore the Environmental Impact of Leisure and Tourism Facilities and Activities

About this element

This element looks at the environmental impact of leisure and tourism facilities and activities. By the end of this element you should be able to:

1 explain the impact of the development of leisure and tourism facilities on the natural environment (performance criterion 8.1.1);
2 describe the types of leisure and tourism activities which use the natural environment (performance criterion 8.1.1);
3 assess the impact of leisure and tourism activities on the natural environment (performance criterion 8.1.1);
4 identify the actions taken in a locality to control the negatives impacts of leisure and tourism facilities and activities on the natural environment (performance criterion 8.1.1).

There is no doubt that we are becoming more aware of our environment and the effect we have on it than ever before. We now expect to use goods and energy at a rate that cannot be sustained if we do not maintain the sources of materials needed for production.

In our domestic lives, we have learnt to recycle our newspapers, bottles and cans. We sometimes remember to choose 'environmentally sound' products – that is, products where manufacture and use does not harm or deplete natural resources. Our government is interested in 'sustainable development' – that is, trying to minimise pollution and use of resources whilst still maintaining production and meeting human needs.

Public concern for the environment has placed increasing pressure on companies to operate in an environmentally responsible manner (becoming 'greener') and some now try to identify environmental effects caused by their company products or processes before they become problems. Wherever possible these companies look for non-polluting technology and practical, energy-efficient methods of recycling materials like plastics.

The leisure and tourism industry is no exception to this green revolution. It is one of the world's largest industries, so its continued development must go hand in hand with principles that protect the environment and minimise use of resources.

What is environmental impact?

General examples of environmental impact include;

- on the sea – pollution from oil;
- in rivers – pollution from dumped chemicals;
- on land – erosion of footpaths from too many walkers;
- in the air – pollution from traffic fumes.

These examples list only the negative effects of our activities on the natural environment. However, environmental impact can be positive, and is not confined to the natural world. Look at the list of the ways in which the leisure and tourism industry create environmental impact and you will see that alterations to human societies are included:

- an increase in crime in holiday resorts as residents perceive tourists as wealthy targets;
- pubs and clubs creating noise in residential areas;
- hotel workers learning new languages to serve foreign guests;
- English pubs appearing on the Mediterranean coast rather than traditional cafés;
- a new leisure centre providing local employment;
- a local café benefiting from an increase in foreign tourists.

The increase in crime as a result of tourism in some destinations is an example of environmental impact on society. Sometimes this crime is committed by the tourists themselves – riotous behaviour and assaults on local property or people, for instance. In other places local crime is increased, particularly where large sections of the resident population are very poor and see no benefit from tourism. As there is no social contact between local people in this position and the tourists, the visitors are often viewed as idle rich and a legitimate target for robbery.

Miami in Florida has received detrimental publicity as a tourist destination as a result of recent crime waves and therefore steps have been taken by the authorities to help protect tourists and with them Miami's economy. A scheme call TRAP, the tourist robbery abatement programme, has been established. It puts more police on the highways looking for tourists who are lost or in trouble. Hire cars can no longer be identified by their number plates and visitors are issued with lists of self-protection tips.

Sustainable development

It is important to remember that the impact of the industries on the human and natural world can be both positive and negative. A new hotel may bring many new jobs to a resort but it may also bring pollution problems to an undeveloped coastline and spoil its beauty.

Look again at the examples of the impact of leisure and tourism given above. It is often difficult to state which are wholly positive and which wholly negative. The creation of a balance between the positive and negative effects human activities have upon the environment is a challenge that industries of every kind now have to face. The achievement of this balance is called sustainable development.

Activity

1   Find examples of the impact of leisure and tourism in your locality; try to find positive and negative examples of each category. Make notes on your research.

2   Now make a chart following the headings given below and complete it with your information.

Leisure or tourism activity	Positive effect	Negative effect

3   Do you think that the positive impact outweighs the negative impact in each case?

The economic impact of leisure and tourism

Direct and indirect employment

Coral reef, in many parts of the world, is under threat as large numbers of tourists swim to it, stand on it and damage it. They also buy it as jewellery causing reefs to be plundered for business. Litter spoils beaches and the natural richness of the marine environment is threatened. Yet these same tourists bring jobs to the people who live around coral reefs, giving their lives greater stability and widening their horizons.

You can see this happening in different forms all over the world. Tourists often have a destructive impact on the very environment that attracted them but they bring a precious benefit to local people – more jobs.

You can see this happening in the UK. Look at the statistics given in Figure 97.

Jobs created by leisure and tourism can be direct, which means jobs actually within the industries or indirect, which means jobs created by the resulting increase in business opportunities.

	June 1988	June 1993	Proportion of total	June 1988/ June 1993
	'000	'000	%	% change
Hotels and other tourist accommodation	281.2	306.0	20	+9
Restaurants, cafés etc.	265.1	298.4	20	+13
Public houses and bars	289.3	322.7	22	+12
Night clubs and licensed clubs	140.5	136.8	9	−3
Libraries, museums, art galleries, sports and other recreational services	373.5	407.3	28	+9
Total	1,349.7	1,471.2	100	+9

FIGURE 97 Employment in tourism-related industries June 1988–June 1993

Note: Figures exclude Northern Ireland. Figures are rounded, so that component figures may not add up to totals.
Source: Employment Department, © 1994 English Tourist Board

Just a few examples of direct jobs created in a new hotel are:

- manager;
- chef;
- receptionist;
- chambermaid;
- waiter;
- cleaner;
- maintenance.

These people are directly employed in tourism.

A few examples of indirect jobs created by a new hotel are:

- local shopkeepers, providing goods for guests;
- butchers, greengrocers and grocers;
- toiletry suppliers;
- milkmen;
- entertainers who perform in the hotel.

These people are indirectly employed in tourism.

Activity   Imagine that a new leisure centre is opening in your town. Consider what kind of jobs will be created. Make a list of these jobs under the heading 'Direct Employment'.

Now consider other businesses, local or national, which might benefit from the building of the new centre. Make a list of these jobs under the heading 'Indirect Employment'.

The balance of payments

All industries, and that includes the leisure and tourism industry, contribute to their country's balance of payments. Balance of payments is the term given to describe the difference in value between a country's imports and its exports. Exports, broadly, are what we sell abroad; imports are the goods that we buy from other countries.

When a country exports more than it imports it is in effect making more money than it is spending in its business dealings with other countries. It is then said to have a 'surplus' balance of payments and the economy is considered to be in a healthy state. However, when a country imports more than it exports (spends more than it earns abroad) it is then said to have a 'deficit' in its balance of payments.

Examples of goods that we export from the UK are textiles, arms and ships. Examples of goods that we import to the UK are coffee, electronic components and cars. We also, of course, 'export' tourists to spend their money abroad. To balance this outflow of money we hope to attract tourists from other countries here and also to persuade as many UK people as possible to spend their money holidaying at home.

The travel balance

If we look at tourism in particular it is possible to measure what the country earns from tourism and balance that against what a country's residents spend by travelling abroad. The difference between these two figures is known as the 'travel balance'. A healthy travel balance will help boost the balance of payments.

Tourism is an invisible export – that is, it is not goods which are physically sent abroad in exchange for cash. Rather it is a service which visitors come here and buy, bringing in valuable income to the country.

Take the example of Mary and Sam Jones, who go to Spain for their holidays. They travel with Iberia, a Spanish airline. They stay in a villa and pay the villa owner in pesetas. They change some of their own money into pesetas to spend whilst they are here. All the money they spend is money lost to the UK economy and flows into the Spanish economy. This money detracts from the UK travel balance but is good for the Spanish economy.

Sandrine and Pierre Gautier come from France to England for their holidays. They travel by P & O ferry with their car. Here, they stay in hotels, eat in restaurants and buy souvenirs in shops. The money they spend contributes to the UK economy.

Currently, UK residents spend more abroad than foreign tourists spend here, resulting in a deficit in our travel balance. There are two ways this can be rectified. Firstly, more foreign tourists can be encouraged to come to the UK. The opening of the Channel Tunnel will help with this aim. The British Tourist Authority is the body whose role it is to promote UK tourism overseas. Secondly, people from the UK can be encouraged to spend their holidays here, thus keeping their money within the economy. To achieve this second aim major investment is required: many of our resorts must be made more attractive and welcoming while hotels need to be more competitively priced. Unfortunately, nothing can be done about the weather!

 Activity   Carefully read the newspaper article given in Figure 98 below. Now answer the following questions.

1 What factors have contributed to the increase in deficit in our travel balance of payments?

2 Why do you think UK holiday makers choose to go abroad rather than holiday here?

3 The USA earns more than $53 billion a year from tourism. What are the attractions of that country for the tourist?

4 What are tourism receipts? Why are they expressed in dollars?

The UK Fights to Regain International Tourists

The British Tourist Authority (BTA) has just revealed a £3.1 billion deficit for the tourism industry for 1993. Britain's share of the international tourist market had slumped from 6% in 1987 to 4.3% by 1993.

The deficit means that more money is spent by UK travellers overseas than by visitors spending in Britain. Only 45% of British holidaymakers choose to stay in Britain. The BTA also says that the industry needs to start a new offensive to promote itself overseas; government funding to the BTA was cut by 35% in three years so it has less funds for promotion.

Although Britain earns $14 billion in international tourism receipts, this is way behind France with $25 billion and the United States with $53.9 billion.

The BTA intends to lead the tourist industry in attracting visitors from abroad so that Britain may regain its international position

FIGURE 98 Stopping the decline in UK holiday income

The multiplier effect

When the Gautiers spend money in the UK they are bringing income to businesses like shopkeepers, or hotel owners. These people in turn spend their income on goods and services locally, generating income for other people in the region.

Example: Sandrine's £200

Sandrine Gautier spends £200 on clothes in a local woollens shop.

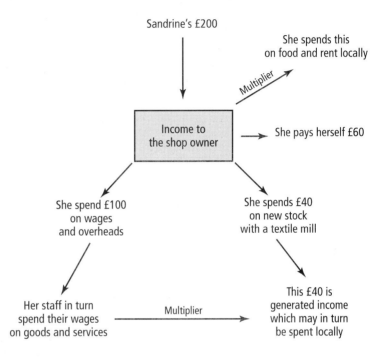

FIGURE 99 The multiplier effect

As tourists we can help to make this effect happen by buying local goods and eating in local restaurants when we are on holiday, thus ensuring that we benefit the economy. It is possible, however, to spend a great deal of money on holiday without bringing much economic benefit to the local community at all. This happens when the money spent flows out of the local economy without buying local goods and services and is known as 'leakage'. Leakage can occur in a number of ways.

Let's go back to the Gautiers and see how leakage might occur if they went about arranging their holiday in a different way.

This time they book their transport to the UK with Air France, a French airline – money flows back into the French economy.

They choose to stay in a hotel which is owned by a company from the USA – money flows from the UK economy to that of the USA.

Their souvenirs are manufactured in and imported from Japan, even though they depict the UK. Even the money they spent in the wool shop can leak away if the stock is imported and if the staff choose to send their wages to family abroad.

You can see in this example how unwittingly the Gautiers fail to benefit our economy.

The worst cases of leakage happen in resorts where tourism is dominated by all-inclusive hotel complexes. These are popular in Jamaica and some other Caribbean islands. Customers buy their holiday from a tour operator to include transport, accommodation and all meals, snacks, drinks and entertainment. As everything the tourist could possibly want is to be found within the hotel complex there is no need for the tourist to go out and explore the local area, and in fact they are often discouraged from doing so. The hotel will gain revenue from this kind of tourism but if the hotel is foreign-owned then once again leakage will occur. Even if the hotel is owned by nationals, local people often come to resent the apparently wealthy tourists who holiday in their resort but do not spend money in restaurants or in shops.

Element 8.2 Investigate Environmental Initiatives in Leisure and Tourism

About this element This element looks at environmental initiatives in leisure and tourism. By the end of this element you should be able to:

1 describe and give examples of environmental initiatives undertaken by private sector organisations in leisure and tourism (performance criterion 8.2.1);
2 describe and give examples of environmental initiatives undertaken by public sector organisations in leisure and tourism (performance criterion 8.2.2);
3 describe and give examples of environmental initiatives undertaken by voluntary sector organisations in leisure and tourism (performance criterion 8.2.3);
4 describe sources of funds for environmental initiatives (performance criterion 8.2.4);
5 assess environmental initiatives undertaken by leisure and tourism organisations in a locality (performance criterion 8.2.5).

Private sector initiatives to protect the environment

Sustainable tourism

You will find many examples of leisure and tourism activities in your area which affect the environment.

Consider the following situation.

It is a warm Sunday in June. Friends and families are glad to see the sun and looking forward to spending a day out.

There are many things they may choose to do.

One family decides to visit a local stately home. They are likely to travel by car, which will add to pollution as we have seen, and there may be congestion on the roads as traffic builds up in the locality of the stately home. Too many visitors to the site cause wear and tear to the fabric of the building and furnishings. However, the visitors will be learning about their heritage and helping to preserve it through their financial contribution and their interest.

A group of friends chooses to go jet skiing on a nearby lake. They have a wonderful time and create employment for the people who hire and maintain the equipment, but there is considerable noise and pollution from the jet skis which disrupts the peace of the local park.

Another group of friends decides to go motor cross riding in the countryside. Again this is great fun but churns up areas of ground, destroying wild plants, frightening wildlife and possibly endangering walkers.

Once again, you can see from these examples that it is difficult to balance the positive and negative impacts of leisure and tourism activities.

Green Flag and Eurocamp
We have already discussed the term 'sustainable development' on pages 219 and 221. When this concept is extended to the tourism industry, it is known as 'sustainable tourism'. Companies who practise this acknowledge that tourism can damage the environment and are consciously taking measures to protect the environment whilst still promoting tourism. A private sector organisation was founded in 1990 in the UK to help organisations practise sustainable tourism. This is Green Flag International, whose job is to advise the UK leisure and tourism industry on integrating environmental issues into business planning. Green Flag is paid for by the organisations who commission their research or otherwise use their services.

One organisation which has been assisted by Green Flag is Eurocamp, a well known camping holiday specialist. Eurocamp is committed to the protection of the natural environment, and has therefore worked in partnership with Green Flag International to consider how they can best achieve this as part of the day-to-day running of their business. Green Flag carried out an environmental audit of Eurocamp's business and as a result Eurocamp set several targets covering all aspects of their business. These included:

- recycling tents;
- using environmentally-friendly cleaning products on site;
- using farmed timber for brochures;
- recycling waste paper;
- environmental suggestion awards for staff;
- 'green issues' training for staff;
- sponsorship of local council's recycling directory.

There will be further stages of the campaign designed to involve those not directly employed by the company, such as suppliers and campsite operators.

Eurocamp is proud of its efforts in sustainable tourism (also called green tourism) and promotes these policies, through brochures and other activities, as evidence of its responsible, caring attitude.

GREEN FLAG INTERNATIONAL is the symbol of conservation working in partnership with the tourism industry to make improvements to the environment worldwide

FIGURE 100 Green Flag logo and objective statement

Other sustainable tourism initiatives

Other UK companies are also taking steps to practise sustainable tourism. British Airways has senior managers to develop in-house environmental policies, and the tour operator Kuoni includes suggestions in its brochures to help tourists 'protect the natural beauty, culture and wildlife of the destinations visited'.

Activity

Read the extract from Kuoni's brochure given in Figure 101 and then answer the following questions.

1 How do Kuoni's policies and projects contribute to sustainable tourism?

2 Choose examples and state whether you think these policies will have a long term impact.

Public sector initiatives to protect the environment

Traffic pollution

The main form of travel in the UK is by car. The volume of motor traffic grew by 44 per cent in the decade 1982 to 1992 and there are now over 20 million vehicles on our roads.

Fumes

Car exhaust fumes contain lead and where lead levels in the air are high breathing it is a danger to health. Drivers are now encouraged to use unleaded petrol; it is on sale at a lower price than leaded petrol as a result of a government decision to place lower tax duty on it.

Car and lorry exhaust fumes also produce carbon monoxide, hydrocarbons and nitrogen dioxides. The latter have been linked with asthma: in December 1991, during a week of

CARING FOR OUR WORLD
HOW WE CAN ALL HELP

FEATURED IN THIS BROCHURE ARE SOME OF THE MOST BEAUTIFUL COUNTRIES IN THE WORLD. AT KUONI, WE BELIEVE TOURISM SHOULD WORK POSITIVELY TOWARDS PROTECTING THE NATURAL BEAUTY, CULTURE AND WILDLIFE OF THE DESTINATIONS WE VISIT SO THAT FUTURE GENERATIONS OF VISITORS AND RESIDENTS ALIKE CAN CONTINUE TO ENJOY THEM. WE WOULD LIKE TO MAKE THE FOLLOWING SUGGESTIONS:

Caring for People

- Support the local economy wherever possible by buying local produce and services.
- Respect the traditions and culture of the local people, particularly when taking photographs.
- Many countries are actively starting projects to protect their heritage and environment eg the Cayman Islands National Trust and the Barbados Environmental Association. Support their efforts by visiting museums, buildings, historic houses etc.

In addition, we are pleased to support an exciting project in Sri Lanka:

Sri Lanka is a beautiful country, a land of golden tropical beaches, spectacular hill country scenery, tea plantations, temples and, most memorable of all, a welcoming, friendly people.

But the infrastructure of the country is underdeveloped, and as a result facilities, particularly for the children of Sri Lanka, are inadequate.

In conjuction with the UK registered charity, PLAN International UK, Kuoni supports the following projects in Sri Lanka. A donation of £2 on behalf of every passenger travelling with us to Sri Lanka will be our 1995 contribution to PLAN International's work in Kandy and Badulla. This enables us to support the following:

- Clinic construction project – the aim of this project is to bring health facilities into the rural communities around Kandy, in the heart of the island's hill country. In 1995, we hope to be able to build 6 clinics in the area which will improve the health standards of some 5,000 children and their families.

- School construction project – the aim of this project is to provide better educational facilities for children by building new schools and undertaking repairs on existing schools in the villages of Badulla District, some 20 miles east of Nuwara Eliya in central Sri Lanka. In 1995, we hope to be able to build 6 schools in the area which will benefit some 1,200 children.

Kuoni customers will be welcome to visit the projects in Kandy and Badulla, by arrangement with PLAN.

Should you wish to make an additional contribution to PLAN International (you may sponsor a child in any one of 30 developing countries in Africa, Asia, Latin America and the Caribbean from only £12 a month), more information is available from:

**PLAN International UK
5-6 Underhill Street
London NW1 7HS
Telephone: 071 485 6612
Registered Charity No: 276035
(Patron: HRH The Duchess of Gloucester)**

. . . Thank you for your help in supporting Sri Lanka's children.

Children of Sri Lanka

Kuoni's support for Friends of Conservation, Kenya

Precious marine life in the Maldives

Caring for the Environment

- Coral reefs are fragile living environments on which a number of marine species depend. Do not stand on them as they can be easily damaged, or collect corals (or shells) as in many countries this is illegal.

- Take your litter home – especially cans, bottles and plastics (sun tan lotion bottles, film cannisters etc). Leaving your litter where you dropped it is both unsightly and a danger to wildlife.

- On safari or in forests and jungles, keep to established roads and tracks to avoid damaging vegetation unnecessarily. When conditions are dry, beware of starting fires with discarded cigarettes.

- Support local efforts to protect and improve their environment by visiting marine parks, nature reserves, etc.

- "Take only photographs; leave only footprints".

Caring for Wildlife

- Never buy products made from ivory, spotted cat furs or sea turtle shell – international trade in all of these products is prohibited.
- Respect the habitat and natural behaviour of wildlife when you are in their environment.
- Support local wildlife conservation projects by visiting turtle farms, elephant orphanages, orang utan sanctuaries, etc.

In addition, we are pleased to continue our close co-operation in Kenya with:

Kenya is home to some of the most spectacular game parks in the world – it is here that many of our client's experience the thrill of seeing at first hand, wildlife roaming free.

But if the parks and the wildlife they support are to survive, the Kenya Wildlife Service needs help. The Game Parks and Reserves of Kenya are under intensive pressure from a rapidly increasing human population and unless they can be proven to be worth saving, they will be forced to yield to this pressure. We believe that tourism can help stop this disaster from happening.

In conjunction with the registered UK charity Friends of Conservation, Kuoni supports the joint projects of Friends of Conservation and the Kenya Wildlife Service, under the personal management of Dr. David Western.
A donation of £2 on behalf of every passenger travelling on safari with us to Kenya will be our 1995 contribution to the Kenya Wildlife Service. This enables us to support the following:

- Wildlife Protection Unit: Tasks include anti-poaching activities, rescuing injured animals, monitoring of tourist vehicles relative to animal harrassment and care of wildlife.

- Rhino Translocation and Wildlife Veterinarian Programme: support for veterinary expertise and the translocation of endangered rhinos into protected sanctuaries.

- Community Conservation and Educational Projects: support for local conservation groups and the production of educational material for use in schools.

Should you wish to make an additional contribution to the Kenya Wildlife Service, more information is available from:

**Friends of Conservation
Sloane Square House
Holbein Place
London SW1W 8NS
Telephone: 071 730 7904
Registered Charity No: 328176
(Patron: HRH The Prince of Wales)**

. . . Thank you for your help in supporting Kenya's Wildlife.

11

FIGURE 101 Extract from Kuoni's brochure

severe smog caused by high levels of nitrogen dioxide and other air pollutants from traffic fumes, there was a 22 per cent rise in those dying from asthma and severe lung disease. The Department of the Environment asked people not to use cars during this period to try and reduce the smog. Ironically, many asthma sufferers prefer to travel by car when pollution is high in order to avoid the polluted air.

Acid rain
You may have heard of acid rain. This forms when air pollutants combine with water vapour to form nitric and sulphuric acids. Acid rain is harmful to both animal and plant life. Some of the nitrogen oxides which contribute to acid rain come from traffic exhausts.

Clearly it is important to make cars cleaner and more efficient, but it is also necessary to have in place measures which reduce the use of cars, both in day-to-day life and in tourism.

What can be done?
First, the public can be encouraged to use public transport but they will only do so where service is regular and reasonably priced. For instance in Manchester an enormous investment has been made in the Metrolink tram system but the investment has paid off: public use of the trams has by far exceeded expectations. Secondly, rail fares should be cheaper: UK fares compare unfavourably with those charged in the rest of Europe. Thirdly, local city councils can encourage drivers to stay away from city centres with the use of park and ride schemes or by banning cars from the city centre altogether. These schemes are often popular with the public: in 1994 a Friends of the Earth survey showed that 84 per cent of people in Oxford wanted cars permanently restricted in their congested and fume-ridden city centre.

Changes in transport policy
A report published in 1994 by the Royal Commission on Pollution recommends drastic changes in the government's transport policy. The report says that petrol prices should be increased so as to double the real price of fuel by 2005, that road building should be cut to half the current levels, that there should be stronger protection for wildlife sites from road building and that the government should give bigger subsidies to railways, support tram schemes like the one in Manchester and help local councils create safe cycling routes.

Activity   Study the charts given in Figure 102 on the next page carefully and then answer the following questions.

1   Which countries have the highest and lowest use of public transport? Suggest reasons for why this should be so.

2   How many billion passenger kilometres per year by car were there in 1994? Why is this steep rise in car use alarming?

3   If petrol prices are greatly increased what will be the effect on road freight transport? What other methods might be used?

In some towns, particularly new towns like Milton Keynes, the provision of cycle lanes encourages the public to go by bike rather than by car. Car sharing schemes are also a good idea, although these have had limited success in the UK. Tourists too can be persuaded to use public transport. In Disneyworld in Florida extensive free bus services mean it is easier to travel by bus than by car. In some of our own city centres we have tourist (guide) buses from which to see the sights with an accompanying commentary. This is much easier for tourists than trying to find their way round a strange city in their own cars.

Coastal pollution

It has been estimated that 42 per cent of sewage from coastal towns goes straight into the sea. Even where sewage is treated, methods can be very crude. For example, solids may be screened out by a wire grid before the sewage is dumped in the sea. Chemical treatment may be carried out, but there are doubts about the efficiency of these methods. Coastal sewage pollution is therefore a big problem for the UK tourist industry as tourists only add to the disposal problems. As a result of swimming in polluted water people contract diarrhoea and gastroenteritis. Add to this beaches spoilt by dog droppings, cigarette ends and litter and it is easy to understand why tourists are suspicious of some UK beach holiday resorts.

What can be done?

There are European Union standards which bathing beaches must meet. Almost 80 per cent of UK beaches currently meet these standards, but some say they are not stringent enough. One such pressure group is Surfers Against Sewage, a group in the frontline of the fight against pollution by coastal sewage. European ministers themselves consider the standards too

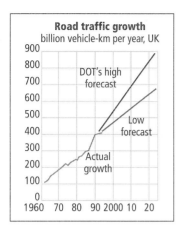

Road traffic growth
billion vehicle-km per year, UK

DOT's high forecast

Low forecast

Actual growth

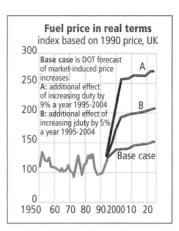

Fuel price in real terms
index based on 1990 price, UK

Base case is DOT forecast of market-induced price increases
A: additional effect of increasing duty by 9% a year 1995-2004
B: additional effect of increasing duty by 5% a year 1995-2004

A

B

Base case

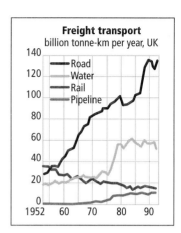

Freight transport
billion tonne-km per year, UK

Road
Water
Rail
Pipeline

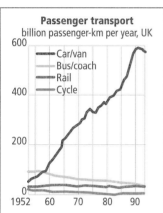

Passenger transport
billion passenger-km per year, UK

Car/van
Bus/coach
Rail
Cycle

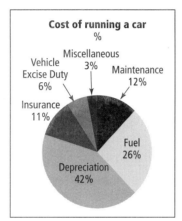

Cost of running a car
%

Miscellaneous 3%

Vehicle Excise Duty 6%

Maintenance 12%

Insurance 11%

Fuel 26%

Depreciation 42%

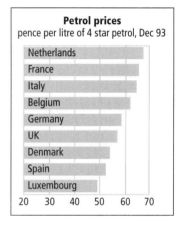

Petrol prices
pence per litre of 4 star petrol, Dec 93

Netherlands
France
Italy
Belgium
Germany
UK
Denmark
Spain
Luxembourg

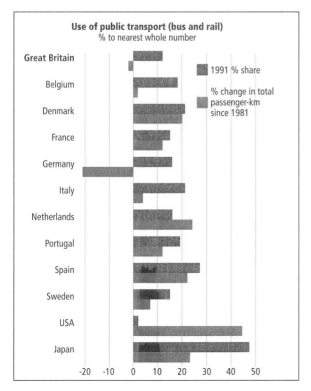

Use of public transport (bus and rail)
% to nearest whole number

Great Britain
Belgium
Denmark
France
Germany
Italy
Netherlands
Portugal
Spain
Sweden
USA
Japan

1991 % share

% change in total passenger-km since 1981

FIGURE 102 Public transport statistics

lax, and propose to tighten them; if this was done, only 50 per cent of UK beaches would meet the tighter standards. It is proposed that sea bathing be banned where discharges of sewage are at unsatisfactorily high levels: beaches at Brighton and Blackpool would be under threat from this proposal.

Full treatment of sewage is possible and Welsh Water have proved this with a full treatment and disinfectant policy for all their coastal discharges. In the future all treatment of sewage should be improved as the UK government strives to meet the European Urban Waste Water Directive: this sets the standards of quality required for the treatment of all significant quantities of sewage destined for discharge.

Rivers

Our rivers, too are subject to legislation. The UK government's Water Resources Act 1991 makes it an offence to discharge any polluting matter into controlled waters. The National Rivers Authority was formed in 1989 to manage water resources, to protect land and property from flooding, to promote recreational activities and to maintain and develop inland fisheries.

Countryside

Our government recognises that the countryside is of recreational value to those living and working in towns besides being important economically to those who live in rural areas.

There are 120,000 miles of rights of way in England to give access to the countryside. The most famous walker's path is the Pennine Way in the Peak District.

Although it is desirable to attract tourists and leisure walkers to the countryside, their presence can cause problems for local people. Visitors may leave gates open, allowing animals to stray, dogs may worry sheep or other animals and thoughtless walkers can spoil crops.

Many people enjoy bird watching and studying plant life, but large numbers doing so disturb natural habitats. Walkers may pick flowers and plants without realising that some are very rare and as such they are protected. Some visitors to the countryside leave the debris from their picnics behind, or light fires which get out of control. Footpaths are becoming eroded in popular areas like the Lake District because of the sheer number of walkers following them.

What can be done?

A number of measures are in place to help conserve the countryside for the enjoyment of visitors and to protect the plant and animal life that we go to enjoy.

Firstly, there are many organisations set up to protect the countryside.

The Countryside Commission

The Countryside Commission is one; its objective is 'to conserve and enhance the beauty of the English countryside and to help people enjoy it'. The Countryside Commission publishes a number of leaflets to this end. An example is 'Out in the Country', which gives advice on what can and cannot be done in the country. An extract is given in Figure 103.

The Nature Conservancy Council

The Nature Conservancy Councils are national bodies, that is English Nature, the Countryside Council for Wales and the Nature Conservancy Council for Scotland. They liaise with local authorities. The Wildlife and Countryside Act 1981 gives Nature Conservancy Councils the duty to identify important wildlife and geographical areas. These are known as Sites of Special Scientific Interest (SSSIs). The Act also protects a large number of threatened species; 92 species of plant and 529 birds and animals are given special protection which means there are heavy fines for actions or behaviour which threaten their survival.

National nature reserves

In the UK we have over 240 National nature reserves, and two newly established marine nature reserves at Lundy Island in the Bristol Channel and at Skomer in South Wales. These areas are designated under the same wildlife legislation as the SSSIs and allow for conservation of the natural habitat. Local authorities also have the power to declare local nature reserves and there are now also over 240 of these.

National Parks

About 9 per cent of the total area of England and Wales is an area of National Park. National Park Authorities run these areas, looking after the many visitors to the park and ensuring the interests of conservation. In Scotland, National Heritage areas are similarly protected. The government has also declared 39 Areas of Outstanding National Beauty (AONBs). These areas are protected from unsuitable development by particularly strict planning controls.

PRINCIPLES FOR TOURISM IN THE COUNTRYSIDE

The Countryside Commission, English Tourist Board and Rural Development Commission recognise that:

Tourism in the countryside is a desirable activity of economic benefit to the nation and local communities, and of personal benefit to the individual.

The quality both of the environment and of the tourist experience can be threatened by excessive and insensitive tourism development and activity.

The Countryside Commission, English Tourist Board and the Rural Development Commission believe that tourism in the countryside should be guided by the following principles:

Enjoyment

The promotion of the tourists' enjoyment of the countryside should be primarily aimed at those activities which draw on the character of the countryside itself, its beauty, culture, history and wildlife.

Development

Tourism development in the countryside should assist the purposes of conservation and recreation. It can, for example, bring new uses to historic buildings, supplement usage and incomes to farms, aid the reclamation of derelict land and open up new opportunities for access to the countryside.

Design

The planning, design, siting and management of new tourism developments should be in keeping with the landscape and wherever possible should seek to enhance it.

Rural economy

Investment in tourism should support the rural economy, but should seek a wider geographical spread and more off peak visiting both to avoid congestion and damage to the resource through erosion and over use, and to spread the economic and other benefits.

Conservation

Those who benefit from tourism in the countryside should contribute to the conservation and enhancement of its most valuable asset - the countryside, through political and practical support for conservation and recreation policies and programmes.

Marketing

Publicity, information and marketing initiatives of the tourism industry should endeavour to deepen people's understanding of and concern for the countryside leading to fuller appreciation and enjoyment.

English Tourist Board

RURAL DEVELOPMENT COMMISSION

COUNTRYSIDE COMMISSION

FIGURE 103 Principles for sustainable tourism in the UK countryside

Charities and voluntary bodies

Charities and voluntary groups play an important part in protecting our countryside.

One very well-known charity which is concerned with the protection of our natural and man-made heritage is the National Trust, now 100 years old.

The National Trust is not a government body, it is an independent charity, although it does claim government grants for some of its work. The bulk of its income comes from membership fees; it has over 2 million members. The Trust is now the country's largest private landowner and nature conservationist, owning more than 250 important buildings and several hundred miles of coastline. Thus it is both one of our most successful leisure and tourist industries and a significant force for the protection of our countryside.

An active voluntary body is the British Trust for Conservation Volunteers. They carry out a number of conservation projects in the UK giving volunteers an opportunity to have a very cheap working holiday. You can examine their work more closely in the next activity.

 Activity

BTCV, the British Trust for Conservation Volunteers, offers holidays with a difference.

A group of volunteers takes a working holiday with food and accommodation included for a very low price. The holiday is spent working on some kind of countryside conservation project, for example, clearing footpaths.

The extract in Figure 104 shows examples of the holidays available. Study these carefully and then answer the following questions.

1 Explain the various symbols and abbreviations appearing in the brochure.

2 List the activities, mentioned in the brochure, which you might pursue when not working.

3 Think of a suitable local project which might be suitable for this kind of holiday scheme. Write a descriptive paragraph suitable for the BCTV brochure. Add symbols as appropriate.

For further reading on the countryside see 'The Countryside' published by the Department of the Environment available from your local library.

Visitor management

Maintaining the balance between attracting tourists and protecting the attractions that they come to see is known as visitor management. A government task force set up in 1990 categorises the measures for visitor management as follows:

Controlling the volume of visitors, either by limiting

numbers to match the capacity, or by encouraging them to come outside peak periods, or to visit an alternative location.

Modifying the behaviour of visitors by channelling them along certain routes, separating them from their cars and encouraging responsible behaviour.

Adapting the resource in some way to enable it to cope with the volume of visitors and sustain less damage.

Source: *Tourism and the environment: maintaining the balance*

July

078 The lost gardens of Heligan, Cornwall
13-20 July

Extending over 1,000 acres, Heligan continues to be the largest restoration project in Europe. Since 1991, painstaking work has recovered many of its hidden treasures such as Victorian glasshouses, rare plant species, walled gardens and a tropical ravine complete with palms and giant tree ferns. Join us for phase three of our 1996 project during which we will continue to clear vegetation out of a valley basin to recover a large lake, thus encouraging the return of unusual wildlife to the area.

Accom	Simple	£43
Pick-up	St. Austell 🚍 & 🚶	6.00pm

079 Stepping through the moors, North Yorkshire
13-20 July

Enjoy a week in the heart of the North York Moors National Park, surrounded by the largest expanse of heather moorland in England which is incised by picturesque valleys of patchwork meadows and woodland. Help improve one of the popular moor routes by constructing a well-drained path and steps which will reduce the likelihood of visitors trampling vegetation and causing erosion. On your day off why not walk on the Moors or visit the historic town of Helmsley with its magnificent castle and tea-shops.

Accom	Simple X	£33
Pick-up	Thirsk 🚶	6.30pm

080 Weaver wanderers, Cheshire
13-20 July

The historic and picturesque River Weaver, running through the Borough of Vale Royal in Cheshire, is the focus of much attention as efforts are made to improve the water ~~quality~~ of the ~~~~ Mersey

635 Canalside fencing, Lancashire
4-11 May

This unusual break will involve protecting an old hedgerow and woodland area by erecting a post and wire fence. Our accommodation for the week is on board the Lancashire Enterprise Canal Boat, which will be moored a short drive from the worksite on the Leeds and Liverpool Canal. On your day off you will be able to take a pleasure cruise along the canal, enjoying the scenic countryside of the Pendle area.

Accom	Standard 🛏 🍴	£55
Pick-up	Blackburn 🚶	6.00pm

636 Portland cream tea special, Dorset
4-11 May

The Isle of Portland is an alluring small island delicately attached to the Dorset Coast by the unusual Chesil Beach. Portland limestone is famous throughout the world as a quality building material. We will be using it to construct a dry stone wall in the traditional Dorset style with the added attraction of another local tradition – a traditional Dorset cream tea on site! On your day off you can enjoy a walk along the Heritage Coast or do some wildlife spotting – the dolphins, seals, and puffins all wait to delight you.

Accom	Simple 🍴	£32
Pick-up	Weymouth 🚶	6.30pm

637 Grizedale Forest, Lake District
11-18 May

Grizedale is a working forest, but is also famous for its sculpture trail and theatre in the forest. Apart

FIGURE 104 Extracts from the BTCV holiday programme

You will find many examples of successful visitor management in your local tourist industries. For example, most castles and large houses in the UK are carefully managed using specially marked routes laid out with signs and rope barriers. Guides give information but are also there to keep a vigilant eye on what is happening; they are authorised to prevent visitors touching and possibly damaging precious items.

**Assignment
activity
Unit 8**

You should keep all your assignment work, clearly labelled, in your Portfolio of Evidence. This work provides evidence of coverage of all the elements and performance criteria covered in Unit 8.

1   You are to research leisure and tourism development and activities in your area and determine their impact on the local environment. You should present your findings in a report suitable for submitting to the leader of your city council.

   a Find out about local leisure and tourism development. General examples are the building of a new tennis court, the provision of a children's playground, the opening of a new hotel or the extension of existing facilities. You will find your own examples by looking through local newspapers.

   b When you have found your examples, write a short piece assessing the environmental impact of these developments on your local area. You may wish to summarise this in the form of a chart as on page 221 with columns for both positive and negative impacts. Attach your chart to the report as an appendix.

   c Using the local newspapers again, find examples of leisure and tourism activities in your area. The weekend newspapers often have 'What's On' sections which are useful for this exercise. Again, write a short piece assessing the impact of these activities on your local area. You can summarise these findings in the form of a chart as before.

   d Choose one of the activities to research in more detail. Go along and either participate in the activity or watch. For example, you might visit a local wildlife centre. Comment on whether your assessment of its impact was correct. Discuss your assessment with a member of staff if possible. Find out what action has been taken to reduce the negative impacts of the impact, for instance reduction in traffic congestion, control of litter.

Now write up your findings as the third part of your report.

2 For this task you must choose one of the following organisations if they operate a conservation initiative in your locality. Otherwise, choose a local organisation (e.g. in London: Friends of Highgate Cemetery, who raise funds, and have volunteers to conserve the old cemetery).

- English Heritage
- Greenpeace
- Friends of the Earth
- Royal Society for the Protection of Birds
- Worldwide Fund for Nature
- British Trust for Conservation Volunteers

a Find out the following information:

- the name and address of the organisation;
- how to join it;
- how much it costs to join.

b Describe in detail:

- the local initiative (e.g. what is happening; who is doing the work; are they paid, or are they volunteers?);
- the aims and objectives of the organisation (e.g. preservation, improvement of facilities, prohibition of trespassers).

c Now provide answers to the following questions:

- What is the role of the community?
- Where do the funds come from?
- How do locals know about the project?
- What is the long term impact on the community?

Present your findings in the form of an article to raise public awareness of the organisation. This must be suitable for publication in your local paper.

Revision Questions

Leisure and tourism facilities

1 Which is an example of a facility in the voluntary sector?
   a a leisure centre
   b a travel agency
   c a gym
   d a youth hostel

2 Leisure and tourism facilities can be put under the following headings.
   a accommodation, catering and hospitality
   b entertainment and education
   c travel and tourism
   d sports and recreation

Under which headings do these facilities fit?
   A An arts centre and a night club
   B A football stadium and a swimming pool
   C A camp-site and a guest house

The economic and environmental impact of the leisure and tourism industry

3 A new leisure centre is to be built in your area. Which is a positive, direct social impact of the new complex?
   a an increase in leisure opportunities for local residents
   b the employment of more local people
   c other centres will lose business
   d the amount of traffic will be increased

4 Pleasure cruisers can have a negative environmental impact on canals and waterways. What is the reason for this?
   a they make waves which wear away the banks
   b they are difficult to steer in a straight line
   c they cost a lot of money to hire
   d their engines are noisy

5 The local council is planning to develop an old quarry into a nature reserve with a small visitor centre. Which is a positive environmental impact?
   a jobs will be created
   b families will be attracted to the nature reserve

c an ugly landscape will be improved

d the visitor centre will be a useful source of information

6 The remains of a Roman villa of great historic interest are to be opened to the public by a private company. Which will be a positive economic impact on the local area?

a extra traffic will cause additional pollution

b tourists will be attracted to the area

c local schools will be able to make educational visits

d the local council will earn money from entry charges

Jobs and job roles in leisure and tourism

7 You work for an airline and your main role is to help customers during their journey. What is your job?

a reservations assistant

b airline pilot

c air traffic controller

d flight attendant

8 What is the job title of a person who takes tourists on a walking tour of a city?

a receptionist

b guide

c coach

d porter

9 You are a lifeguard working in a leisure centre. To which job are you most likely to be promoted?

a recreation assistant

b receptionist

c pool area supervisor

d general manager

Education, training, skills, knowledge and training

10 You work for a travel agency and want to gain an NVQ in Travel Services. What will this involve?

a going to college full-time

b taking GCSEs

c studying and learning while working

d taking a part-time job

Marketing and promoting leisure and tourism products

11 A new theme park is opening this summer. What is the main role that marketing will play?

a giving information to potential customers

b meeting customer needs

c ensuring prices are fixed at the right level

d carrying out research into customer satisfaction

12 A squash club has just increased its membership fees. Which component of the marketing mix is this?
  a price
  b product
  c promotion
  d place

13 A travel agent is giving free balloons and stickers to children who visit the branch with their parents. What type of activity is this?
  a advertising
  b public relations
  c sales promotion
  d personal selling

14 The management of a theme park is carrying out research using information gathered from turnstiles at the entrance. What type of information does this give them?
  a the age of visitors
  b information about other theme parks the customers have visited
  c the number of visitors
  d the level of satisfaction of the visitors

15 Tour operators sell a range of holidays to suit many different market segments. One market segment is young employed singles. Which type of holiday is most likely to be targeted at them?
  a a cruise to Scandinavia
  b a long stay package holiday to Portugal
  c a continental coach tour
  d a two week package to Ibiza

16 As part of a promotional campaign, a theme park advertises in a regional tourist guide. What is the main objective of this advertisement?
  a to improve the image of the theme park
  b to inform regular visitors of their opening hours
  c to be competitive with other theme parks
  d to attract new visitors to the theme park

17 A theatre puts up colour posters around the town announcing the start of its pantomime season. Due to rehearsal problems the start is delayed by a week. What should theatre management do about this?
  a redesign and reprint the posters with the new date
  b put up a notice in the foyer apologising for the delay
  c print stickers with the new date and put them on the posters
  d cancel the pantomime

18 An hotel offers special discount rates for a limited period to increase the number of guests. Which is the best way to measure the success of this promotion?
   a talking to the guests
   b checking the occupancy records
   c count the guests as they check in
   d talking to the staff

Customer service

19 The policy of a tourist office is to give the same customer care training to all its counter staff. What is the main reason for this policy?
   a to make the staff work harder
   b to create a consistent standard of service
   c to avoid complaints
   d to keep staff happy

20 A theatre box office closes every Saturday. What is the most likely effect on customers arriving at this time?
   a customers will come back on Monday
   b customers will turn up for the performance without tickets
   c potential customers will be lost
   d customers will buy tickets on Friday

21 A theatre has questionnaires in the foyer for customers to fill in. What is the reason for this?
   a so that customers can see what is on at the theatre
   b to give customers something to do
   c to find out if customers are satisfied with the service provided
   d to find out who the customers' favourite actors are

22 The management of a leisure centre has trained staff in customer care to both external and internal customers. Internal customers are
   a a group of schoolchildren swimming
   b tourists visiting the facilities
   c staff who do routine maintenance in the centre
   d members of the leisure centre

23 On a winter's afternoon a dry ski slope is very busy. Which of the following customer needs would be given priority as most urgent?
   a the chair lift breaks down with passengers aboard
   b the restaurant has run out of coffee
   c a bus collecting a scouts group has not arrived
   d people are complaining about the queue to use the slope

24 The fire alarm in an hotel is sounded every Tuesday for ten seconds at 11 a.m. What is the main reason for this?
 a to see how long it takes for the fire brigade to arrive
 b to ensure all the guests are up and about
 c to test if the alarm system is working properly
 d to make sure guests know the fire drill

25 Travel agents need to know if they are making a profit or a loss. Which is the most important set of records they need to obtain this information?
 a invoices from tour operators
 b details of enquiries from customers
 c bureau de change receipts
 d records of payments and receipts

26 Badminton racquets are sold for £20 before VAT. What is the cost of a racquet if VAT is 17.5 per cent?
 a £16.50
 b £18.25
 c £21.75
 d £25

Answers to selected questions

1	d	6	b	13	b	20	c
2	A b	7	d	14	c	21	c
	B d	8	b	15	d	22	c
	C a	9	c	16	d	23	a
3	a	10	c	17	c	24	c
4	a	11	a	18	b	25	d
5	c	12	a	19	b	26	d

Answers for the activity on page 149, Figure 59.

Declining	Increasing	Stable/little change
Snooker	Walking	Swimming
Darts	Keep fit/Yoga	Horse riding
Golf	Cycling	Cricket
Running	Weight-lifting	
Soccer	Ten-pin bowls	
Tennis		
Fishing		
Bowls		
Squash		
Table tennis		

Useful Addresses

To help with your research, here are some useful addresses and telephone and fax numbers.

Amateur Swimming Association. Tel. 01509 230431; fax 01509 610720.

Association of British Travel Agents (ABTA), National Training Board, 11 Chertsey Road, Woking GU21 5AL. Tel. 01483 727321; fax 01483 756698.

Association of Independent Museums, PO Box 68, Chalon Way, St Helens WA9 1LL. Tel. 01744 22766; fax 01744 22599.

Association of National Tourist Office Representatives (ANTOR), 42d Compayne Gardens, London NW6 3RY.

British Airports Authority (BAA). Tel. 0171 932 6653; fax 0171 932 6659.

British Association of Tourism Officers. Tel. 01273 550523; fax 01273 550523.

British Sports Association for the Disabled, 13 Brunswick Place, London N1 6DX. Tel 0171 490 4949.

British Tourist Authority (BTA). Tel. 0181 846 9000.

British Waterways. Tel. 01923 201239; fax 01923 226081.

Central Council of Physical Recreation. Tel. 0171 828 3163.

Civil Aviation Authority (CAA). Tel. 0171 832 5620; fax 0171 240 1153.

Countryside Commission, John Dower House, Crescent Place, Cheltenham GL50 3RA. Tel. 01242 521381; fax 01242 584270.

Department of Transport, 2 Marsham Street, London SW1P 3EB. Tel. 0171 276 3578; fax 0171 276 0818.

English Tourist Board (ETB). Tel. 0181 846 9000.

Forestry Commission, 231 Corstorphine Road, Edinburgh EH12 7AT. Tel. 0131 334 0303; fax 0131 334 4473.

Hotel and Catering Training Company. Tel. 0181 579 2400; fax 0181 840 6217.

Institute of Baths and Recreational Management, 36 Sherrard Street, Melton Mowbray LE13 1XJ. Tel. 01664 65531.

Institute of Leisure and Amenity Management (ILAM), Ilam House, Lower Basildon, Reading RG8 9NE. Tel. 01491 874222; fax 01491 874059.

Museums and Galleries Commission, 16 Queen Anne's Gate, London SW1H 9AA. Tel. 0171 233 4200; fax 0171 233 3686

National Express. Tel. 0121 456 1122.

National Playing Fields Association. Tel. 0171 584 6445; fax 0171 581 2402.

National Rivers Authority. Tel. 0171 734 1921; fax 0171 582 8240.

Tourism Society, 26 Chapter Street, London SW1P 3ND

Youth Hostels Association. Tel. 01727 855215; fax 01727 844126.

Index